Organization Development
in Public Administration

PUBLIC ADMINISTRATION AND PUBLIC POLICY

A Comprehensive Publication Program

Executive Editor

NICHOLAS HENRY

Center for Public Affairs
Arizona State University
Tempe, Arizona

Publications in Public Administration and Public Policy

1. Public Administration as a Developing Discipline (in two parts)
   by Robert T. Golembiewski

2. Comparative National Policies on Health Care
   by Milton I. Roemer, M.D.

3. Exclusionary Injustice: The Problem of Illegally Obtained Evidence
   by Steven R. Schlesinger

4. Personnel Management in Government: Politics and Process
   by Jay M. Shafritz, Walter L. Balk, Albert C. Hyde, and David H. Rosenbloom

5. Organization Development in Public Administration (in two parts)
   edited by Robert T. Golembiewski and William B. Eddy

Other volumes in preparation

Developmental Editors

Library of Congress Cataloging in Publication Data

Main entry under title:

Organization development in public administration.

(Public administration and public policy; v. 5)
Includes index.
CONTENTS: Pt. 1. Organization properties and
public sector features.
1. Public administration—Addresses, essays,
lectures. 2. Organizational change—Addresses,
essays, lectures. I. Golembiewski, Robert T.
II. Eddy, William B., 1933-   III. Series
JF1411.0725   350   77-27574
ISBN 0-8247-6667-9

MARCEL DEKKER, INC.
270 Madison Avenue, New York, New York 10016

Current Printing (last digit):
10 9 8 7 6 5 4 3 2 1

PRINTED IN THE UNITED STATES OF AMERICA

Organization Development in Public Administration

(IN TWO PARTS)

Part 1

ORGANIZATION PROPERTIES
AND PUBLIC SECTOR FEATURES

EDITED BY

Robert T. Golembiewski
The University of Georgia
Athens, Georgia

William B. Eddy
The University of Missouri
Kansas City, Missouri

MARCEL DEKKER, INC.   New York and Basel

83390

PREFACE

This set of two volumes represents an effort whose time certainly has come. Indeed, if anything, these two books are long overdue. The editors plead guilty to neglect but only because they were busy contributing to the growth of Organization Development and its associated technology that this necessary project kept being postponed to attend to more basic research and applied issues.

Despite the intense concern with organization development, that is, no volume has yet been targeted specifically to the public sector audience. The oversight of the public administration audience is not trifling. For the latest statistics tell us that as many as two employees out of every 11 work for a public agency or governmental unit. Moreover, there are some 20,000 first-year students in our nation's several programs awarding the Master of Public Administration degree. And numerous other public employees are involved every year in in-service seminars, and the like, which focus on organizational change and development. Similarly, OD has become a major topic at professional meetings of public administrationists, having been first emphasized at a convention of the International City Management Association six or eight years ago and now having attained the status of a common topic at meetings of the PA clan at local, regional, national, and international levels.

For the first time, then, such variegated users will have book-length resources in organization development tailored to their own needs and environments, with much of its content drawn from public sector experience. Reasonable coverage requires two volumes on the common theme Organization Development in Public Administration:

    I. OD Properties and Public Sector Features

    II. Public Sector Applications of OD Technology

Specifically the first part contains two major sections which provide generic perspective on OD as well as direct attention to issues particular to public sector usage. The first three chapters are basically generic, and the fourth emphasizes motivators and constraints more or less specific to the public sector. These major chapters deal with:

Descriptions and definitions of OD

Normative or value concerns about OD

Basic empirical processes or dynamics in OD

Some specific factors relevant to the choice of whether or not to use OD in a public agency

Specifically, also, the second part has a dual focus. Thus numerous OD designs are described, and their consequences are detailed. Moreover, applications of these designs in public agencies are illustrated in some detail. The second part, then, emphasizes both the what and the where of OD applications.

As usual, such efforts are clearly dependent on the wit and will of many contributors. Such debts in this volume are especially great, in fact, because many of the selections below reflect the commitment of many employees and managers trying to make a better worksite for themselves, and a better quality of public service for their clients. Special thanks go to Sandra Daniel, who again provided indispensable service at several stages of this volume's progress toward publication.

Robert T. Golembiewski
William B. Eddy

CONTENTS

v

83390

CONTENTS OF PART 2

Chapter 1

WHAT IS ORGANIZATION DEVELOPMENT?
Basic Descriptions and Definitions

Readings

S. A. Culbert and J. Reisel, "Organization Development: An Applied Philosophy for Managers of Public Enterprise" 56

W. B. Eddy, "Beyond Behavioralism?: Organization Development in Public Management" 103

J. J. Sherwood, "An Introduction to Organization Development" 205

R. R. Blake and J. S. Mouton, "Strategies of Consultation" 29

It would be easy to overload this chapter with question marks. Does the term Organization Development (OD) refer to a specific method, or does it encompass a potpourri of approaches and techniques? Is it sensitivity training done inside an organization? Is it a faddish relabeling of old techniques, or is there something new? Is it based on scientific evidence, or does it depend on slick consulting and training tactics? Are special skills necessary, or can anyone do it? Is it based on newer and more useful notions about how organizations actually function and how they might function better, or is there too heavy a dose of pie in the sky humanism? Is there evidence that it works?

Major questions certainly exist in OD, but this chapter seeks to provide a positive approach. The purpose here is to introduce the reader to the multiple complexities that must be encompassed by any working answer to these questions. The approach will take two tracks. One suggests why OD has been difficult to get a handle on. The other shows the reader how several selections reprinted in this volume can begin the job of providing a definition of what OD is and does.

Some Difficulties in Describing OD

Organization development has been a difficult phenomenon for both scholars and administrators to grasp. Those who practice it usually have a reasonably clear notion about what they are doing and why. And they can communicate fairly well with other practitioners. But the questions above, and many others similar to them, continue to arise.

In part, the difficulty of defining OD derives from its complexity. This complexity inheres in what OD seeks: some definition of what is desirable and useful in organizations, and specific ways of achieving what is desirable and useful. No wonder, then, that fundamental differences of opinion exist about what OD is, what goals it seeks, and how it proposes to go about achieving them. OD deals with some fundamental issues of life, both empirical and ethical. So no wonder that many major questions remain unanswered.

Many of the problems of getting a conceptual handle on OD also derive from its mixed parentage, as it were. There is no establishment—no one university, professional society, or consulting firm—which "owns" OD and therefore has the more or less exclusive right to define it. The term appeared in the 1960s out of the work and writing of behavioral scientists. They came from many disciplines—social psychology, education, sociology, anthropology, political science, social work, management sciences, and many others. And OD practitioners had many different kinds of experiences and training. Basically, they were united only by a problem: how to apply knowledge to increase the efficiency of organizations and to heighten the growth and satisfaction of employees. Many of these founders, but far from all, were associated with the National Training Laboratories, or NTL. But that is about the only home they had in common.

Popularity of OD brought another source of diversity to what OD was said to be. Once OD became an increasingly fashionable thing to do, and it is now *very* fashionable in some prominent circles, all manner of consultants and researchers began to advertise that what they were doing was "into OD." Similarly, many organizations set up OD units, often with prodigious energy and commitment, but sometimes by just rechristening an existing unit of organization and its personnel.

Given its truly interdisciplinary heritage, and given the many who newly identified with it, no wonder that OD is described kaleidoscopically. Indeed, no agreement exists even about who first used the term, or how it was applied. It is probable that the concept came into common use to refer to several quite different activities.

This much seems certain about OD. Widespread dissatisfaction existed with Management Development, a term in longstanding usage which referred to a broad array of activities. Management development approaches focused on the technical and human relations skills of individual managers, and these failed to have much real impact on the organization. This major inadequacy became more and more obvious to many observers, especially beginning in the 1950s.

Clearly, there was a need to go beyond development of individual managers and to find ways to bring about improvements in the total group or system. Hence organization development was a notion whose time had come.

But OD is not simply playing with words. Its common usage coincided with the development of a growing number of techniques for working with groups and systems. Group dynamics, t-group training, survey research, consulting skills, and other approaches emerged. They gave variegated content to the words "Organization Development," but variation around some major central tendencies that will be emphasized in the four articles reprinted in this chapter.

Although there are points of difference in the articles that are introduced below, then, there is at least agreement that OD focuses on improving or changing the organization, or some coherent subsystem thereof. This contrasts with attempting to deal individually with organization members.

Some Ways of Describing OD

It is possible to go far beyond this elemental agreement, fortunately. The approach here is both convenient and revealing.

We now introduce four selections as a sample of those which seek to define OD. The selections are generic, as well as specific to Public Administration. Two articles were chosen because of their focus on the public sector: Samuel A. Culbert and Jerome Reisel, "Organization Development: An Applied Philosophy for Managers of Public Enterprise" and William B. Eddy, "Beyond Behavioralism?: Organization Development in Public Management." The piece by John J. Sherwood, "An Introduction to Organization Development," is a widely used brief description of the OD process, and it is most likely to be known among students of business administration. A fourth selection, "Strategies of Consultation" by Robert R. Blake and Jane Srygley Mouton, was chosen because it provides kaleidoscopic insight and illustration about the numerous specific kinds of OD interventions as well as about the several levels at which they are applied.

These four selections usefully represent several major themes in OD descriptions and definitions. At the level of general definition, Culbert and Reisel focus on the management of change and adaptation to dynamic internal and external realities. Sherwood sees OD as an educational process aimed at enhanc-

ing the utilization of human resources for organization renewal. Eddy emphasizes the use of applied social science techniques to assist in coping with some
of the chronic problems of public bureaucracies. All view OD as an ongoing
process which focuses on the human or social systems crucial to organizational
functioning. Emphasis is placed on interpersonal processes—including teamwork, communication, collaborative problem solving—rather than on structure,
procedure, or technology.

Another distinguishing characteristic of the field involves the role of the
OD consultant, often called change-agent or intervenor. In the articles that
follow, the practitioner performs a variety of functions. There are, however,
several consistent trends. Primarily, OD consultants tend not to act as experts
who provide the organization with advice or scientific data regarding the resolution of subatantive problems. Nor do they take a dominant role in developing plans or making decisions. OD consultants are more likely to be oriented
toward helping members of the client systems improve their own problem-
solving capabilities, as well as toward increasing the effectiveness of interpersonal
and group processes. Important and subtle skills inhere in this role. Interpersonal skills such as group facilitation, interviewing, counseling, building trust, and
dealing with conflict are seen as significant.

Another common thread in OD emphasizes application of a problem-
solving approach with significant help from the scientific method. This constitutes a powerful combination, to be sure, but it is not an unmixed blessing. It
is both boon and bane. The intended blending causes very real differences and
tensions in OD, for the demands of science and immediate problem solving may
be quite inconsistent. The one urges doing something that will work, even if
for the wrong reason, and the scientific attitude encourages laborious testing of
alternative hypotheses of why and how phenomena are orderly. To make matters even more complicated, OD adds a significant dimension to the standard
research approach, in that members of the client system often participate with
the behavioral scientist in planning, implementing, and evaluating the study.
Charges of contamination of results consequently can be made.

OD does not take the easy way out, however. Its practitioners, more or
less determinedly, seek that subtle marriage of science and immediate problem
solving. Illustratively, many descriptions of OD indicate a progression of phases
that include recognition of symptoms indicating problems within the organization, collection of data for testing and diagnosis, interventions designed to resolve problems, and evaluation of results. Survey-feedback and action/research
approaches (discussed more fully in other parts of the volume) are examples of
the explicit use of the scientific method.

The selection by Robert R. Blake and Jane Srygley Mouton, "Strategies
of Consultation," provides more specific and highly useful discussion of *what*
a change-agent does and *where.* Specifically, Blake and Mouton distinguish five

kinds of interventions and five settings or levels at which the interventions may be made. The five cases of what and the five of where, as it were, generate a matrix with twenty-five cells. Blake and Mouton essentially describe and illustrate OD efforts that can be classified in those twenty-five cells. In a basic sense, OD is best defined by the diverse content with which Blake and Mouton fill their matrix. They call it a D/D Matrix, for Diagnosis/ Development.

Chapter 2

NORMATIVE ISSUES RELEVANT TO ORGANIZATION DEVELOPMENT
Preferred Conditions and Critical Questions

Readings

All technologies generate three related concerns: that knowledge is power; that power can be perverted; and that, consequently, the greater the knowledge, the greater the possible perversion. This is the common dramatic theme of much literature, both powerful and puerile, from Goethe's *Faust* to Shelley's *Frankenstein*. The scientist goes mad in his lust for knowledge, and somehow sells his soul to the spirits of darkness for their aid in acquiring it. The outcomes are tragic. The scientist pays a stiff price for his lust for knowledge, whose major contribution is to raise merry hell with the otherwise comfy lives of his fellow men.

We should pay some attention to such popular wisdom. Knowledge *is* power, of course, and it *is* wise to be concerned about power and thus about accumulating knowledge. That there can be too much of even good things, therefore, is a useful warning to which we should pay considerable attention.

That knowledge can be perverted has encouraged some unwarranted conclusions, however. Some imply, or even state explicitly, that the only sure way to avoid perversions of knowledge is not to seek knowledge. Some otherwise reasonable persons thus have argued for a kind of return to the Dark Ages as the basic remedy for such awesome facts as the knowledge that nuclear fission has permitted the threat of annihilation of large parts of the world's population. Typically, such approaches also imply some prior attractive condition—before the bomb, or industrialization, or urbanization, or the steam engine—that could be recaptured, only if we had not been so obsessed with seeking knowledge.

OD does not take such an easy way out. It takes a harder route, in at least three senses. First, this volume acknowledges that any technology involves normative issues, and has to deal with them for what they are. They are statements of where we want to go, and how. And they are central in determining what the human condition will be.

Second, normative issues are very complicated in OD, in large part because OD is an eclectic composite of three broad and sometimes inconsistent systems of philosophy: rationalism, pragmatism, and existentialism. As Friedlander conceives today's tensions in OD:*

> Rationalism pushes contemporary OD toward becoming more scientific, more theoretical and conceptual, more logical, more mathematical; toward abstract models; toward building theories; toward understanding the determinants of our organizational, social, and personal worlds. Pragmatism pushes OD in the direction of becoming more useful—how does OD increase effectiveness, performance, productivity . . .? Existentialism within OD pushes the organization to become more humanistic, more aware, more emerging, more person-growth oriented. The rationalist learns by thinking; the pragmatist by doing; and the existentialist by becoming aware.

The ideological pieces do not always fit together nicely. Indeed, their several thrusts create considerable tension and forces in opposition. A more detailed sense of the philosophic integration attempted in OD is reflected in Figure 1.

Third, OD is an applied science. Hence it faces in very immediate ways any gaps between what is preferred and what exists or can be delivered. These two points, in fact, serve to organize the rest of this introduction to four selections that seek to provide broad normative perspectives on OD.

Some Preferred Conditions

That OD is, and should be, value loaded could be demonstrated in numerous ways. They all boil down to pretty much the same point, however. In the long

*Reproduced by special permission from *The Journal of Applied Behavioral Science.* "OD Reaches Adolescence," by Frank Friedlander, Volume 12, Number 1, pp. 7-21. Copyright © 1976 NTL Institute.

	Rationalism	Pragmatism	Existentialism
Purpose	Discover truth	Improve practice	Experience, choose, commit
Basic activity	Think (knowledge-guilding)	Do (acting)	Exist (being)
Learning paradigm	Conceptualize → define → manipulate ideas	Practice → experiment → valid feedback → improvement	Experience → choose → commit
Terms	Precisely defined	Tentatively defined	Need not be defined
Meaning emerges from	Definition (concepts)	Practice (results)	Experience (perception)
Ingredients for learning	Concepts, assumptions, logic	Practice, experiment, feedback	Awareness and confrontation of one's existence
Locus of knowledge	The conceptual model	The organizational practice	The individual experience
Reality	Objectivity and truth	Workability and practice (validity)	Subjective perception
Causes of good communication	Semantic precision	Consensual listening and understanding	Shared feeling and resonance

Figure 1 Three systems of philosophy that impact on organizational development. Reproduced by special permission from *The Journal of Applied Behavioral Science*, "OD Reaches Adolescence," by Frank Friedlander, Volume 12, Number 1, p. 14. Copyright © 1976 NTL Institute.

run, OD works toward a greater mutuality between what people need to function as full individuals, and what organizations need to perform effectively. The overall image is one of an exchange, a trade-off.

What does this greater mutuality mean, more specifically? Robert Tannenbaum and Sheldon Davis provide useful perspective on this crucial question, given that nothing like a complete answer is now possible. Their "Values, Man, and Organization" is at once a first approximation, and yet quite specific about the preferred conditions in a humanistic organization. But do not lose sight of their goal. They not merely define an organizational condition in which individuals will somehow be more comfortable. The implied exchange is that as individuals can approach those multiple humanistic values in organizations, so also will they be fuller and freer contributors to the organizational task as well as to their own development. OD does not contemplate some kind of a free ride, in short.

The approach taken by Tannenbaum and Davis to making explicit the values that guide their vision of OD is direct. They see a transitional world. OD values are moving away (for example) from an emphasis on humans as essentially bad, and those values also are moving toward a view of humans as basically good. Tannenbaum and Davis focus on thirteen such transitional values, in all, and incisively discuss both their implications and applications.

One point underlying their analysis deserves especial emphasis here. Their thirteen transitional values are not the result of scientific demonstration. No science can tell us what we should prefer, of course.

But neither are those thirteen values inconsistent with scientific work.

Quite the opposite, in fact. Much empirical research—some of which is sprinkled throughout the pages of this volume—testifies to two critical points.

First, it is an empirical fact that nearly all organization members prefer the transitional pole of the values that Tannenbaum and Davis emphasize, and nearly all informants agree that their organizations provide too little of what is preferred. For example, organizations variously reflect too much of a view that people are essentially bad, and too little of the view that people are basically good. This empirical gap between preference and reality patently provides major motivation for OD efforts.

Second, overall, available research implies that organizations based on the transitional values often produce attractive outcomes in terms of participant satisfaction and output. Much of this scientific support for OD values is also found throughout this volume, especially in the materials covered in Chapters 3 and 4. We clearly do not yet know what outcomes are most probable under which specific conditions. But the knowledge is accumulating, and the character of that knowledge will be critical in how far and how fast OD will develop.

Some Critical Normative Issues

Whatever happens in the long run, of course, we live in the short run. Hence pie in the sky, by and by, may seem attractive. But what of the normative problems that must be faced, day by day, as we struggle to get from here to the humanistic future?

Two selections especially respond to this central, practical question. First, getting from here to there inherently implies difficult normative issues. There is no single, easy road.

For example, OD interventionists cannot flee basic normative issues by claiming that they are only technocrats, experts in the application of specific OD designs or tactics. In at least two crucial senses, indeed, that means going from the frying pan into the fire. Simply, being a technocrat runs the risk of being a gun for anyone's hire, and therein can lie serious ethical issues which only the insensitive can ignore.

Assume the validity of the values espoused by Tannenbaum and Davis, to raise a more subtle and troublesome point. Not every means to those ends is thereby justified, of course, to simplify grievously. Richard Walton and Donald P. Warwick develop such ethical issues in satisfying detail in "The Ethics of Organizational Change." That selection deserves thoughtful reading, both by those who "do OD" as well as by those to whom OD is done.

Basically, Walton and Warwick concentrate on the issues of justice and openness. If the OD technology is indeed powerful, that raises the basic issue of its availability to "have-nots" as well as to the "haves." In this regard, as in many others, Walton and Warwick remind us that the world is anything but fair to the have-nots, which raises serious ethical issues for users of the OD technology and OD intervenors as well. Nor is that all. Openness about the power consequences of OD efforts also raises serious concerns, as Walton and Warwick document. Their message is both simple and profound. It is no reasonable defense to emphasize the intent to "do good:" one must be prudently certain as to the fullest range of consequences of an OD design, and not merely secure in the conviction that one's intentions are honorable.

Second, some observers even argue that the whole organizational effort rests on ethical quicksand. The more you struggle and succeed, in short, the worse things may become. David K. Hart and William G. Scott represent this point of view in their "Organizational Imperative."

Hart and Scott present a sophisticated argument, but their essential point is not subtle. The needs of organizations have come to replace human needs, goes the brief of their argument. Hence this basic irony: the more people successfully struggle to meet human needs in organizations, the more likely they are to find that they merely further enslave humans to the "organizational imperative." The whole business has a tragic "Catch 22" quality, as Hart and

Scott see the world. As organizations have come to be more successful in ful-filling certain human needs, so also grows the tendency to serve organizational needs whenever they conflict with even profoundly human needs. The conflict occurs more and more frequently, and with growing intensity, the authors in-form us. So also escalates the danger to human needs or concerns. There is much for OD specialists to ponder in the discomforting argument of Hart and Scott, even for those of us, like the editors of this volume, who understand their position but do not share it.

Chapter 3

EMPIRICAL UNDERPINNINGS OF ORGANIZATION DEVELOPMENT
Some Basic Dynamics and Processes

Readings

J. B. Harvey and D. R. Albertson, "Neurotic Organizations: Symptoms, Causes and Treatment" 170

G. L. Lippitt, "Transition Management–Coping" 189

G. W. Dalton, "Influence and Organizational Change" 72

M. R. Weisbord, "Why Organization Development Hasn't Worked (So Far) in Medical Centers" 247

It is not possible here to provide anything but a lick and a promise about why and how OD seems to work. What is now known would fill several volumes the size of this one, and what needs to be known is vast in comparison to what we now know.

But so be it. Although we cannot win here for losing, we also cannot avoid trying. The present limited contribution to outlining the empirical underpinnings of OD will have three emphases

OD Processes within people

OD Processes between people in large systems

Introducing four selections concerning OD dynamics and processes

Together, the three emphases will provide useful perspective on why and how OD interventions work.

OD Processes Within People

From one perspective, OD designs work because they provide organization members with things they need as people. Basically, people need caring and accurate tests of how others perceive them and of how effective they are perceived to be. Hampden-Turner calls this a test of our "experienced and anticipated competence," which for him includes

> The quality of cognition
> The clarity of personal identity
> The extent of self-esteem

To be truly alive, for Hampden-Turner, one must be a willing actor in a "cycle of accumulating human experience," on the model sketched in Figure 2. The

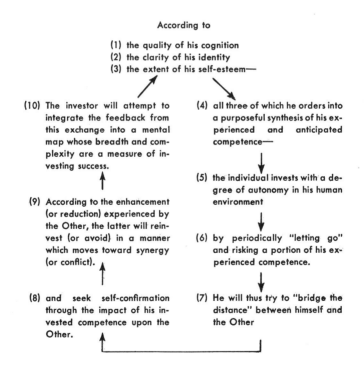

Figure 2   A cyclical model of accumulating human experiences. Reproduced by special permission from *The Journal of Applied Behavioral Science.* An Existential 'Learning Theory' and the Integration of T-Group Research," by Charles M. Hampden-Turner. Volume 2, Number 4, p. 368. Copyright © 1966 NTL Institute.

individual must test his or her competence: a negative test requires that an individual reassess his or her competence, and test again; a successful test can serve as a kind of emotional launching pad for future expansions in individual competence, which also will require further testing.

To put it briefly, OD designs typically provide information that is crucial for this essential human process. OD designs permit, indeed, encourage individuals to perform behaviors that are required for really living, even though that may sometimes be so hurtful that some people might shy away from the information even as they cannot do without it. And that is one powerful reason why some OD designs generally seem to work, and sometimes seem to fail.

OD Processes Among People in Large Systems

OD designs also seem to work because they often improve or reverse what may be called "degenerative interaction sequences" between people in large organizations, which have outcomes that most people prefer to avoid, at least most of the time.

The point requires some stage setting. To oversimplify, two patterns of relationships among people can be visualized, as in Figure 3. Those sequences involve four central variables, only two of which require distinguishing here.

It is possible to be open without owning. Assume that a reader of this volume were to say, "You know, a lot of people think your prose is dry and

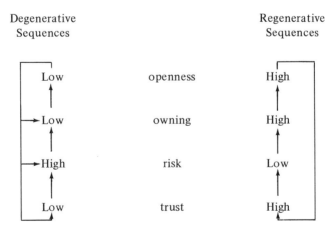

Figure 3   Two idealized patterns of interaction.

dull." That may be an open comment but, if the reader is really one of those having that reaction to the text, the reader is not owning that concern.

Degenerative interaction sequences can have nasty consequences in organizations, as Figure 4 attempts to suggest. The total sense of it is a constipated organization, in which even easy things require major effort to bring off, and apparently firm decisions have a way of becoming unraveled even under slight pressure. Individuals in such organizations would be more preoccupied with developing "just in case" files than in problem-solving, to summarize one implication of Figure 4.

Organization members tend to prefer avoiding such consequences as those in Figure 4 if they can see how that might be done. Many OD designs provide such a way out. And to state a complex story in the briefest terms, that capability of OD designs is a major reason why they often work. The designs provide a way out of undesired conditions, in sum, and thus motivate appropriate behavior from those intent on getting out from under.

Three Perspectives on OD Dynamics and Processes

Before introducing three selections that provide useful perspective on empirical features of OD, let us conveniently provide some general context, from the consultant's point of view. All OD consultants have their own models for testing the health of organizations, a kind of a map of major checkpoints to a very complicated territory. Roger Harrison provides one such map of special interest and usefulness, which Figure 5 briefly summarizes.

Note that comprehensive and subtle quality of OD consultancy reflected by the summary in Figure 5 of Harrison's position. The picture is graphic. Harrison approaches each new organization, his perceptual antennae quivering, as he tries to keep *all* of his analytical categories in mind. After probing, Harrison often decides that *one or a few* of the categories are especially relevant for openers. And as he focuses on that smaller number of categories, Harrison tries to keep in mind the other categories, for at least two reasons. He strives to tailor early strategies and designs in such ways as to facilitate later work, to minimize conflict and work at cross-purposes. In addition, the fuller checklist reminds Harrison of the longer road that can be traveled in extensive OD efforts, even if he can never get around to dealing with them.

Given this comprehensive picture of the scope of OD, four selections can be relied on to provide more detailed perspective on important empirical features of OD designs. Each selection will be introduced briefly.

First, Jerry Harvey and D. Richard Albertson provide important perspective on how and why things can go badly in organizations. Their "Neurotic Organizations" sketches the character and consequences of a serious but com-

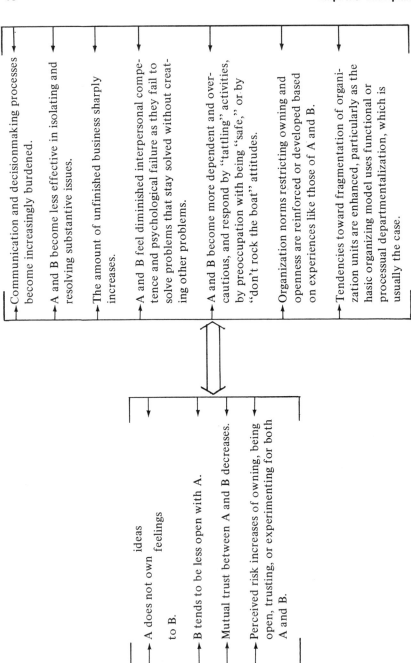

A does not own ideas feelings to B.

B tends to be less open with A.

Mutual trust between A and B decreases.

Perceived risk increases of owning, being open, trusting, or experimenting for both A and B.

Communication and decisionmaking processes become increasingly burdened.

A and B become less effective in isolating and resolving substantive issues.

The amount of unfinished business sharply increases.

A and B feel diminished interpersonal competence and psychological failure as they fail to solve problems that stay solved without creating other problems.

A and B become more dependent and over-cautious, and respond by "tattling" activities, by preoccupation with being "safe," or by "don't rock the boat" attitudes.

Organization norms restricting owning and openness are reinforced or developed based on experiences like those of A and B.

Tendencies toward fragmentation of organization units are enhanced, particularly as the basic organizing model uses functional or processual departmentalization, which is usually the case.

Figure 4   Some consequences of degenerative interaction sequences.

Information System
Modes of communication
(written, group, individual, etc.)
Informal groupings
Information channels

Technical System
Work process—technology
and organization of tasks
Responsibility and authority
for specific things
Types of decisions which are
made

Points of Entry
System members' own change
and improvement goals
Role conflicts and concerns
of members
Members' blocks to job
effectiveness
Conflicting goals of sub-
systems
Satisfaction of members with
their jobs
Performance evaluation and
appraisal of organizational
units
Performance evaluation and
appraisal of individuals

Power System
Formal authority structure
Informal reward system
Responsibility and authority
for major types of decisions
Types of decisions
Types of decisions which are
made

System Objectives
Goals of system
Priorities among system
objectives
Goals of subsystems: espe-
cially those which conflict

Ideology
Organizational culture:
norms and values of
system members
Control systems

Figure 5 Harrison's model for organizational diagnosis: categories and sub-categories. Harrison's categories were derived from his response to a portion of the Hornstein and Tichy "Change Agent Survey" questionnaire which instructed respondents to (1) indicate what information (from a list including such things as formal reward structure, goals, control systems, individual satisfactions, etc.) they would seek in order to diagnose and understand an organization, and (2) to arrange the items into categories. Reproduced by special permission from *The Journal of Applied Behavioral Science.* Noel Tichy's "Interview with Roger Harrison," Volume 9, Number 6, p. 707. Copyright © 1973, NTL Institute.

mon malady in collective enterprise. Neurotic organizations cannot win for losing. No matter how hard their members may try, such organizations often induce the sense that they are not even running fast enough or effectively enough to stand still. Problems never seem to get solved, at least not without creating other equal or even greater problems. Their members may have the appropriate information for effective decision making, but the information is either mistrusted, is not used in making decisions, or is reflected in decisions that get made again and again because support for them always seems to come unglued. Such organizations provide real challenges for OD efforts, and constitute a major tribulation for their members.

Second, Gordon L. Lippitt provides detailed counterpoint on a similar central theme: OD consultants must remember the forest as they are busy hacking away at one of its trees. His "Transition Management—Coping" urges such comprehensiveness in useful detail. Lippitt cautions against fixating on any single OD learning design or approach and he encourages OD practitioners to pay attention to the full range of organizational inputs, processes, environments, and outputs. For OD is, above all, *organization* development. The focus is consequently on systems and their complex relationships, as contrasted with learning designs that begin and end with only some amelioration of the condition of individuals or small groups.

Third, Gene W. Dalton puts an analytic microscope on effective OD applications in his "Influence and Organizational Change." This is a classic piece of work, to which no brief introduction can do justice. Basically, Dalton focuses on a group of early studies of organizational change. And he confronts each study with this basic question: What does this research tell us about the conditions and processes that help account for the success or failure of attempts to induce change in organizations?

Dalton comes to some central and detailed conclusions about what seems to work, and when. He relies basically on the three-stage model of Lewin, which focuses on these elements in change

Unfreezing old attitudes, behaviors, and values

Learning new attitudes, behaviors, and values, with emphasis on appropriate skills

Reinforcement of any learning

To this elemental and seminal model, Dalton marshals impressive detail that bears ample testimony to two facts. The processes of organizational change are complex, sometimes paralyzingly so. But those processes of change are not beyond human wit and will; they can be brought off, and in ways that have many basic similarities.

Fourth, Marvin R. Weisbord provides useful counterpoint to Dalton. That is, the latter focuses on the factors that encourage success in OD. And Weisbord's emphasis is clear in his title: "Why Organization Development Hasn't Worked (So Far) In Medical Centers."

Clearly—to judge from the "so far"—Weisbord is still optimistic, but he essentially argues that some organizations present a range of especially difficult problems to confound OD intervenors. His focus is on the medical center, which he defines as a "complex academic center including many training, service, and research activities." Basically, his argument centers around a profound simplicity: that medical centers encompass three primary systems, not the one that he attributes to industry. Weisbord sees the "task system" as common in both industry and in medical centers, but the latter also have complex "identity" and "governance" systems.

One can argue that Weisbord misjudges the degree of uniqueness of medical centers from industry, but it seems inescapable that he also has isolated much that is significant in the differences between alternative contexts for OD applications. For example, the "labor union system" may be a significant one in industry, along with the "task system." And OD applications in socialist countries, just now beginning in Poland, will have to encompass the "party system" as well as the "task system." But such examples do not undercut Weisbord's argument. They suggest that it may have far broader applications, with modifications, than to medical centers. And that is to say that Weisbord did a significant job, and did it well.

Chapter 4

MOTIVATORS/CONSTRAINTS ON
PUBLIC SECTOR ORGANIZATION DEVELOPMENT APPLICATIONS
Perspectives on Whether to Use Organization Development in Public Agencies

Readings

R. T. Golembiewski, "Organization Development in Public Agencies: Perspectives on Theory and Practice"   133

E. J. Giblin, "Organization Development: Public Sector Theory and Practice"   123

W. B. Eddy and R. J. Saunders, "Applied Behavioral Science in Urban Administrative/Political Systems"   113

M. R. Weisbord, "Why Organization Development Hasn't Worked (So Far) in Medical Centers"   247

D. K. Hart and W. G. Scott, "The Organization Imperative"   151

S. A. Culbert and J. Reisel, "Organization Development: An Applied Philosophy for Managers of Public Enterprise"   56

W. B. Eddy, "Beyond Behavioralism?: Organization Development in Public Management"   103

A truism repeated among consultants runs to the effect that all organizations believe their own problems are unique and different, although they are, all, in fact, pretty much the same. This belief represents one of the difficulties in the dissemination of applied behavioral science approaches, as well as other management innovations. Some intervention may have worked in agency X, that is, but our organization is so different.

Public administrators perhaps especially fear that the particular characteristics of their agencies and of public administration diminish the chances of an OD effort. The point of view is often expressed as a general assumption that OD began in private industry, and that its prominence there is due to unique features of that context. Any possible OD application to public and third-sector organizations must therefore be viewed as risky, goes this common line of thought.

There is some sense and nonsense in this common line of thought. Thus many of the early large-scale OD efforts did take place in business organizations, but the record is more mixed than the common wisdom allows. Laboratory training originated largely out of work with educational administrators. Government contractors in aerospace and weapons systems were among the earliest users of OD, and the techniques developed were soon applied to teams of appointed and elected city officials and to state agencies, especially in California, but also elsewhere. The articles discussed in the previous section detail several such cases, and refer to many more public sector applications.

These realities notwithstanding, concern still exists about possible conflicts between OD and values, traditions, and norms common in public agencies. The articles discussed in this chapter explore that concern from three basic perspectives. In turn, that is, emphasis shifts from those constraints on OD applications that are said to derive from specific public-sector features, to those constraints implicit in broad cultural values, traditions, and norms that are often said to act as constraints on public OD efforts, and, finally, to the strong need—perhaps even the special need—for OD in public agencies, the common wisdom about specific and generic constraints on OD applications notwithstanding.

Some Specific Constraints

Four selections below, especially, define some differences between private and public organizations that may bear on evaluating the likelihood of OD success. These selections include: Robert T. Golembiewski, "Organization Development in Public Agencies: Theory and Practice;" Edward J. Giblin, "Organization Development: Public Sector Theory and Practice;" William B. Eddy and Robert J. Saunders, "Applied Behavioral Science in Urban Administrative/Political Systems;" and Marvin R. Weisbord, "Why Organization Development Hasn't Worked (So Far) in Medical Centers."

Whether commonplace or less apparent, several public vs private differences are seen as real constraints on the success of OD applications in the public sector. These constraints are not Go/No-Go criteria. Rather, they raise or lower the probability of the success of an OD application, they make an application more or less complicated. The selection by Weisbord most clearly argues this point in a particular kind of organization, the medical center: many are public agencies in a direct sense and all relate in pervasive ways to the public good. The other three selections, by Giblin, Golembiewski, as well as Eddy and Saunders, seek to generalize about public agencies as a broad class. Both kinds of foci are useful. The degree of specificity provided by Weisbord is clearly greater, while the other three selections seek to gain in breadth what they lose in sharpness of focus.

Specifically, some of these differences between the private and public sectors are obvious and oft-stated: private firms have "the bottom line" as the ultimate measure of performance while public agency success criteria may be "softer"; private organizations often have concrete and measurable units of output while agencies respond to needs/demands, control something, or provide a service for which no market value exists and whose quality may be difficult to assess; and private firms tend to experience less external control over their policies and programs.

Other differences between the business and public sectors are less immediately apparent. But they may be significant in assessing OD's applicability because they bear on basic assumptions about needs, values, appropriate modes of interaction, role conceptions, and problem-solving traditions. These differences, it is asserted, must be understood before one can answer the question: Does OD fit the public sector?

For the editors of this volume, that question is better phrased: Does a very specific OD design fit a particular agency, at its present stage of development, given its planned future evolution, and taking into account relevant features of its institutional context, whether public or business? But we prefer asking the simpler question about applicability, if the only alternative is to ask no questions.

Some Generic Constraints

David K. Hart and William G. Scott's "The Organizational Imperative" raises a somewhat different set of possible constraints which are also significant and challenging for the OD practitioner. Pressures within society, they argue, are forcing the development of norms related to organizational membership and role which run counter to the humanistic values underlying most OD approaches. OD, then, may be flying in the face of current trends representing an organizational imperative.

The prognosis is not favorable, Hart and Scott note. Even if OD is successful at making organizations more productive and the people in them more satisfied, they note, that will only further bloat the organizational imperative. You can't win for losing on this one.

Hart and Scott's main point might apply with equal or perhaps even special force to public administration. That is, public administrators are probably quite susceptible to such societal norms. Public administrators often are pressured to make their organizations more controlled, rational and pragmatic, that is to say, and OD efforts tend to have biases toward greater employee freedom and spontaneity. For their part, OD practitioners may decide to revise their approaches somewhat in order to buy into the organizational imperative with their public sector clients. Or they may attempt to use OD to fight the imperative's normative system, thus risking problems for themselves and their clients. Again, you can't win for losing on this one.

Some Compelling Motivators

Other selections below focus on the characteristics of public agencies which indicate special need for OD, constraints or no. For example, consider the emphasis on the processes of *planned change* in two selections below: Samuel A. Culbert and Jerome Reisel, "Organization Development: An Applied Philosophy for Managers of Public Enterprise;" and William B. Eddy, "Beyond Behavioralism?: Organization Development in Public Management." A common charge levied at public bureaucracies is that they are unusually skilled at mobilizing massive resistance to even needed change. OD offers the possibility of helping overcome such resistance, as well as contributing to a more creative planning process. This characteristic of public administration implies the especial need for OD. Similar arguments might be made concerning other features of our public agencies and their institutional contexts.

Taken together, of course, the selections emphasized here do not answer the question of whether OD fits public-sector organizations, or of whether specific public-sector organizations especially need OD. And the reason for this apparent failure to provide answers is simple: there is no general answer to what is not a very useful question. That is, there are wider differences on almost all dimensions among public organizations than between any given public and private organization. Moreover, some problems are relatively similar and comparatively easy to solve, such as poorly conducted and ineffective team meetings, whether they occur in public or business agencies. Other problems tend to be much harder to get at, in contrast, such as autonomous departments competing for budget dollars and blocking each other in the process. Again, this is true whether the context is in business or government.

Rather than answer an unanswerable question, then, this part of the volume has more humble ambitions. It seeks to (1) highlight some public and private differences and their possible consequences in OD, (2) identify areas in which OD may contribute to public organizations, and (3) raise awareness about some serious value issues related to doing OD in public agencies.

STRATEGIES OF CONSULTATION*

Robert R. Blake and Jane Srygley Mouton

In the process of our studies we have come to recognize that five different kinds of interventions characterize what applied behavioral scientists do as they work with people in organizations. They intervene, in any of these five ways, in five different settings or units of change. So a matrix of twenty-five cells is necessary to describe the significant change efforts that are going on. We would like to explain what these cells are, provide a brief bibliography to pinpoint work going on in each, and provide a few examples that describe the respective intervention/ development assumptions that each contains.

You will notice that Figure 1 is called the D/D (Diagnosis/Development) Matrix. This is because diagnosis and development are two aspects that are more or less interdependent in planned change efforts, although occasionally they need to be separated for purposes of analysis.

The *rows* of the matrix represent types of interventions. One is acceptant. The next is catalytic. A third is confrontation. The fourth is prescriptive. The fifth and last includes use of principles, theories and models as the determinants of change. Selection of any particular intervention, of course, is a judgmental decision taken on the basis of prior diagnosis.

The *columns* of the matrix refer to settings within which change occurs. The first column identifies the individual *per se* as a unit of change. The second,

*Originally titled "The D/D Matrix," by Robert R. Blake and Jane Srygley Mouton. In Adams, John D. (Ed.) *Theory and Method in Organization Development: An Evolutionary Process.* NTL Institute for Applied Behavioral Science, 1974. Reproduced by permission.

Types of Intervention	Unit of Change				
	Individual	Team (group project, department)	Intergroup (interdivisional, headquarters-field, union-management, etc.)	Organization	Society
Acceptant	A	B	C	D	E
Catalytic	F	G	H	I	J
Confrontation	K	L	M	N	O
Prescriptive	P	Q	R	S	T
Principles, Models, Theories	U	V	W	X	Y

Figure 1 The D/D matrix. This way of organizing intervention strategies led us to introduce a third dimension called *focal issues*. There are four: power/authority, morale/cohesion, norms/standards, and goals/objectives. See R. R. Blake, and Jane Srygley Mouton, *Consultation* (Reading, Mass.: Addison-Wesley, 1976). Copyright © Scientific Methods Inc., 1972. Not to be reproduced with permission.

or team, column refers mainly to small groups, projects, departments, and managerial "family" groups, but it also includes interpersonal relations on a one-to-one basis. The third column is for intergroup relationships. Examples of intergroup diagnosis/development units are interdivisional, headquarters-field, union-management, and other relationships between any organized groupings within or semi-external to the organization. The fourth column refers to the organization considered as a whole or as a system. The fifth we have labeled "society" because of the broader implications of training and development for planned change of society at large.

Acceptant Intervention

Now let's go along the top. What an "acceptant" intervention does is to enter into contact with the feelings, tensions, and subjective attitudes that often block a person and make it difficult for him to function as effectively as he otherwise might. The developmental objective is to enable him to express, work through and resolve these feelings so that he can then return to a more objective and work-related orientation. This is not the whole area of counseling as it relates to therapy. It is that aspect of counseling which takes place within the framework of organizations and which is intended to help a person perform better. Certainly it is a very important application of counseling.

Here is an example of counseling with individuals from Cell A in the matrix. During the 1930's, at the Hawthorne plant of the Western Electric Company, it was discovered that many employees were blocked, taut, seething with tensions of one kind or another. Generally these tensions were either work-focused or home-focused, or an intricate combination of both. For some years Hawthorne management provided a counseling service that enabled people to be aided through counseling to discharge the emotion laden tensions. We say "to discharge" tensions, as distinct from resolving them more or less permanently. The procedure was, in effect, "Any time you feel overcome by tension, get a slip from your supervisor and go see a counselor." This is comparable—if we adopt an oil-industry analogy—to "flaring off" subterranean natural gas rather than piping it to wherever it can be productively used.

In the peak year of the program, 1948, Hawthorne's department of counseling was manned by fifty-five people. That's a large complement of counselors. This very interesting experiment has been documented by its originators, who were able to return to the scene of their effort and to study the consequences thirty years after the program began.

An example I would like to paraphrase for you is from their book (Dickson & Roethlisberger, 1966, 225-226). The situation takes place in the counselor's office. Charlie enters. He is a semi-skilled worker who has been with the company for some time but has recently been transferred to a new inspection job from another one he had formerly mastered and enjoyed. He is unhappy with his new job.

Counselor: Hi 'ya Charlie, how are you?
Charlie: Glad to see you. We all set to go?
Counselor: Sure, any time you're ready.
Charlie: Well, I'm ready any time to get out of this g.d. place. *You know, you get shoved around from one place to another.*
Counselor: You mean you don't have one steady job?
Charlie: Steady, hell. When I came from the first floor I was supposed to do this particular bank job. I stayed on that for two or three weeks, not even long enough to learn it, then I got transferred up here. . . . Of course you know what I got. It got me nothing, just this job here which was a cut.*
Counselor: Then all that work didn't pay off?
Charlie: Pay off? There's no payoff at all.

As you can see in this brief example, Charlie is ventilating his feelings and frustrations and the counselor is "reflecting"; trying to aid Charlie to clarify them by feeding him back a summary of those tensions so that Charlie might get an understanding of what they are, rather than just feeling the hurt and distress of them. You will notice that the counselor is not attempting to help Charlie solve his "transfer with pay cut" problem. That's one point of application that involves counseling with an individual to promote catharsis.

In recent years—and "way out" from Hawthorne—the continuum of learning through experience has been extended and enriched through experimentation with action oriented, non-verbal approaches. An advantage here is that the modalities through which an individual is able to experience himself in situations are increased. Results and experiences can be more directly, *felt,* in the sense that words are unnecessary to convey whatever emotions are involved. The way in which any particular approach is used, of course, determines its location in the matrix. One of the most common uses of "encountering" is in the effort to promote personal growth through individual cathartic experiences (Watson, 1972, 155-172).

Now let's look to Cell B. This involves acceptant interventions at the team or group level. Here the idea is that before a team can do an effective job of dealing with its work problems, it may have to deal with emotional tensions and feelings that exist within and between its members.

Gibb has for a considerable time been aiding teams to discharge tension in a cathartic way. This example is from his account of his methods (Gibb, 1972). He describes how, in the process of team building, he may begin with

*In his hourly rate of pay.

what he calls a "preparation meeting." He brings together the people who are going to be leaders of different teams in order to prepare them for their experience. Why does he start this way? "The primary constraint," he says, "... is, of course, fear. Participants are given ... perhaps the first half-day to share and fully explore as many of their fears as they are able to verbalize." What help is this? "Fears dissipate as they are brought into awareness, shared with others, lived with, listed on the board, made public, and made acceptable. The public expression of the fear may take many forms." (Gibb, 1972, 38). So the effort begins with group exploration which aims to remove these constraints so that constructive sessions can take place.

Cell C identifies approaches to planned change utilizing catharsis at the intergroup level. For example, I am sure that many readers have experienced the tensions and emotions that underlie many union-management relationships. Bickering at the bargaining table is a constant feature and, many times, the topics discussed are not the relevant ones that need to be resolved. Sometimes the relevant ones can't even be expressed! Rather, the issues that people concentrate on seemingly are brought to the table in order to provoke a fight. Often such intergroup dynamics emerge from emotions and frustrations which never get uncovered but stay beneath the surface. Catharsis at the intergroup level has as its purpose to uncover feelings that are barriers to problem-solving interaction; to provide the opportunity for them to be made public; and, in this way, to escape from their hidden effects.

Here is an example from a union-management situation we happen to be familiar with. Contract bargaining was underway. It was hopeless. It was going nowhere. We heard management voicing its frustrations and bitching about the union, and we suggested that perhaps the needed activity was to get *away* from the union-management bargaining table and to sit down together in a special conference for the sole purpose of exploring the feelings these groups held toward one another. This was done. The tensions discharged in those three days were destructive, deep-rooted, intense. The grudges and fantasies from the past that were blocking present effectiveness finally got unloaded, and this freeing-up permitted bargainers to get back to their deliberations.

Here is just one example of the many fantasies unveiled during these days. At one time, actual events which were the source of the fantasy had occurred, but now the "truth" of these events was a matter of history. At the present time the varied feelings about these events were in the realm of fantasy.

"In 1933," (this cathartic session took place in *1963*) the union told the management, "you s.o.b's had us down and out because of the depression. And what did you do? You cut everybody's pay in half and, having done so, then you turned us out into the yard to dig up all the pipe and repack it. How do you expect us to bargain with a bunch of cutthroats that would do that to human beings who are down?"

The managers, hearing this, did a retake and said, "Oh, but golly, that was not *us;* that was five dynasties of management ago!" But this disclaimer didn't mollify the union. Eventually, 1963 management walked the 1963 union back through the time tunnel in an attempt to reconstitute the thinking that 1933 management had undertaken. This was "We shouldn't let people go home with no job. We should keep them 'whole.' We can't employ them full time because we don't have that much production scheduled—market demand is way down. Rather than laying off people *en masse,* the humane thing to do is to keep everyone on the payroll, but to make the cost burden bearable by reducing wages. Also, we have to keep them occupied somehow. With operational activities currently at such low levels, the only thing we can do that has long-term utility to it is to dig up the yard pipe and repack it."

So the 1933 management's intentions were probably well-meant, but the union's legend regarding those intentions portrayed them as very malicious. Yet eventually the 1963 union, after reconsidering that management's dilemma, agreed that it had taken the most humane alternative open to it. So the old legend dissolved away. Only by getting this kind of emotional muck out in the open and discharged was it possible for these union and management representatives to get back to a businesslike basis of working toward a contract. That's an example of acceptant at the intergroup level.

There are many examples of acceptant interventions at the organization level, Cell D.

In another company the entire management engaged in an "acceptant" experience prior to bargaining. The reason was that even though management, at an intellectual level, desired to interact on a problem-solving basis with the plant's independent-union representatives, there were many deeply-rooted antagonistic attitudes which continually surfaced and stifled the effort. Why? The ostensibly humane attitudes of people who have received formal education sometimes only serve as a mask for deeper feelings of resentment and antipathy. Often there is a lot of hate among managerial people toward the work force. Such feelings are particularly prevalent among engineers, supervisors and foremen who have, in their own careers, only recently risen above the level of the "blue-collar stiff."

The consultant determined that to work solely with the bargaining committee would be insufficient as they could only move in a problem-solving direction if they had the support of the rest of management. Thus a series of conferences were held. Participants were the top 100 members of management, who represented all levels of supervision except first and second line foremen. The stated purpose of these meetings was to develop shared convictions in regard to answering the key question, "How can we create better relations between union and management?"

Participants were put into three "cross-section" groups during each conference. Quinn, the plant manager, sat in one group. Van, the operations super-intendent, sat in another group and Wes, the personnel chief, in a third. The groups struggled with the problem of how to improve union-management relations. It was fascinating to watch because a fairly substantial cross-section of the managerial group considered the key question a hopeless one to answer. "There is no way to bring about any improvement vis-à-vis the thugs, thieves and crooks who presently are running the union. How can you cooperate and collaborate with such a rat pack?"

Then as the question got debated, their deep-lying attitudes and feelings were expressed in detail and were looked at from many points of view. A new concept began to appear. Consciousness dawned that one can never look forward to an improvement in union-management relations unless this governing attitude—namely that the union is composed of thugs, thieves and crooks—is erased or at least given an experimental adjournment in the minds of management. After the discharge of emotions was completed, it was concluded in group after group, "Regardless of what the union officers are personality-wise and what their history has been, the only conceivable way of bringing about a resolution of conflict is through treating the union officers as officers and according them the dignity and respect due to people who are duly elected. It is not our place to judge the people who have been chosen by their membership as lawful representatives. This is not our role. Our role is to meet with these people and to search for whatever conditions of cooperation and collaboration are possible."

As a result of this cathartic experience, it was possible thereafter for management's bargaining team to take a more collaborative stance (Blake & Mouton, 1973).

At the level of society shown in Cell E, there also are mechanisms that provide for catharsis. Religious institutions are one example. More so in American history than now, but still persisting, is the role of the clergyman as one of the persons to whom people turn when in deep emotional trouble, with the expectation of his providing the disturbed person an opportunity to talk through his feelings. In addition, the doctor, teacher, and school or private counselor are often turned to for help during periods of emotional turmoil, as indeed may be true for parents as well. Beyond these, whenever there is a trauma in society it frequently happens that *ad hoc* mechanisms are created which help people work through their distressed emotional feelings. Well remembered American examples include the two Kennedy funeral processions that were carried by television to many parts of the world. These occasions aided people to mourn. Mourning, in this sense, means working through and discharging tensions of a painful emotional character which currently are preventing people from going on living in their customary ways. As is true in the individual case, societal catharsis mechanisms may not have any direct and systematic connection to potential problem-solving steps, although they sometimes stimulate remedial action of one kind or another.

Catalytic Interventions

Let's move to the next row down: catalytic interventions. "Catalytic" intervention means entering a situation and adding something that has the effect of transforming the situation in some degree from what it was at an earlier time. That's quite different from catharsis. When a training manager or consultant is acting to induce catharsis, he is reflecting or restating the problem—or perhaps simply listening in a fashion that gives empathic support. But when a person makes a catalytic intervention, he might provide a suggestion that causes the problem to be seen in a different and more relevant perspective. Or he might suggest a procedure that will lead to a different line of action being adopted.

Here is a catalytic intervention at the individual level, Cell F in the D/D Matrix. In one particular company they have a career-planning project. A young man who had been employed for some time came in to talk about his career hopes. The interviewer said, "What are your aspirations? Where would you like to end up in the company?"

The young man replied, "Well, I think I would like to be president or chairman."

Now then, the interviewer might have said something in a cathartic or reflective way. But he didn't. He said, "Well, that's an interesting aspiration. I would like to think it through with you. How many years of education do you have?"

"Six."

"How many promotions have you had in the last two years?"

"One small wage increase."

"Have you taken any courses on your own initiative?"

"No."

And as the discussion continued, the young man began to see the unrealism in his aspiration to be president. Currently there was *no* realistic possibility either in terms of some evidence of upward progression, or of autonomously achieved preparation, or in terms of anything else he was doing. The consultant thereby brought him to the choice point of whether he was prepared to make the additional sacrifices necessary for him to generate upward movement, or whether he was simply content to go on projecting an unrealistic career fantasy (Gould, 1970, 227-228). That's a catalytic intervention at the *individual* level.

Another example, which uses a laboratory setting for life/career planning, is premised on catalytic intervention at the individual level (Fordyce & Weil, 1971, 131-132).

Catalytic intervening at the *team* level, Cell G, is one of the most popular applied behavioral science developments of the past twenty-five years, and has become a central intervention in industrial life. There are a whole host of names that come to mind at this point. There are people who engage in team-building sessions where the purpose of their interventions is not to direct the team or merely to reflect back members' feelings, but to facilitate the interaction process so that the team comes to have a better understanding of the problems and pitfalls it's gotten into, and so on.

The following is an example of Schein, a consultant, facilitating group action by focusing attention on how the agenda for meetings was determined.

> In the Apex company I sat in for several months on the weekly executive-committee meeting, which included the president and his key subordinates. I quickly became aware that the group was very loose in its manner of operation: people spoke when they felt like it, issues were explored fully, conflict was fairly openly confronted, and members felt free to contribute.

> What did this mean to Schein?

> This kind of climate seemed constructive, but it created a major difficulty for the group. No matter how few items were put on the agenda, the group was never able to finish its work. The list of backlog items grew longer and the frustration of group members intensified in proportion to this backlog.

> How did members themselves diagnose the situation?

> The group responded by trying to work harder. They scheduled more meetings and attempted to get more done at each meeting, but with little success. Remarks about the ineffectiveness of groups, too many meetings, and so on, became more and more frequent.

> But what did it look like to Schein?

> My diagnosis was that the group was overloaded. Their agenda was too large, and they tried to process too many items at any given meeting, and the agenda was a mixture of operational and policy issues without recognition by the group that such items required different allocations of time.

> So what did Schein propose?

> I suggested to the group that they seemed overloaded and should discuss how to develop their agenda for their meetings. The suggestion was adopted after a half-hour or so of sharing feelings.

> Was Schein passive and reflecting or active in a facilitative way?

> It was then decided, with my help, to sort the agenda items into several categories, and to devote some meetings entirely to operational issues while others would be exclusively policy meetings. The operations meetings would be run more tightly in order to process these items efficiently. The policy questions would be dealt with in depth. (Schein, 1969, 106).

Another example of facilitative or catalytic interaction occurs between boss and subordinate as they engage in "management by objectives." Quite frequently, however, in the introduction of MBO in an organization, people other than just the boss and subordinate are used to develop and facilitate the program. Here is a description of what such facilitators do. It is taken from Humble's work with management by objectives (Humble, 1967, 60). He calls these internal people "company advisers."

> Company Advisers must be selected and trained to a highly professional standard in the various techniques. . . . An Adviser is a source of professional advice on the whole programme. He develops suitable techniques and methods with managers; counsels each, individual manager in the Key Results Analysis preparation; is present at first Reviews; helps to analyse training plans. He is an "educator" and "catalyst," *not* a man who states what the standards should be, nor what the priorities are and how the problems should be solved. That is management's task.

In this description we see a clear distinction between what we later on call prescriptive interventions—where the intervention is for the purpose of telling people what to do—and the facilitative or catalytic type of intervention where the goal is to aid a process of change or development to occur.

Data-gathering procedures frequently are used in a catalytic way. This is where data are intended to add something to the situation in order to change it (Likert, 1961). When these data are returned to their users, the expert's own personal participation is best described as catalytic. Usually he doesn't tell people what the data mean, but he does ask them questions that aid them to probe meanings more directly.

Next to Cell H, intergroup. Catalysis here denotes adding something *between* two groups, in order to enable existing difficulties to rise to the surface or be placed squarely on the examining table so that they can be dealth with.

An intergroup intervention example is described by Beckhard. What he describes is a situation where people from a higher level meet with people from a lower level. The goal is to aid the lower-level people to communicate with the higher-level managers, or discuss specific problems with them, or to bring forth their feelings, attitudes, opinions and ideas regarding what actually is happening in some existing situation. Usually they have been unable, on any prior occasion, to communicate their ideas directly through organizational channels.

The person who organizes and leads the meeting is acting in a catalytic way. He is inserting a procedure into the situation that is facilitating in the sense that it helps the situation to develop toward resolution. In the following description, the meeting leader gives an assignment to each of the groups—say, to a top level group and a middle management group. He does not give directions as to what specifically should be discussed, but he indicates a way to get started on a facilitative discussion.

Think of yourself as an individual with needs and goals. Also think as a person concerned about the total organization. What are the obstacles, "demotivators," poor procedures or policies, unclear goals, or poor attitudes that exist today? What different conditions, if any, would make the organization more effective and make life in the organization better? (Beckhard, 1967, 154).

Then each unit goes off and discusses this separately. Beckhard's instructions are sufficiently general to permit people to put into their discussion whatever it is that is specifically troubling them in their particular jobs and situations. Then the meeting leader, from there on, continues in his procedurally facilitative role by helping the two units collect their data, analyze their feelings and facts, evaluate and compare them, and generally make progress. A similar example of catalytic intervention with multiple membership groups is provided by Bennis (Bennis, 1970, 158-160). Sometimes this approach is called a confrontation meeting, but this is a misnomer, because it entails no confrontation of the sort correctly described by Argyris (Argyris, 1971) which will be discussed later. Rather, the proceedings have a "group suggestion box" quality.

At the organization level (Cell I), intervention by an "ombudsman," who is empowered to bypass ordinary channels when he problem-solves on behalf of people who are burdened with difficulties because of some mistake or lack of response on the part of his particular company or government department, is catalytic in character, particularly in its facilitative aspects (*Commerce Today,* 1972, 29; Foegen, 1972, 1972, 289-294).

At the level of society there are many endeavors that are essentially catalytic, as specified in Cell J. We wish it were possible to say they were being systematically implemented within comprehensive and coherent frameworks of development. But there are some that, considered individually, have become quite systematic by now. Taking a census every five or ten years, one which describes the state of the nation "as of" a given point in time and permits comparisons to be made across several decades, is one way of aiding citizens to review their situation, of aiding national leadership to formulate policy, and of aiding industries to see the contemporary shape of markets, population trends, and many other things. The census is a powerful force in society. So are opinion polls. These are becoming ever more significant in the eyes of the public. Unfortunately their uses are somewhat limited to political affairs, but there are many other points of application that are possible for polling mechanisms, ones that can have a catalytic effect in terms of how society sees itself conducting its affairs.

Confrontation

Let us now look along the next row, which deals with *confrontation* strategies. These represent quite different intervention styles from catalysis and very different from cathartic interventions. Confrontation has much more challenge in it. It's a much more active intrusion into the life experience of other people than could possibly be implied by a catalytic approach, and certainly much more than would be implied by a cathartic one.

There's another distinction here. As you move from catharsis and catalytic approaches into the next three, what you find is that, under the first two, there is no challenge of the *status quo* by the intervener. In other words, he accepts the definition of the problem, and the associated values and attitudes usually as these are given by the client, and then helps the client to adjust better to the *status quo.* Under a confrontation mode you frequently find a shifting across some kind of "gap"—the existence of this gap having been identified in the locus of the challenge that the intervener implies.

In different ways, each of the next three approaches is much more likely to cause people to challenge the *status quo* and to reject the existing situation as being less preferable than a stronger situation that could be designed to replace it. That's a very important shift in thinking—from simply aiding people to conform or adjust, to assisting people to redesign the situations in which they live and work.

First, we'll describe a confrontation type of intervention at the individual level (Cell K). This occurred in a multinational company where the New York president visited the subsidiary president and said to him, in effect—though it was a whole day in the doing—"Look, Henry, I want you to know that we're very unhappy with how your company is operating. As we look at it, in comparison with other companies in our worldwide group, your profit performance is far below the best, and we just don't see you taking the vigorous action necessary to solve your problems."

Henry *said*—that is, he didn't reply to the specifics of that statement: he couldn't hear them—"If you'll look at our 1949 figures and then look at our latest performance records relative to 1949 when I took over, you'll see that over the years we have made a dramatic shift for the better."

An so they went at it, this way and that, all day, and neither heard the other. From the New York Headquarters president's point of view, this was a company they would willingly sell, because they couldn't exert influence upon it. From the subsidiary president's point of view, a valiant effort over many years that had produced betterment was being disregarded. Now the confrontation was this.

The next day, one of us said to Henry, "My hearing is that two quite different *perspectives* are being employed to evaluate this company's performance.

The perspective of the New York president is a here-and-now perspective. He doesn't care what you did for him yesterday, he is asking, 'What are you doing for me today?' By comparison, your perspective is historical. You're saying, 'How much better we're doing now than yesterday and last year and five years ago.' So unless you two can get onto a common perspective and reason from there, I see very little possibility of any collaborative effort occurring." Well, they did eventually get onto that common perspective basis. Once both of them understood what the central issue was, and that they weren't just totally unresponsive to each other, then some very significant changes took place in the subsidiary company, ones which are continuing to have enlivening effects. That's a confrontation that has caused development to get underway. And the *status quo* has been radically changed from what it previously had been.

Gestalt approaches, several of which are engineered to dramatize an encounter between the participant and an absent person, between two or more imaginary people, or even to dramatize ambivalent feelings within the person's own personality, are confrontational in character, even though cathartic elements are present. Conflicts, contradictions, incongruencies, and so on, are focused by the situation as the intervener structures it—or directly through the intervener's own words—in such a way as to permit more insightful resolutions through the elimination of contradictions, rationalizations, etc. (Herman, 1972).

Now let's examine confrontation at the team level (Cell L). An example of this comes during a team-building session conducted by Argyris. During this team-building session, and for the last several hours, members had been insisting that the company has a soft, manipulative, ineffective philosophy. Yet they had not really pinned down examples but were just talking in terms of generalities. So he said, "It is difficult to deal with such an answer, namely that the whole company is at fault. Could you give a specific example?" Nobody could. He continued very directly, saying, "OK fellows, are you going to be soft on these issues? You speak of integrity and courage. Where is it? I cannot be of help, nor you for that matter, if all you do is accuse the company of being ineffective. You said you were ready to talk—OK, I'm taking you at your word." (Argyris, 1971, 84) He is confronting them with the discrepancies between what they can be specific about and the abstractions.

Confrontation at the intergroup level (Cell M) usually involves each in coming to terms with the other. This interaction is not in terms of discharge of emotional tensions—as in the example of union and management given earlier—but in terms of gaining a shared and realistic sense of what their relationship is.

Here is an example. This one involves the headquarters' Division of Manufacturing in a large company and its major plant, which is located thirty miles away. The Division is headed by a vice president. A general manager runs the plant. These two had gotten more and more out of phase with each other over the years until they had nearly reached total impasse. It was very difficult for anyone to see how their misunderstandings had originated and grown into crisis proportions.

Eventually it was arranged for the vice president of manufacturing, and eight or ten people who reported to him, and the plant's general manager and the twelve people who reported to him to get together to study their relationship. The task was for each group to describe what the relationship between headquarters and the plant would be like if it were really a good one. Thereafter, they were to describe what the relationship actually was, here and now. The vice president of manufacturing's group worked in one room and put on newsprint a description of what, from their viewpoint, an ideal relationship would be like. The plant manager's group did the same thing, but in another room. Then they came back together and put their newsprints on the wall so that it could be seen by all what both sides thought a sound relationship would be like. The descriptions were similar and this similarity gave a lot of encouragement. Differences were discussed and resolved.

The next step, working separately, was for each group to describe the relationship as it actually existed here and now. They did this, and brought back their newsprints. Now it seemed like the relationship being described, as viewed from the headquarters point of view, was "totally" different from the relationship being pictured from the plant point of view. These dramatic divergences stimulated confrontation between the two groups on the issue of what, in fact, did characterize their mutual relationship. For several days, with close management of this situation and the interaction maintained by the interventionist to avoid an uncontrolled explosion, they thrashed through many aspects until a more accurate picture of the present relationship emerged. Now it became possible for both groups to see the many deep problems that in fact existed. They then designed some strategies for improvement steps that could lead toward resolution.

There is a comprehensive description of confrontation at the organization (Cell N) level (Jaques, 1951). The project was one of the innovative applied behavioral science interventions of the early post-war period and took place within the Glacier Metal Company in England. Jaques describes how he and others on his research team continually confronted the organization with the character of its internal relationships and objective performance.

At the societal level are found a good many institutionalized as well as informal mechanisms through which problems are confronted. What these are is a function of the kind of society you are looking at. The two-party system provides way of confronting issues by challenging what's going on. When one party publicizes its point of view, the other side is confronted with the necessity of either accepting the point of view as expressed, or identifying flaws in it. This is not to imply that in *any* political system this is done particularly well. We are only suggesting that two-party mechanisms, as these link into and work through a nation's executive branch, legislatures and public media, constitute one important way of confronting the problems of society and getting them into definition so that actions can be taken in behalf of solving them. Furthermore, the spread of the union-management confrontation mechanism into government, school, university and professional settings has resulted in this mechanism of intervention taking on social dimensions. Beyond that the entire legal system provides mechanisms by which confrontation with redress of injustice is provided for.

Prescriptive

Now let's consider the *prescriptive* row. These are the most forceful types of intervention, ones which I rather doubt are widely practiced by training and development people. But they are widely applied by outside consultants in conjunction with managers in industry, commerce, and government. Higdon describes the prescriptive approach as used in various consulting firms such as McKinsey and Company; Arthur D. Little; Booz, Allen and Hamilton, and many others (Higdon, 1969). The basic procedure is that management asks an expert in, and he and his associates study the situation and provide a recommended solution. The "mainstream" consultant is not working with emotions in a cathartic sense. He is not working catalytically. He is not confronting. He is telling. His recommendations would be directions, if he had the authority of rank. But he is certainly prescribing, and these prescriptions sometimes are very complete and fundamental. Often they involve changing an organization's structure, or getting out of one product line and into another, or applying a more efficient theory of business. Many times they involve firing or laying off people, and so they can have impactful consequences on the development of an organization. Sometimes the prescription is rejected out of hand. Sometimes, when taken, it results in a healthful bracing up of part or all of the organization. There have been numerous instances, however, of consulting prescriptions becoming very frustrating to the organization in terms of the difficulties and side effects left in their wake. These include lowered morale, people leaving because they no longer can give their commitment, and so on.

Here's a description of prescriptive strategy at the individual level (Cell P). It is where a consultant is trying to hold up a mirror in front of a manager to help him see what he is like, and then to prescribe, in concrete and operational terms, what he'd better do. The client is a plant manager who has trouble with his chief accountant, who is a rather "cold and formal" individual. To obtain better results than he was presently getting from this man, the plant manager—a genial fatherly person who likes to develop warm personal relations with his subordinates—was advised to take a forceful, direct, impersonal approach with him. This, the consultant predicted, would resonate much better with the accountant's psyche than the manager's more typical approach had been doing. On the matter of delayed reports the manager was to say the following, "I want your report on my desk at nine o'clock Friday morning, complete in every detail, and no ifs, ands, or buts about it." Having delivered that ultimatum, he was to turn around and leave. The plant manager did just that, although, being the kind of person he was, it was hard for him to do. The new approach brought striking results. The report came in on schedule and it was one of the finest the plant manager had ever received (Flory, 1965, 158-159). The client had been told specifically how he should act and he followed it through in strict accordance with the consultant's plan. In this case it produced effective results. Incidentally, the developing area of "behavior modification " (Krumboltz, 1965) is a training strategy that has prescriptive qualities.

An example of a prescriptive intervention at the group level (Cell Q) is offered by Cohen and Smith. They think this kind of intervention is most suitable toward the end of a group experience. At that time the total group is divided into subgroups of four or five members who are given the following instructions.

> . . . In each subgroup one person will leave the room for ten minutes. During that time the remaining members will first diagnose this person's typical style of interacting with others, and secondly try to pinpoint definite, specific, helpful suggestions as to how he might be helped to engage in atypical but productive behavior both for himself and the group. I must stress the terms 'definite' and 'specific.' Don't make abstract generalizations like 'you're too much of an introvert, so try being an extrovert for a while.' Instead, give him definite and specific prescriptions to carry out that are generally atypical but productive. Thus, one person might be told to express anger toward the group more directly and verbally instead of remaining quiet. The process continues until everyone has been given a 'behavioral prescription.' We will all meet back here in 'X' minutes to see what sort of changes have occurred. (Cohen & Smith, 1972, 103)

Robert's Rules of Order are prescriptive rules for conduct at the group or team level [Robert (1876), 1970]. They tell the leader how to operate meeting procedures. This rather mechanical set of criteria, if followed, prescribes the process parameters of the meeting, provides for expressions of differences, and offers a voting mechanism for resolution.

The third party arbiter is used at the intergroup level to provide for the resolution of differences, and to speed thinking toward further progress (Cell R). Typically, it operates in the following way. Two groups—say, management and a union—reach an impasse. Both agree to submit the disagreement to binding arbitration. The arbitrator, characteristically a disinterested outsider, hears evi-

dence or otherwise studies the case and renders his decision. This usually takes
the form of a prescription which both sides in the dispute are obligated to take
(Linke, 1968, 158-560; Lazarus *et al,* 1965).

Prescriptive approaches at the organization level are shown in Cell S. One
is vividly described in a case study from *Fortune.* Top management of Philco
had engaged an outside firm to study the organization and to propose needed
changes. Here's how a crucial meeting was described.

James M. Skinner, Jr., president of Philco Corp., (arrived) . . . for a momen-
tous meeting that had been six months in the making. Waiting for Skinner in
suite 1808 were nine somewhat apprehensive men from Arthur D. Little, Inc.,
the technical consulting firm of Cambridge, Massachusetts.

. . . Donham spoke first, outlining in general terms what A.D.L. hoped to
accomplish with its reorganization plan. What he was proposing, in brief, was a
massive reorganization of Philco's marketing setup, which would: make the job
of marketing all of Philco's consumer products the responsibility of one division;
fix profit responsibilities at precise points in the company; get day-to-day pressures off the backs of men who should be doing long-range planning; and provide
much closer support for Philco's independent distributors and dealers. (Thompson, 1959, 113-114).

Levinson, operating out of a psychoanalytic tradition, has described his
model of organization diagnosis in step-by-step terms. The approach he depicts
is prescriptive in character, as demonstrated in the following excerpt which gives
a few of the diagnostician's recommendations regarding the improvement of
personnel practices at "Claypool Furniture and Appliances."

The recommendations to be made, following the logic expressed in the
last discussion, are as follows:

Personnel Practices The company should establish descriptions and standards and objectives for all positions. It should develop orientation and training
programs to properly prepare people for their jobs and provide appraisal devices
by which personnel and their superiors can assess progress and training needs.
Positions and training in supervision and management are to be included in this
process. A procedure for identifying prospective managerial talent should be
evolved. The representative council should be abolished, and it should be replaced by employee task forces appointed to solve specific intraorganizational
problems. Such groups, to include stock personnel, would end the isolation of
the stock people and contribute to organizational identification and group co-
hesion.

A continuous and open evaluation of the wage and salary structure below
the managerial levels should be undertaken, with the intention of creating and
maintaining an equitable and competitive salary structure. . . . (Levinson, 1972,
491).

The Hoover Commission was an effort to use prescriptive techniques of diagnosis and development at the societal level. Ex-president Herbert Hoover and other members of the commission comprised a prestigious group. The presumption was that the voice of their authority behind recommendations would be sufficient, along with a responsive incumbent President, to bring about the recommended reformations in terms of restructuring the design and operations of the executive branch of the government.

The usual procedure, applied on all levels of government in the United States, is to set up a formal inquiry into existing conditions, in the hope of bringing forth concrete recommendations with a fair chance of adoption. Inquiries of this type on the federal level include the President's Committee on Administrative Management with Louis Brownlow as chairman (reporting in 1937) and the (first) Commission on Organization of the Executive Branch headed by former president Herbert Hoover (reporting in 1949). (Wilson, 1968, 632)

Principles, Theories, and Models

The first row of the matrix identifies diagnostic and developmental efforts which focus upon aiding people to acquire insights derived from principles, theories, or models. The assumption is that deficiencies of behavior or performance can be resolved best when people responsible for results use relevant principles, theories, or models in terms of which they themselves can test alternatives, decide upon and take action, and predict consequences. It is an approach which emphasizes intervention by concepts and ideas rather than by people.

With regard to Cell U, the particular significance to an individual of theory, principles, and models is that they are capable of providing a map of valid performance against which actual behavior and actual performance can be contrasted. When gaps exist between theory specifications for sound conduct and actual behavior, then change can be introduced which reduces the gap by increasing the congruence between the two. In this sense—and also, importantly, in the sense of removing self-deception—systematic concepts involving theories, principles, or models constitute a "theory mirror" which has the unique power of enabling people to see themselves, their present situations or future potential more clearly than if reliance is on subjective notions that something feels "right," "natural," or "okay," or simply that others "approve" it. Here are some examples:

Transactional Analysis is a conceptual formulation which provides a mirror into which people can look as a way of seeing themselves. Training designs have been created which enable participants to identify "Parent," "Child," and "Adult" oriented behavior both directly and with the benefit of colleague feedback and to study and practice ways of shifting toward more adult-like behavior (Blansfield, 1972, 149-154).

Also at the individual level, there is the Kepner-Tregoe system which provides managers with a model through which to design an analysis of any given problem and evaluate the quality of decisions they make. The objective is to reduce impluse, spontaneity and reliance on past practice and to shift to a rationality basis for problem analysis and decision making (Kepner & Tregoe, 1965).

There are a variety of theories, principles or models regarding individual behavior, some of which are accompanied by intervention strategies calculated to make the models functionally useful in concrete situations. Some of the more widely known include Theories X and Y (McGregor, 1960), Grid® formulations (Blake & Mouton, 1964, 1968, 1970; Mouton & Blake, 1971), and Systems 1 through 4 (Likert, 1967). However, the approach described by Likert does not involve man-to-man feedback on actual performance. Thus provisions are unavailable for penetrating and correcting self-deception.

Examples of theory orientation at the individual level include four Grids: Managerial, Sales, Customer, and Marriage; each of which describes several alternative models—9,9, 9,1, 1,9, 5,5, and 1,1—as well as mixed, dominant and backup theories. Once a person has learned the various theories, they can be used to diagnose his own behavior. In addition, he can select any theory as a model to change toward, but the most likely endorsed one is 9,9. He can then study and practice ways of increasing the congruence between his actual behavior and the model (Blake & Mouton, 1968, 34-66).

Some approaches to team building (Cell V) use principles, theories and models as the basis for diagnosing and feedback and for implementing development activities. Central issues, which, for the top team of a large chemical plant, demonstrated the gap between a diagnosis of their present ways of functioning and a model of what they considered ideal, are shown in Figure 2. This actual/ ideal comparative diagnosis was used for designing strategies of change to be implemented within the next four months (Blake & Mouton, 1968, 120-157).

Theory, prinicple and models also have proved useful in strengthening intergroup relations (Cell W). Phase 3 of Grid Organization Development, for example, begins with two groups convening for the purpose of describing what would be an ideal model for their particular relationship. This ideal model is itself based on theories of intergroup conflict and cooperation (Blake & Mouton, 1964; Blake, Shepard & Mouton, 1964). It culminates with an *in situ* design which spells out the properties of a sound and effective relationship in a particular, concrete setting. The modeling stage is followed by implementation strategies for converting "what is" to "what should be." An example of the properties of an ideal management-union relationship as described by one company is shown in Figures 3 and 4.

The development of an Ideal Strategic Corporate Model in Phase 4 of Grid Organization Development is an example of the use of models at the organization level (Cell X). Phase 4 enables a top group, particularly, to isolate itself from the *status quo* long enough to design what would be an "ideal" company, given

Actual	Ideal
Persons only do what is expected of them. Each man runs his own shop. The boss calls the shots.	Synergism is exploited, issues are talked through, and solutions and decisions based on facts are fully thrashed through to understanding and agreement.
Plans come down from the boss without opportunity to review, evaluate, or recommend changes by those who implement them.	Plans based on analysis of facts permit real issues to be treated soundly; plans are produced jointly by those who should be involved; individual responsibilities are clear.
Traditional ways of doing things are rarely questioned; they represent the tried and true operating standards.	Elements of culture are continually evaluated in the light of requirements for peak performance and, if necessary, they are modified or replaced through thoughtful discussions and agreement among team members.
Results are what count, no matter how achieved.	Team members are fully committed to excellence, results are achieved because members are motivated to exceed.

Figure 2 Actual vs. ideal top team culture in a chemical plant. Copyright © Scientific Methods, Inc., 1972. Not to be reproduced without permission.

The Management Would

Maintain open communications with the union in the following areas:
    Economics of industry and company
    Goals and objectives of company
    Long range company plans
    How company profits handled and distributed
    Problems facing company
    Growth opportunities—company and individual
    Security and development of employees
    Employee induction and orientation—where person fits in total scheme of
        things
Participate in prebargaining discussions to:
Identify and clarify current economic climate
    Identify and understand company's competitive position
    Assess and evaluate indexes for productivity
    Identify and agree upon appropriate and objective cost of living standards

(Figure 3 continued)

The Management Would (continued)

Participate in prebargaining discussions to:
  Identify and understand employee attitudes and concerns
  Assess strengths and weaknesses of present contract
  Identify possible obstacles and barriers that could arise during negotiations
Adopt bargaining strategy to:
  Develop frame of reference for agenda
  Explore problem areas jointly
  Explore opportunity areas
Have more joint problem solving—e.g., on:
  Evaluating impact on employees from operational changes
  Work simplification
  Benefits and pension programs
  Techniques of training
  Job safety
Handle complaints and grievances as follows:
  First line supervisors would discharge responsibility for resolving complaints
    and grievances and act with dispatch
  Participate in continuing joint efforts leading to clear interpretation and uni-
    form application of contract clauses at working level
  Maintain open door policy—union executives have free access to management
    executives and vice versa
  Establish and maintain open, upper level labor-management dialogue—ongoing
    critique
  Endeavor to understand problem confronting union officers within their frame
    of reference in their relationship with membership.

The Union Would

Develop comprehensive understanding of specific nature of the business and concern for it
Understand and consider nature of competition as it relates to company perfor-
  mance and needs for change
Develop understanding of relationships of productivity to wages and benefits
Because of peculiar nature of industry, understand long range impact on both
  company and employees from work stoppages
Recognize implications of taking fixed positions in approaching problems—win-
  lose trap
Recognize harm in intragroup (within union) conflict resulting in company and
  employee backlash
Subdue personal interests in favor of overall company and union objectives
Accept responsibility to communicate facts to employees without prejudice.

Figure 3   What a sound union-management relationship would be as described
by management. Source: Blake, R. R. & Mouton, J. S. *Corporate excellence
through grid organization development: A systems approach.* Houston: Gulf
Publishing, 1968, 181-182. Not to be reproduced without permission.

The Management Would

Exercise authority on complaints, grievances, questions, decisions needed, etc.,
    without needless delay, particularly first level managers
Adopt uniform education program for all supervisors, vertical and horizontal, on
    understanding, interpreting, and applying the contract
Interpret the contract in an honest and aboveboard way
Consult employees on changes in working schedules, shifts, transfers, location, etc.
Apply a system of seniority and rotation without favoritism, e.g., assigned over-
    time, easy jobs, time off, vacations, best working schedules, etc.
Rate employees' performance on a uniform, systematic, and fair basis and with
    employees told where they stand
Coordinate and communicate effectively between department supervisors to pre-
    vent needless work by employees and cut down costs and wasted effort.

The Union Would

Represent all employees fairly
Communicate problems, complaints, contract infractions to management
Have access to top management without runaround at lower levels
Be concerned with costs and amount of production
Insure employee has correct rating for skills he has and that he is paid for job he
    does, not the classification he has.
(Union had insufficient time remaining to complete this activity.)

Figure 4   What a sound union-management relationship would be as described
by the union. Source: Blake, R. R. & Mouton, J. S. *Corporate excellence
through grid organization development: A systems approach.* Houston: Gulf
Publishing, 1968, 183. Not to be reproduced without permission.

its realistic access to financial resources. Issues considered include, "What should
be the key financial objectives that the company should strive after?" "What
should be the nature of the company's business, and the nature of its markets?"
"What should its structure be?" "What policies should it operate under?" Finally,
"What are development requirements for getting from where it is to where it
would go if it were to approach the ideal model?" An example of the change in
thinking about financial objectives at the corporate level during Phase 4 is shown
in Figure 5.

The use of principles, models and theories also can be seen at the level of
society (Cell Y). The Magna Charta is a well-known historical example. The U.S.
Constitution describes the kind of behavior, freedom and control which American society was expected to be modeled after. Over nearly two centuries, several
constitutional amendments have updated the model in the light of contemporary
perspectives. Legislative and executive actions are always being tested against
the Constitution.

From	To
Maintain or increase market share while living within a budget.	Optimal 30, minimum 20 percent pretax return on assest employed with an unlimited time horizon.
Dollar profit should improve and not fall behind last year. Return on investment computed and discussed on an after-the-fact calculation which exerted little or no influence on operational decision making.	Each business should have a specified profit improvement factor to be calculated on a business-by-business basis. The objective should be an earnings per share level which would within five years justify a price-earnings ratio of 20 to one or better.
	Share of market objectives should be established within the framework of return on assets and cash generation objectives.

Figure 5   Genuine concern with the organization's earning capacity results from designing an ideal strategic model. Source: Blake, R. R. & Mouton, J. S. *Corporate excellence through grid organization development: A systems approach.* Houston: Gulf Publishing, 1968, 233. Not to be reproduced without permission.

Lilienthal's work in Iran can be viewed as intervention at the societal level to bring about change through assisting the eventual users to design models of "what should be" as the basis of specific implementation plans. Lilienthal is a notable industrial statesman who led first the Tennessee Valley Authority and then the U.S. Atomic Energy Commission in their beginning years. He has described his later consulting work (Lilienthal, 1969) when, with his own and his colleagues' vast knowledge of hydro-electric engineering, community rehabilitation, and agri-business, they helped the Iranian government design a model for water and electric-power resources for the future of its then undeveloped Khuzestan province. That model is being systematically implemented through the building of dams, power irrigation systems, and so on, as well as infrastructure developments such as agricultural advisory programs, health and educational facilities, etc. This is an example of how a consultant can work, not in a prescriptive mode, but as a skillful teacher in aiding people to learn to design and implement complex models. Lilienthal thus has enabled a vast development to occur, one that otherwise would have been piecemeal, suboptimizing and possibly impractical.

Skinner's recent writings about society are derived from theory and principles and also rest on a model concept (Skinner, 1971).

Summary and Conclusions

The D/D Matrix provides a way of encompassing a wide range of activities now underway for strengthening human performance through diagnosis and development. Illustrations of each approach have been provided without trying to be inclusive.

Using this matrix, anyone who wishes to do so can identify the assumptions underlying his own work, and evaluate their probable consequences for increasing the effectiveness of individuals, groups, groups in relationships with one another, organizations, and society. The acceptant approach of emotional barrier-reduction and the catalytic approach of helping people to make progress in dealing with given situations are most likely to aid individuals and groups to do a better job within the existing *status quo*.

Confrontation and prescription are useful in a "fixed" or "frozen" situation. They provide alternatives to those currently present in the *status quo*. Both rely heavily on outside expertise.

The history of society and its capacity to identify and grapple with complex and interrelated problems of the physical environment, new technologies, and community development is significantly linked with the production and use of principles, theories and models for understanding, predicting—and, therefore, managing—natural and human environments. Approaches to diagnosis and development which rely on the use of principles, theories, and models for understanding emotional, intellectual and operational events provide the most powerful and impactful approach to the implementation of planned change.

It is highly unlikely that any single approach will be based solely on one intervention mode. Rather, the likelihood is that several intervention modes will be included, with one of them being central or dominant. For example, the Dickson-Roethlisberger counseling program appears to have been a very "pure" individual-cathartic approach, with minor reliance on counseling as catalytic intervention. Process consultation, as depicted by Schein, relies heavily upon catalytic intervention, with some use of acceptant interventions and very infrequent use of the confrontation mode, Schein makes practically no use of the prescriptive mode, and makes theory interventions only after the fact.

The intervening in T Groups is mainly catalytic, with secondary reliance on the cathartic mode. "Encounter" relies very heavily on catharsis. Grid OD concentrates on theory, principles and models; but it also provides at key points for confrontation, catalytic intervention, and cathartic release. Other approaches can be analyzed in a similar manner.

No one can say, in an abstract sense and without regard to a particular situation, that there is "one best way." While principles, theories, and models constitute the strongest approach, they may lack feasibility until emotional blockages have been reduced through cathartic intervention. Or, perhaps, opening up the possibilities of systematic OD may take little more than a timely catalytic intervention which enables managers to see possibilities not previously envisaged. Statements of a similar character can be made with regard to confrontation and prescription.

In the final analysis, however, acceptant, catalysis, confrontation or prescription constitute means to an end, rather than ends in themselves. The ultimate goal is that people become capable of effective living through utilizing principles, theories and models as the basis of human enrichment.

References*

Argyris, C. *Organization and innovation.* Homewood, Ill.: R. D. Irwin, 1965. *L*

Argyris, C. *Intervention theory and Method.* Reading, Mass.: Addison-Wesley, 1970. *L*

Argyris, C. *Management and organization development.* New York: McGraw-Hill, 1971. *L*

Beckhard, R. The confrontation meeting. *Harvard Business Review,* March-April, 1967, 149-155. *H*

Bennis, W. G. Organization development: What it is and what it isn't. In D. R. Hampton (Comp.) *Behavioral concepts in management* (second edition). Encino, Calif.: Dickinson, 1972. Pp. 154-163. *H*

Blake, R. R. & Mouton, J. S. *The managerial grid: Key orientations for achieving production through people.* Houston: Gulf Publishing, 1964. *U*

Blake, R. R., Shepard, H. A. & Mouton, J. S. *Managing intergroup conflict in industry.* Houston: Gulf Publishing, 1964. *W*

Blake, R. R., Sloma, R. L. & Mouton, J. S. The union-management intergroup laboratory: Strategy for resolving intergroup conflict. *Journal of Applied Behavioral Science,* 1965, *1,* 1, 25-57. *C*

Blake, R. R. & Mouton, J. S. *Corporate excellence through grid organization development: A systems approach.* Houston: Gulf Publishing, 1968. *U, V, W, X*

Blake, R. R. & Mouton, J. S. *The grid for sales excellence: Benchmarks for effective salesmanship.* New York: McGraw-Hill, 1970. *U*

Blake, R. R. & Mouton, J. S. *How to assess the strengths and weaknesses of a business enterprise.* Austin, Tex.: Scientific Methods, Inc., 1972, 6 vols. *X*

Blake, R. R. & Mouton, J. S. *Journal of an OD man,* Forthcoming, 1973. *D, I*

Blansfield, M. G. Transactional analysis as a training intervention. In W. G. Dyer

---

*Italic letter following the reference indicates the Matrix Cell discussed.

(Ed.), *Modern theory and method in group training.* New York: Van Nostrand Reinhold, 1972. Pp. 149-154. *U, V*

Cohen, A. M. & Smith, R. D. The critical-incident approach to leadership in training groups. In W. G. Dyer (Ed.), *Modern theory and method in group training.* New York: Van Nostrand Reinhold, 1972. Pp. 84-196. *Q*

Commerce Today, 2, April 3, 1972, 29. *I*

Dickson, W. J. & Roethlisberger, F. R. *Counseling in an organization: A sequel to the Hawthorne researches.* Boston: Division of Research. Graduate School of Business Administration, Harvard University, 1966. *A*

Flory, C. D. (Ed.) *Managers for tomorrow.* New York: The New American Library of World Literature, 1965. *P*

Foegen, J. H. Ombudsman as complement to the grievance procedure. *Labor Law Journal,* May 1972, *23,* 289-294. *I*

Fordyce, J. J. & Weil, R. *Managing with people: A manager's handbook of organization development methods.* Reading, Mass.: Addison-Wesley, 1971. *F*

Gibb, J. R. TORI theory: Consultantless team building. *Journal of Contemporary Business,* 1972, *1,* 3, 33-41. *B*

Gould, M. I. Counseling for self-development. *Personnel Journal,* 1970, *49,* 3, 226-234. *F*

Herman, S. M. A. Gestalt orientation to organization development. In W. Burke (Ed.) *Contemporary organization development: Approaches and interventions.* Washington, D. C.: NTL Institute for Applied Behavioral Science, 1972. *K*

Higdon, H. *The business healers.* New York: Random House, 1969. *S*

Humble, J. W. *Improving business results.* Maidenhead, Berks.: McGraw-Hill, 1967. *G*

Jaques, E. *The changing culture of a factory.* London: Tavistock, 1951. *N*

Kepner, C. H. & Tregoe, B. B. *The rational manager.* New York: McGraw-Hill, 1965. *U*

Krumboltz, J. D. (Ed.) *Revolution in counseling: Implications of behavioral science.* Boston: Houghton Mifflin, 1965. *P*

Lazarus, E. *et al. Resolving business disputes: The potential of commercial arbitration.* New York: American Management Association, 1965. *R*

Levinson, H., with Molinari, J. & Spohn, A. G. *Organizational diagnosis.* Cambridge, Mass.: Harvard University Press, 1972. *S*

Likert, R. *New patterns of management.* New York: McGraw-Hill, 1961. *G*

Likert, R. *The human organization, its management and value.* New York: McGraw-Hill, 1967. *U*

Lilienthal, D. E. *The journals of David E. Lilienthal.* Vol. IV. *The road to change, 1955-1959.* New York: Harper & Row, 1969. *Y*

Linke, W. R. The complexities of labor relations law. In R. F. Moore (Ed.), *Law for executives.* New York: American Management Association, 1968. *R*

McGregor, D. *The human side of enterprise.* New York: McGraw-Hill, 1960. *U*

Mouton, J. S. & Blake, R. R. *The marriage grid.* New York: McGraw-Hill, 1971. *U*

Robert, H. M. *Robert's rules of order* (newly revised). Glenview, Ill.: Scott, Foresman, 1970. First published, 1876. *Q*

Schein, E. H. *Process consultation: Its role in organization development.* Reading, Mass.: Addison-Wesley, 1969. *G*

Skinner, B. F. *Beyond freedom and dignity.* New York: Knopf, 1971. *Y*

Thompson, E. T. The upheaval at Philco. *Fortune,* February 1959, 113-116+. *S*

Watson, G. Nonverbal activities—why? when? how? In W. G. Dyer (Ed.), *Modern theory and method in group training.* New York: Van Nostrand Reinhold, 1972, Pp. 155-172. *A*

Willson, F. M. G. Government departments. *Encyclopaedia Britannica.* Vol. 10. Chicago: Encyclopaedia Britannica, Inc., 1968. *T*

ORGANIZATION DEVELOPMENT
An Applied Philosophy For Managers of Public Enterprise*

Sameul A. Culbert and Jerome Reisel†

As this decade commences it is already quite apparent that both public and private enterprise will have to deal with the challenges of survival, consolidation, and growth in ways that differ markedly from those that prevailed as recently as ten years ago.[2] The ranks of key executives who seek to manage an organization sheerly as a technical system become thinner with each passing year. The once comfortable and comforting image of the world as mechanism, the image of the world as operating in terms of discoverable and controllable cause-effect relationships, is clearly outmoded and in the process of being replaced. The contemporary manager is coming to see the world as one in which variability, uncertainty, and probabilism are the predominant dimensions.[3] Though mechanistic concepts continue to have utility, these are no longer seen as central and totally explanatory: further, the applicability of these concepts to the management of human resources is at best negligible.

What will characterize the top-level manager of the 1970's will be a redefinition of role and function; a redefinition that will find him responsible for the direction of an organization where his skill in dealing with human systems is seen as equally relevant to his skill in dealing with technical systems. Thus, he will be an integrator of the human and the technical. Where his predecessor

*Reprinted from *Public Administration Review,* Vol. 31, No. 2 (March/April 1971), pp. 159-169.
†NTL Institute for Applied Behavioral Science.[1]

was an expert in reacting for purposes of stability, the executive of the '70's will be an expert in proaction, in the seeking out of innovative processes for purposes of adapting to change or for initiating it. Insofar as the management of enterprises are concerned, be they public or private, this means that the image of the organization as a closed system with fixed boundaries, structures, and functions is, to all intents and purposes, quite dead. Therefore, the viability of both managers as well as their enterprises will henceforth be dependent on open-system approaches, approaches in which continued though varying interchange with a variety of environments, internal as well as external, will have to be anticipated, planned for, and confronted.

Organization development (OD) can be defined as a process of planned . change. Used correctly by managers, it is an approach that enables an enterprise to adapt effectively to the demands of internal and external reality. An enterprise geared to the requirements of reality is likely to be appropriately responsive, flexible, and innovative, thereby enhancing its viability. Viability, quite obviously, is the predominant concern of any enterprise. OD is therefore an approach keyed to the basic responsibility of managerial practice for the '70's; preserving the viability of the enterprise. OD, however, is relevant in terms of the times as well as the enterprise. By means of its basic concern with change it links the manager and the enterprise with the probabilistic world view. Not only is it new, contemporary, and pertinent, but at this point in the 20th century it is also futuristic.

It is our purpose here to establish the relevance of OD as an applied philosophy for the manager of public enterprise. We should like to acknowledge that while OD in use is apt to differ according to the setting in which it is applied, OD in principle is constant no matter where employed. To reiterate, OD is an approach for planning change in order to maintain the viability of an enterprise.[4] How OD is used is always situationally determined.

The first part of this presentation will deal with the identifying characteristics of OD and with the relevance of these for managers. Examples will be used to illustrate the kinds of situations in which OD interviews can be effective for coping with the conditions cited. A second section will be devoted to a demonstration of how OD works in practice. In this latter section we shall select a prototypical case of OD processes in its initial applications in a public enterprise.

Characteristics and Relevance

OD, as a particular instance of applied behavioral science, addresses itself to a certain range of organizational issues, and it brings to these issues a characteristic point of view. To establish the relevance of OD as a managerial approach, some of the characteristics that define this method will be discussed and amplified by examples illustrating problems OD is designed to handle. Before proceeding, however, it is important to note that the term, organization development, by its very nature denotes a *process*.[5] One does not, therefore, apply OD to an enterprise; rather one engages in OD, involves himself in OD, participates in an OD process. As we have said earlier, while the process of OD may vary from one enterprise to another, its basic principles remain constant.[6] It is to these that we now turn.

1. OD Focuses on the Internal Environment of an Organization

For present purposes the internal environment of an organization is defined as that aspect of an enterprise that is some function of its human components and the aggregate interactions that take place between them. OD takes these elements as being central to its interest. This should not be taken to mean that a process of OD ignores issues that involve the external realities faced by an organization. It means, quite simply, that the OD process begins with a focus on the internal environment and will maintain that focus until circumstances indicate it would be appropriate to do otherwise.

At its beginning point OD looks at the balance that an organization maintains between its needs for survival, consolidation, and growth and similar needs among the human beings who are part of it. It does this with a particular point of view: that most organizations have sufficient latitude in functioning to meet human needs for growth and expression while simultaneously realizing its own needs for productivity and invention. In fact, OD makes the point (yet to be exploded as mere idealism) that meeting these needs can be mutually facilitating. In addressing itself to the organization's internal environment, OD seeks to establish the degree to which personnel perceive a convergence of personal and organizational objectives over the long run. To the extent that management sees such a convergence as desirable and attainable, OD processes can be accelerative and facilitating. Conversely, management might eschew such a convergence on the grounds that it is utopian and chimerical. Under such circumstances, the utilization of OD processes of the kind referred to here will be a contradiction in terms.

Example:[7] The enterprise was among its country's most successful. Its board of governors had evolved a method of operation that insured success. Innovation, long hours, and hard-driving competition characterized middle-managerial levels. Routine decision making, concerned with shaping new operations to fit established procedures, characterized the duties of the senior managers. Although the middle managers were constantly irritated by senior managers whose "stabilizing" actions amended their projects, they were also envious of these higher managerial positions and competed vigorously to be promoted.

Board members were privately amused at this condition, because it was the key to their enterprise's success. In fact they constantly were finding ways to make the senior roles more attractive: retirement benefits, salary increases, free time, company cars, etc. Since senior managers generally held their positions until retirement, the enterprise was under constant internal pressure to expand, thereby, creating more senior positions.

Example: It took a while before someone recognized that the resignations for "personal reasons" of four senior managers over a two-month period not only represented a 400 per cent rise in attrition at that level, but broke a precedent since "no one ever resigns," they merely retire. Unconcerned about losing senior personnel, top management wondered about the effect this would have on motivation at middle levels.

2. OD Employs a Systems Approach to Organizations

OD views an enterprise as a network of interacting systems. Thus, the individual, the work group, or a large organizational segment are never seen solely as entities isolated and independent from one another or the total system that the enterprise as a whole represents. Further, OD does not neglect to consider the enterprise as part of an even broader system: the culture. Focus on the internal environment therefore represents a concern for bringing about more effective integration of human resource systems in the enterprise.

Example: The clients of a social service institution were complaining that the services offered them were no longer pertinent to their needs. They were demanding a voice in the planning. Similarly, the workers having closest contact with these clients were complaining to management that only about 50 per cent of the services they had to offer, on behalf of the institution, were relevant. Management, however, didn't see things this way. Their charter, from a political body, specified exactly what they were supposed to offer and their job was "to administer the institution," not to try to change the minds of legislators.

3. The Entry Point for OD Is Each Person

OD is workable only when those involved are interested in viewing the human dimensions of their jobs. A manager committing his organization to an OD process makes two major assumptions: (1) an important aspect of the job is the challenge it presents to expand personally in ways which are enriching to all aspects of one's life; and (2) work associates have an important part to play in providing learnings that facilitate personal and professional development.

To assert, then, that the entry point for OD is each person is to acknowledge the interconnection between one's life at work and one's life more generally.

Care should be taken, however, not to read "each person" to mean that the person is viewed as an isolated entity in the OD approach. OD uses the individual as the basic organizational unit for the type of change and growth that will ramify eventually into activities that will enable the enterprise to fulfill its specific mission.

Starting with *each* person, the OD process examines the individual in a variety of ways. He is looked at in terms of his task responsibilities and the factors facilitating or inhibiting the fulfillment of these. The individual provides the necessary data for constructing an image of the organization through his eyes. The information provided by the individual is vital to the design of relevant OD programs. Thus such matters as personal and task needs are brought into view; interrelations of these with corresponding ones among his peers, superiors, and subordinates are identified; the intermix of power, responsibility, and communication systems with their connection to the broader issues of interprise strategy and programs—all of these begin with the recognition of the individual as the core unit.

Although all dimensions of organization life can be examined using the person as the OD working unit, quite frequently OD programs accomplish their objectives by focusing on particular systems in the enterprise where modifications will have the broadest impact. Thus, if those interviewed provide impressions that indicate a need for improving task-group productivity, OD intervenes in that sphere. There are times when the issue becomes identified as one of power conflict within or between work groups. Sometimes the issue is one of data flow (communication-system efficacy), and its relationships to climates of trust, openness, and risk taking within a group or the organization at large. Leadership style and its effectiveness may prove to be a key issue. The OD process might intervene to deal with problems on any of these levels. OD activity is flexible enough to deal with local issues without losing sight of the system, environmental, or human dimensions of any of its interventions.

Example: Most of the senior managers working with George, a member of the top-management group, made the same assumption: "the only way to get things done is to make an 'end-run' around George." George was in the unfortunate position of standing between production in the field and the technical specialists in the central office. The managers were either in the position of running around established procedures or being frustrated and confused by their transactions with George's office. While a more secure personality than George would have "flagged" this structural problem earlier, George was a case of being promoted beyond his competence and, at a personal level, was struggling to maintain his existence in the organization.

Example: The president of an enterprise, well known in financial circles for its rapid success, requested an OD consultation. He stated as his problem troubles caused him by noncollaboration among his top management group.

However, the beginning point for the consultation was not the managers, it was the president himself. Money no longer a prime motivation, the president mostly valued the freedom he had to make deals on his own. He demanded this freedom and it was given to him based on his reputation for always being right. Later he would tell his board of directors and get their rubber stamp approval and advise his top management group for their follow-up and execution.

4. OD Seeks To Build Strategy and Design Capabilities in the Enterprise

OD works essentially with the power-influence systems in an enterprise. It attempts to influence opinion leaders and thereby multiply its impact. This means that OD processes are involved initially and continually with the top and uppermost levels of management, although eventually all managerial segments can be involved in some measure. OD is not merely an occasion for identifying problems and working to solve them. Its role also is viewed as an opportunity to develop management's capabilities for generating strategic programs that maintain enterprise momentum in the face of new or unexpected challenges to its growth and renewal.

Looking for opportunities to increase the strategy and design capabilities is of constant interest to the OD consultant, particularly as he works with top-level management or with an organizationally based liaison person for OD work, often referred to as the "inside consultant." As the OD process proceeds, various problems are identified, programs for solving the problems are developed, and evaluation takes place. These problem-solving sequences provide an experience-based opportunity for managers to broaden their skills in developing human potential while solving problems related to the job. Thus, OD processes continue long after an outside consultant has left the scene. Indeed, one sign of successful OD consultation is that of a client acquiring many, if not all, of the strategy and design capabilities that initially were seen as belonging solely to the consultant.

For the most part, the OD process works to generate an expanding effect in the enterprise. As the managerial system, from the top downwards, increases its capabilities for developing problem-solving strategies and designs, there is an exponential result; managerial competency takes the form of systemwide effectiveness.

Example: The refinery was just completed. It had a much greater capacity than others already in operation and its production was counted on to play a big role in the country's economic expansion. Existing refineries were operating below projected capacity and their management seemed incapable of learning from the experiences of one another. In an attempt to improve this condition, the board of governors had initiated a system of rewards which placed each refinery's management in competition with the management of the other refineries. Placing its hopes on the new refinery, the board of governors recruited a high-quality staff from the smaller refineries. Although each recruit was expert in his field, these men had a history of not learning from one another and recently had been competing with one another.

5. OD Has the Future as Its Major Time Reference

OD methodology utilizes the zest managers exhibit when offered assistance in solving immediate problems to provide them, simultaneously, with the kind of perspective that will enable them to solve equally difficult problems, without consultant help, in the future. One might say that the meta-goals of all OD activity are learning from one's own experiences and learning how to learn from one's experiences. OD continually focuses the manager on the learning to be extracted from the problem and its solution. To this degree, OD is future oriented.

On another level, the future emphasis of OD takes the form of building long-term capabilities into the managerial structure while working with short-term, problem-solving technologies. The degree to which a manager can envision consequences in the future while at the same time meeting immediate demands is a particular orientation established in the OD process.

Finally, it can be said that OD is concerned with inculcating a proactive-adaptive stance in managerial resourses rather than simply reactive-curative posture. Pro-action has a definite future thrust inasmuch as it implies an initiating innovating set of activities.[8]

In summary then, the future time reference of OD is concerned with (1) preparing the manager to learn from the present so that future applications are available; (2) inculcating an assessment of long-term consequences both in managerial planning and programming, and (3) valuing a proactive-adaptive philosophy as a means of maintaining a managerial stance that moves on both a future as well as concurrent basis.

Example: The annual long-range planning meeting is, as usual a half-hour late in starting. All other meetings begin on time, but no one is ever in a hurry to begin the predictably frustrating process of trying to gain consensus about what will be needed five years from now. Invariably there is "flighty" behavior, talking about today's details, and a shallow last minute attempt to get something down for the board of directors. The same people who give this management group solid direction on other topics are embarrassingly ineffective during this meeting. Nothing is different this year and it's now safe to predict nothing will be different next year.

With some of the salient characteristics of the OD process outlined, and with examples presented to illustrate the conditions under which these might apply, we now turn to a presentation of what OD is like in action.

How OD Works

Although there are many different ways in which OD methods can be applied, all make use of a common sequence. The initial step is diagnosis; next there is a phase in which alternative action programs are explored and a course decided upon; then the action program is followed out; and, finally, there is an assessment of the steps taken. This leads to a second-level diagnosis, thereupon initiating a recycling procedure. This sequence applies irrespective of the organizational elements involved. Thus it would be employed if one was examining: (a) the total organization as it faced productivity issues; (b) a management team establishing criteria for wage and salary administration; (c) arbitration of conflicts stemming from personal differences between two top managers; or (d) career planning with an executive who had reservations about accepting a promotion because it entailed a geographical change, etc.

Typically there are three key roles in the OD process. People undertaking these roles combine with additional personnel to form a task force for approaching the issue of organization development.[9]

The first of these key roles belongs to the manager who takes the lead in noticing that there is a persisting problem, usually within his jurisdiction, that has either resisted permanent solution, or for which indigenous resources are unavailable. The manager's main responsibilities are to get the specific dilemma resolved and, in the process, upgrade the problem-solving capabilities of his work group. Since his main concern is with the immediate, his presence on the OD task force insures a high degree of face validity for each stage of the OD sequence. At the same time, the degree of his commitment to the longer-range aspects of the OD process will, in large measure, enhance the prospects of a favorable outcome.

A second important role in the OD task force is that of the "inside consultant." This role is taken by an individual having staff responsibility to the manager and possibly to others in the enterprise as well. Generally his major job requirements are to develop the organization's unused human potential and at the same time concern himself with upgrading of managerial capabilities. Cognizant of the specific problems evoking managerial concern, his responsibility is to bridge between the manager and the resources which seem needed to mobilize an OD task force. On a day-to-day basis, the inside consultant has a major role to play as an integrating-linking element between the manager and the other resources recruited for the project. Over the long run, he has a crucial part to play in insuring the kind of continuity that will enable gains to be maintained. This generally takes the form of continued utilization of the organizational resources developed in the process of solving organization problems.[10]

The third key role is that of the outside consultant. Usually this is a person who pools a professional OD expertise with the objectivity that comes from being free of daily organizational pressures. Consulting may be his primary occupation or, as is frequently the case, it is an activity he combines with his job as a university professor. The outside consultant has the vital responsibility to uncover information relevant to both the definition of the problem and the formulation of action alternatives. In addition, his task is to use the information acquired to help develop innovative problem-solving procedures. Parenthetically, the outside consultant often has an explicit commitment to transfer his understandings and his technical knowledge to the inside consultant. Such a commitment adds to the outside consultant's level of interest in his task. It also leads him to make inputs that clearly have longer-term reward value for the organization.

The outside consultant is usually an expert interviewer.[11] As he goes about acquiring necessary information, he is also interested in identifying the personal motivations that underlie what is being said. OD specialists are thus interested in pinpointing the amount of distortion in the data given them. In this way they can begin to envision how the organization uses data and what strategies might be required to reduce a distortive use of data in the problem-solving process. OD consultants are strongly committed to reality-based behavior and are looked upon, albeit sometimes reluctantly, as important check points in this regard.

Lastly, interviews provide opportunities for the outside consultants to identify the various systems in the enterprise that are pertinent to a particular problem focus. The understanding attained by the outside consultants often lead to broadened perspectives for the rest of the task force. Hence the process of diagnosis is not only important in gaining an accurate definition of the problem, but it also has the additional characteristic of serving as an "organizational mirror." This mirroring function generates a reflective attitude in other members of the task force when they must confront the image of their organization as seen by others outside of it.

The OD Process: An Illustrative Example

The following example, designed to give the reader a feel for the OD process in action, restricts itself essentially to the diagnostic phase in the OD sequence. We do not believe that this is a serious constraint inasmuch as our objective of demonstrating the nature of OD technology should be evident to the reader at the conclusion of the presentation.

Background

Some years prior to the initiation of OD consultation, a developing state had passed a land-reform law. Arable land had been made available to members of the poor lower class. The objective of this land-distribution law was to set in motion the development of a middle-class farmer community structure that could play a vital role in the country's social, economic, and political progress. The government established a number of agencies to administer and support the land-reform program. Some of the programs developed by these agencies were funded by foreign governments interested in the country's economic improvement.

The problems confronting each agency were multitudinous and complex. The great majority of the new landowners were illiterate and lacking in knowledge of modern farming technology. Roads and schools needed to be built, cooperatives capable of competing in open markets had to be formed, sanitation and public health programs had to be initiated, and local leadership capabilities had to be identified and utilized.

The OD project was initiated by the top manager of an agency centrally involved in community development when it became apparent to him that a key program, training for local leadership, was failing. The collapse of his agency's leadership program would seriously damage the credibility of other agency programs and could, in fact, jeopardize its chances for fulfilling its long-range mission. As a means of coping with this problem, OD consultation was sought.

Diagnosis

The first step in the OD process is diagnosis. Diagnosis is a process of collecting, arraying, and analyzing data in order to achieve an accurate definition of the organization's problem. It also provides the basis for developing programs to resolve the problem.

The diagnostic process begins with obtaining the manager's formulation of the problem. Part of his formulation generally deals with the resources he needs that are otherwise not available in his organization. The OD consultants (outside and inside working together) take the manager's statement as a working hypothesis in determining their mission. Their information-collecting activity begins by contacting others whom the manager identifies as concerned with the issue. As the interviewers proceed, they often identify information sources who might offer additional perspectives. They, too, must be interviewed for a complete picture of the issue. These varied sources provide a basis for discovering where conflicting opinions exist about what needs to be done.

In understanding that the OD consultants, whether inside or outside, will not be accepting his or anyone else's formulation of the problem as a matter of course, the manager's behavior often exemplifies a type of openness that is crucial for the inception of OD processes. The manager's openness is based on his need to obtain help in finding an accurate description of the critical issues facing his enterprise. The question for him becomes less a matter of being "right" than it is of instituting processes, via the consultants, designed to involve others in improvement actions. By involving others in the early planning and diagnostic procedures, he starts a process of strengthening their commitments to change.

The manager sought help because he felt that the leadership training aspect of his community development program was vital to its overall success. He reasoned that OD technologies would be of immediate assistance in upgrading his agency's leadership training activities. Contact with the outside consultants was established through a third person, a member of the agency staff, who would serve as the "inside consultant."

The outside OD consultants sought the manager's cooperation in determining which people would be useful sources for the information needed in doing a diagnosis. In agreeing to an initial data collection, the top manager was somewhat apprehensive. This was understandable, inasmuch as he was clear about what had to be done and the consultants' request for additional data seemed a needless delay to him. He wanted the consultants to upgrade the leadership training skills of the technical specialists assigned to this task.

Working together, both inside and outside consultants recognized that the manager was motivated by a desire for a quick solution to a problem that for him was self-evident. The pressures of his situation limited his concern for the longer-term consequences of a makeshift solution. The consultants were able to buy the time for a diagnostic study when the manager accepted the notion that an "effective" program rather than "any" program was what he wanted.

Included in the interviews and later to be included in decision making were those members of the manager's central staff who were most concerned with leadership development. This staff, together with the top manager, the inside consultant, and the outside consultants (a two-man team), met as the OD task force to plan an interview schedule designed to include all those whose points of view were seen as relevant to the task at hand.

Additional interviews were held with field personnel of the agency, farmers who were involved both in the agency's programs and programs of other agencies, and managers of other government groups doing work in rural community developments. Also, there were interviews with certain political officials who had viewpoints on the priorities attached to the development of these farming communities. In striving to understand each viewpoint and not having a viewpoint to sell, the interviews conducted by the OD consultants were useful not merely as sources of information but also as a means of building a more cooperative climate within the agency, and a friendlier attitude among those external to it. Those involved all seemed very eager to have their outlooks accurately represented in the client agency. This need became a prominent point in the eventual diagnosis.

Outside consultants recognize that once their diagnostic work is completed, the rest of the contract is renegotiable. Sometimes an OD consultation comes to a conclusion with the completion of the diagnosis. Frequently the diagnostic findings represent a picture different from that initially presented by the manager. Next steps might be indicated that are not of the kind management is desirous or willing to pursue; or it is possible that the diagnostic result is one that suggests programs that management is capable of covering with its own resources.

There is no such thing as an absolute diagnosis. Typically, an OD consultant will present his conclusions together with the data that led to those conclusions. Much as the OD consultant is reluctant to accept, on faith, formulations offered him, his method also requires that the task force not take him on faith. Moreover, in displaying the data that led to his formulations, misinterpretations can be identified and clarified.

The data-collection phase of the diagnostic process took eight days. Because a substantial amount of traveling was involved, late-night sessions were needed to discuss and sort out the information the interviewers had collected. As new leads to understanding emerged, the consultants would follow up on them. The key resources in this process were the initiating manager and the members of the OD task force.

Arraying and analyzing the data took an additional two days. The analysis was then presented to the task force for inspection. A general summary of the report is presented here in order to familiarize the reader interested in the nature of OD procedures.

The diagnostic survey uncovered a number of pressures which apparently were forcing this agency to take a less than optimum course with respect to leadership training. Each of these pressures were carefully identified in the report.

It appeared that leadership training was a hot item. Various agencies were involved in it and there was considerable competition among them. The countrywide result was a considerable amount of duplication of effort with the consequence that other key areas of community development were being neglected. Since each agency prized and guarded its autonomy, each acted as if little was to be gained by integrating one's efforts with those of other agencies.

There were at least three major reasons for this interagency competition:

1. To be identified and trained as a community leader was highly prized in the culture.

2. The results of most community development projects were longer term and less visible than "number of leaders trained."

3. There appeared to be a definite political advantage to having one's agency affiliated with communities that were now organized and had a well-delineated local leadership system.

Inside the agency with which the consultants were working there was considerable loyalty and good feelings towards the top administrators. Nevertheless, there was evidence to suggest that there was much waste of time due to personnel's ignorance of where they fit into the agency's big picture. In some cases this lack of clarity led staff to define their roles quite narrowly and to carry these out regardless of its relevance to the farmers with whom they dealt.

The farmers were polite in acknowledging the value of the staff in helping to train them, but they weren't quite sure how to proceed when training was completed. Follow-up to training seemed needed.

The OD consultants arrayed their information so that the major charactersitics of the agency's work in leadership training could be seen clearly. Each characteristic posed certain issues to the agency and each issue, in turn, posed certain action alternatives to the agency. All of these data were included in the presentation to the task force.

Once the diagnostic survey results are made available to the remaining OD task force, the role of the outside consultant shifts somewhat. Skilled in procedures of group decision making and collaborative problem solving, the consultant has an important part to play in helping the task force to formulate action alternatives and then to decide on which course to take. This role is a somewhat precarious one since familiarity with the problem and expanded knowledge of the client's organizational capabilities leads him to have personal preferences about feasible courses of action. For him to assume a posture of utter neutrality when in fact he does not feel that way is to fall victim to just the kind of reality distortion that he is concerned with eliminating in his client's system. For this reason, the diagnostic report is a point in time that can lead to a renegotiation of contract. It is the OD consultant's responsibility to provide resources in helping the client members of the task force to reach consensus on action alternatives, but if their decision is one that appears indicative of irreconcilable value differences, he is free to terminate his contract.

Usually the diagnostic descriptions presented by the OD consultants make immediate sense to most members of the task force. Despite this, some will claim that nothing new was learned. The latter comment often is true from many perspectives, with the exception being that when outside viewpoints remind them of what they already know, people tend to act with greater responsibility. This inevitably leads to important dialogue. Most frequently though, each person sees previously missing parts that complete the picture they had been trying to construct for themselves. Fitting all the parts together takes time, but the result is a new preparedness for action.

The task force used two days to develop action plans based on the data given them in the diagnostic survey. Included in their work were some interpersonal confrontations that proved highly productive in that they were freed of historical differences in order to be collaborative in the present. They ended in a position of seeing what could be learned from the past and applied to the future.

Perhaps the major outcome from the two days of meetings was an openness to the possibility of collaborating with other agencies in community development projects. It was decided that the senior administrator would initiate discussions with the heads of other agencies, and then with this additional information in hand prepare a plan for this group to consider. The next directions taken by the OD task force would also include consideration of what the future involvements of the outside OD consultants might be.

As it turned out, this agency decided not to continue its leadership training programs as they had been constituted. Based partly on the top manager's discussions with other agencies and partly on the internal dialogue which took place during the OD consultants' diagnostic report, a new orientation was decided upon. Those in the organization who participated in the OD task force met and decided to build an agency image in two other areas of community development: follow-up to leadership programs carried out in their jurisdiction by other agencies, and youth work. These were areas in which they thought their staff were uniquely qualified to work and had not been covered by the community development programs of other agencies.

Summary and Conclusions

This paper is designed as an introduction to OD as a managerial approach. Like most introductory efforts, it provides a large-scale view, thereby omitting many details. Again, we should like to emphasize that OD is a human resource technology; that it is concerned with marshalling the capabilities of people for meeting their own as well as organizational objectives. It is a process, a process of planning and implementing change in such a manner that enterprises have increased capacity for survival and growth. As its base the OD process seeks to inculcate organizational climates in which human needs and organizational objectives are seen as convergent. Such a climate is one in which alternative views are valued, innovative efforts are encouraged, and an active concern for renewal and growth are characteristic. The enterprise is seen as serving the natural growth tendencies in the individual, the realization of which mean not only organization viability, but also continued development.

In the main body of this paper we have discussed OD as a process that is contemporary, relevant, and workable. We do not wish to convey the idea that it is a panacea for troubled managers, not that in practice it is either simple or obvious. Our focus on the diagnostic aspect of OD represents only one of a variety of OD interventions. In addition, OD can intervene to deal with issues of:

1. *Team development*—working with task groups, including individual members, to upgrade their output by focusing on those internal issues that might increase effectiveness.

2. *Intergroup relations*—developing plans and procedures for maximizing collaboration among groups that must work together.

3. *Issue-centered groups*—these groups focus on ways of learning how to increase their effectiveness by engaging in job-related problem solving. Here the objective is to provide actual work problems and to carry learning from these into new problem situations.

4. *Changes in organizational structure*—startups, acquisitions, mergers, managerial shifts, and reorganization often produce increased stress and tension in an enterprise. Preparing for problems by confronting anticipated difficulties is thus an aspect of OD intervention.

On the whole, the OD process offers the possibility of producing innovative change on a wide or narrow level, as the case might be. OD is never concerned, however, with change for change's sake alone. Ultimately, its concern is with meaning—meaning as an important aspect of human life, meaning as an important aspect of enterprise objectives and procedures. OD processes might enter on organizational levels where efficiency is sought, but its essential utility comes when realizing human potential is prized.

Notes

1. The NTL Institute for Applied Behavioral Science (associated with the National Education Association), a nonprofit organization, conducts a year-round program of training, consultation, research, and publication. Its programs are created and conducted by a faculty of 300 carefully selected and trained social scientists located at over 60 universities throughout the world.

   Two social inventions were born out of a determination on the part of the NTL Institute to link social science and social action to bring the fruits of behavioral research to the immediate service of man: *laboratory method,* an experience-based training process that can change outlook and behavior; and the *behavioral science network,* an innovative organizational pattern which has produced a uniquely flexible and creative resource for change. The NTL Institute includes four program centers, for organization studies, community affairs, the development of educational leadership, and international development; and three divisions serving the centers: research, communications, and professional development. Among the Institute's publications are *The Journal of Applied Behavioral Science, Human Relations Training News,* and monographs, books, and training materials. The Institute maintains headquarters at 1201 Sixteenth Street, N.W., Washington, D. C. 20036.

2. W. G. Bennis and P. E. Slater, *The Temporary Society* (New York: Harper & Row, 1968).

3. E. Trist, "Urban North America: The Challenge of the Next Thirty Years," paper presented at the annual meeting and conference of the Town Planning Institute of Canada, June 26-28, 1968.

4. S. A. Culbert, "Organization Renewal: Using Internal Conflicts To Solve External Problems," in the *Proceedings of the Twenty-Second Annual Winter Meeting,* Industrial Relations Research Association (Madison, Wis.: the Association, 1970), pp. 109-120.

5. E. H. Schein, *Process Consultation: Its Role in Organization Development* Reading, Mass.: Addison Wesley, 1969).

6. W. G. Bennis, *Organization Development: Its Nature, Origins, and Prospects* (Reading, Mass.: Addison Wesley, 1969).

7. Recall that these examples, as well as others in this section, are used to illustrate the kinds of situations in which OD interventions can be effective for coping with the conditions cited.

8. Adaptive behavior has less of a future orientation, but it nonetheless implies some change qualities in order to endure eventual stress situations. Reactive qualities generally suggest response only when stimulated by some external condition. It is thus a term that tends to denote a present response as sufficient. Curative can take on the meaning of crisis intervention. In managerial terms it connotes a brush-fire philosophy and thus binds one solely to meeting present dilemmas.

9. The remaining positions on the OD task force are filled by staff who are involved in the project, either by virtue of their area of responsibility, because they are affected by the project's outcome, or because of their expertise in the area.

10. Sometimes the OD process finds one person combining the roles of initiating manager and inside consultant. This can result in effective, although seldom optimal benefits for the organization.

11. The consultant also relies on additional forms of data collection. Thus he might employ survey methods, questionnaires, relevant reports, etc. However, his skill in collecting information directly through interviews is often his most effective asset in obtaining an accurate diagnosis.

INFLUENCE AND ORGANIZATIONAL CHANGE*

Gene W. Dalton

During the last few years a new term, Organizational Development, has been rapidly finding its way into the organization charts of American corporations. Because of the recency of this phenomenon it is sometimes difficult to ascertain the extent to which the activities carried out under this title are old activities being carried out under a new name or a new set of activities aimed at an old but increasingly urgent problem. But one fact does emerge: there is an increasing number of men in these organizations whose primary function is to foster change. This has always been part of the job of a manager and often a significant part, but now there is an increasing number of men in the organizations who are essentially specialists in the process of organizational change.

Almost inevitably, a part of the requirement of this new role will be an ability to be explicit about the change process itself, for the O.D. specialist will be an advisor and helper more often than an initiator. In this role of counselor, he will need a framework or model for both thinking and talking about the means by which individuals and groups are influenced to change their behavior in organizations. A model has a number of uses. It can help order the available data and clarify discussion. It can provide some much-needed categories so that similarities between similar acts can be highlighted. It can point out the multiple functions which some act performs without forcing us to talk about everything at once.

*Reprinted from Anant R. Negandhi and Joseph P. Schwitter, *Organizational Behavior Models* (Kent, Ohio: Comparative Administrative Research Institute, Kent State University, 1970) pp. 77-108.

For several years my colleagues and I have been studying an organization in which a new director of a research and development center set out to change the behavior of a substantial number of managers and engineers. We observed his efforts over time and attempted to measure their effects. Over a period of a year and a half it became increasingly evident that he had been successful in influencing one part of the men but had had little effect on the others. This result both baffled and challenged us. In our attempt to understand the difference, we examined the studies we could find which described instances where someone had successfully influenced others to change their behavior. From the analysis of these studies and of our own data we constructed an elementary model of the influence process in organizational change. I am proposing that it may serve as a useful point of departure for those engaged in organizational development, as well as for those of us who study organizational life.

Organizational and Individual Change

First I should clarify what I mean by organizational change. As used here, the term refers to any significant alteration of the behavior patterns of a large part of the individuals who constitute that organization. I make a point of this because students of organizations, in their efforts to characterize an organization as a system or organism, too often lose sight of the fact that the "behavior" of an organization is made up of the actions and interactions of the individuals in it. We read so frequently about an organization "adapting" to market shifts, economic conditions, and scientific discoveries that we slide over the internal processes by which an organization does that adapting. The biological analogy of an organism adapting to its environment can be dramatic and conceptually helpful, but students of organizations typically make only partial use of the analogy. They stop at this generalized level of explanation and fail to follow their biologist colleagues, whose concepts they have borrowed, to next step of examining the internal processes by which the system adapts.

Our focus will be on the response within the organization to factors in its environment. Typically, one or more individuals in the organization see something in the environment which calls for different behavior on the part of the members of the organization. He (or they) then tries to move others in the organization to make this change in their behavior. This is fundamentally an influence process and it is the process I shall be representing here. The primary data chosen for illustration comes from our own study plus studies of change in organizational settings by Guest,[1] Seashore and Bower,[2] Jaques,[3] and Blake, Mouton, Barnes and Greiner,[4] and was all focused on the internal change process.

Some of the best reported studies of the influence process, however, were made in non-organizational settings: experimental studies of attitude change, individual and group psychotherapy, religious conversion, and so-called thought reform. In deciding whether to draw from these, I was faced with the question as to whether studies of individual change materially can aid our understanding of organizational change and my answer was affirmative. Certainly, membership in a formal organization places the individual within a potent influence network and any explanation of changes in his behavior and attitudes must take this network into account. But we must not allow ourselves to presume that behavior in formal organizations is discontinuous from human behavior elsewhere. The object of change in planned change programs is the behavior and attitudes of individuals. Within an organization, these attitudes and actions form an inextricable part of larger formal and informal systems but the workings of social processes ultimately take place as intrapersonal and interpersonal processes.

Sequencing

In our study of the events at the Nampa Development Center, one of the first things we noted was the importance of time. Often the most significant fact about a given event was that it followed other events or that it created a condition which influenced subsequent events. This is also the one point on which other students of change agree—that behavioral and attitudinal change takes place in sequential steps or phases.

Probably the most fruitful conception of the change process, judging from the frequency of its use by others and by the research it has stimulated, is the three-step model advanced by Kurt Lewin:[5] unfreezing the system which is operating in a given pattern, moving to a new pattern, and refreezing into this new pattern. Lewin postulated that systems tend to operate in a given pattern or at a given level as long as there is a relative balance of forces acting on the system.

A sequential model serves a number of functions. It provides a dimension along which to order events and draws attention to events and conditions at the boundaries of the phenomena under examination. Too often, I think, those of us managing or studying organizations tend to be historical in our approach. For example, in our own study, when we conceived of "unfreezing" broadly, we were led to examine not only the unsettling effects of the director's changes in the organizational structure, but also the conditions in the organization at the time he became director and the events leading up to them. Using this one dimension, time, we could characterize the change process at the Center, where successful, shown in Figure 1.

Subprocesses

So far, so good. Time is important and a sequential model such as Lewin's is useful in pointing to the tendency toward orderly movement related to prior

Unfreezing		Change	Refreezing
Tension and the need for change was experienced within the organization.	Change was advocated by the new director.	Individuals within the organization tested out the proposed changes.	New behavior and attitudes were either reinforced and internalized, or rejected and abandoned.

Figure 1

events. But, as we compared the successful attempts to exert influence, it also became obvious that there was not one process at work but several, all moving simultaneously. Where influence was successful, changes occurred not only in the way an individual related to the influencing agent, but also to his co-workers and to himself. As interaction patterns were dissolving and reforming, changes were taking place within the individuals involved, changes in their feelings about themselves and in the objectives they sought.

We identified four major subprocesses that tended to characterize successful change in our own study and in the other empirical studies of change we examined.

The four subprocesses are characterized by movement:

Away From	*and*	*Toward*
Generalized goals		Specific objectives
Former social ties built around previous behavior patterns		New relationships which support the intended changes in behavior and attitudes
Self-doubt and a lowered sense of self-esteem		A heightened sense of self-esteem
An external motive for change		An internalized motive for change

A Model for Induced Change

If we combine these four subprocesses with our notion of sequencing, we arrive at the diagram in Figure 2. Following this diagram, we shall look at the two antecedent conditions which were present in each case of successful planned change examined. Then we shall look separately at each of the four subprocesses pictured.

Tension Experienced Within the System	Intervention of a Prestigious Influencing Agent	Individuals Attempt to Implement the Proposed Changes	New Behavior and Attitudes Reinforced by Achievement, Social Ties and Internalized Values—Accompanied by Decreasing Dependence on Influencing Agent
	Generalized Objectives Established	Growing Specificity of Objectives— Establishment of Sub-Goals	Achievement and Resetting of Specific Objectives
Tension Within Existing Social Ties	Prior Social Ties Interrupted or Attenuated	Formation of New Alliances and Relationships Centering Around New Activities	New Social Ties Reinforce Altered Behavior and Attitudes
Lowered Sense of Self-Esteem	Esteem-Building Begun on Basis of Agent's Attention and Assurance	Esteem-Building Based on Task Accomplishment	Heightened Sense of Self-Esteem
	External Motive for Change	Improvisation and Reality-Testing	Internalized Motive for Change
	(New Schema Provided)		

Figure 2   A model of induced change.

Internal Tension as an Antecedent Condition

At the risk of stating a truism, let me point out that one of the most important conditions necessary for the successful initiation of change is a sense of tension or a felt need for change among those who are the targets of influence. In nearly every instance in the studies reviewed where one person or group successfully influenced the behavior of others, those influenced were experiencing a more-than-usual amount of tension or stress.

In our own study, a major project on which many of the men had worked for years had just been discontinued and the technology sold to a competitor. The decision by top management not to manufacture or market the product, which had been announced just prior to the new director's appointment, had generated a sense of disappointment and frustration at the Center, since many had come to identify their own future with the success of the project. The men were also concerned about the falling prices of their division's major product and at the Center's apparent lack of success in recent years at translating their technical capabilities into dramatic new products.

Guest, in his three-year study of leadership and organizational change in an automobile assembly plant, reported that before the arrival of the new production manager who succeeded in "turning the plant around" from the least to the most efficient plant in the Division, there was great tension. Labor grievances were high, turnover was twice that in other plants and the plant was under constant pressure from Division Headquarters.[6]

Seashore and Bower, in their study of an ultimately successful change effort by a consulting-research team from the University of Michigan, reported that in the year prior to the interventions of the team, "Banner (the company) dropped to a very marginal profit position . . . . . Waste, service, and quality problems arose . . . . . There was a sense of things getting out of control, a feeling shared and expressed by many nonmanagerial people."[7]

Elliot Jaques, in his pioneering study of social and technical change in the Glacier Metal Company, reported the impact of a crisis which resulted in a large number of lay-offs and "great anxiety about job security." "The procedure adopted (to handle the lay-offs) had lessened some of the morale problems—but it did not and could not remove everyone's anxiety about job security."[8] Jaques, in fact, concluded that a necessary factor in allowing for a working through of group problems was a "problem severe and painful enough for its members to wish to do something about it."

Blake, Mouton, Marnes and Greiner, describing a major organizational change effort featuring a training program, noted the presence of great tension in the Sigma plant prior to the training consultant's arrival at the plant. A merger had taken place, bringing the plant under a new headquarters staff, and a serious problem arose over the "use of Sigma manpower on construction work of new projects." When the headquarters staff began to "prod Sigma," the plant management "became defensive" and, according to one of the managers at head-quarters, "some of our later sessions became emotional." "Strained relations between different departments and levels within the plant "began to develop."[9] Greiner reported that "plant morale slipped badly, insecurity arose and perfor-mance slumped," while a manager within the plant reported that: "Everything seemed to get out of control."[10]

This uniformity was also evident in other settings where there was a suc-cessful attempt to influence attitudes and behavior. The religious convert usu-ally is experiencing self-doubt and guilt before he gives careful heed to the mis-sionary or revivalist. A need for change is already felt by the person who walks into the Christian Science reading room or the revivalist tent. Certain organiza-tions, such as Alcoholics Anonymous, whose central aim is to induce specific behavioral change, refuse to admit anyone unless he is consciously experiencing distress. An applicant to A.A. must openly admit the failure of previous individ-ual efforts and his need for help.[11] Jerome Frank suggests that in psychotherapy the presence of prior emotional distress is closely related to the results of the treatment. He argues as follows:

> The importance of emotional distress in the establishment of a fruit-ful psychotherapeutic relationship is suggested by the facts that the greater the over-all degree of expressed distress, as measured by a symptom check list, the more likely the patient is to remain in treat-ment, while conversely two of the most difficult categories of pa-tients to treat have nothing in common except lack of distress.[12]

Even in Chinese "thought-reform" prisons, where the interrogator had the power to induce new stresses, the presence of internal tension prior to imprisonment appears to have been a crucial factor in the prisoner's susceptibility to induce an attitude change. Schein and his associates, who studied the Chinese thought-reform program as it was reported by American civilian prisoners in Chinese prisons assigned a crucial role to the sense of guilt experienced by the individual. They reported that "if the prisoner-to-be was susceptible to social guilt, he was particularly vulnerable to the pressure of the cellmates in a group cell."[13]

It is important to note that these are qualitatively different situations, in many ways, from industrial settings; Alcoholics, Communist prisoners, and psy-chiatric patients share an emotional distress and lack of control over their own actions which differentiate them from men working in industrial organizations. But as in the industrial studies, attempts to influence behavior have a high prob-ability of success only when the individuals have been experiencing internal stress.

In an organization, of course, the need for change isn't experienced uni-formly throughout the organization and its locus helps determine the methods used to effect change. If the tension is felt primarily by those at the top of the authority structure but not by those below, change efforts will be exerted through the existing authority structure. Resistance usually takes the form of circumvention and token compliance. If, on the other hand, the tension exists at the bottom of the legitimate power structure, but not at the top, attempts to change the organization take the form of a revolt and an attack on the existing authority structure, as in campus riots and wildcat strikes. The extent and locus of tension also help determine outcomes. In our own study, two groups, the Senior Scientists and Junior Managers, were relatively more frustrated than others at the Center and it was among the men in these two groups that the new Director found the greatest acceptance of the changes he proposed.

Authority and Prestige of the Influencer

The forces for change represented by tension and the desire for change must be mobilized, however, and given direction, while forces acting to resist change in a given direction must be overcome, neutralized, or enlisted. In an organization, unless there is to be protracted resistance, someone must gain the acceptance and possible support of individuals not seeking change and even those who feel threatened by it.

A second prerequisite for successfully induced change, therefore, appears to be that the initiation come from a respected and, ideally, a trusted source. The persons being influenced need confidence that the change can, in fact, be effected, and a large part of this confidence comes initially from their confidence in the power and jusgment of the influencing agent. When men are unsure of their capacity to cope effectively with the situation, they identify with someone whom they perceive as having the knowledge or power to successfully cope with it and who states *where* they need to change. As such, he is then placed in a position where his expectations can become "self-fulfilling prophesies."[14]

In the organizational studies reviewed, successful attempts to change either were initiated by the formal head of the organizational unit involved or were given his strong support. In Guest's study, the initiator was the new plant manager who brought with him a strong repuration for success in his previous position. Furthermore, it quickly became obvious to the other employees that he had the support of the district management.[15] (Pelz reported that upward influence with one's own superior was a necessary condition for influence with subordinates.)[16] Jaques also had the active support of the Managing Director of Glacier Metals.[17]

The changes at the "Banner Corporation"[18] were initiated by the highest official at the plant. He gained support from Rensis Likert and brought in an agent from the Survey Research Center who carried with him the prestige of the University as well as the authority of an experienced manager. The change effort at the Sigma plant had a similar dual sponsorship, receiving active support from the Plant Manager and a consultant, Robert Blake, who "had an impressive reputation with the management in other parts of (the headquarters company)."[19] (As a contrast to these successful change efforts, consider for a moment the many ineffectual training programs for first and second line supervisors in which the top management group did not participate and therefore never fully understood or supported.)

Non-organizational studies show the same link between prestige and influence: individuals tend to believe and do those things suggested by authoritative, prestigeful sources.[20] Goalsetting studies reported by Mace indicated that setting goals for individuals and associating these goals with prestigeful authorities like "scientific progress" or "the advancement of research" tended to have a favorable effect on performance.[21]

Studies of operant conditioning of verbal behavior, where one person reinforces certain verbal signals emitted by another person, indicate that when the conditioner has some prestige or power in the subjects' eyes, the influence tends to be stronger and more consistent. Students were more consistently influenced by their instructors, for example, than by fellow students. (Of course, this was several years ago. Perhaps today instructors over 30 may not enjoy the same influence.)

Another area of study focusing on the persuasive influence of a prestigeful figure is faith-healing and the so-called "placebo effect" in medicine. Jerome Frank reports that even healers regarded by the community as charlatans or quacks, were able, in some instances, to bring about change and symptom relief among persons who regarded them as sources of authority and power. Their success appeared to rest on their ability to evoke the patient's expectancy of help. In medical treatment, the fact that relief and healing can be brought about solely by the patient's expectation of help from the physician, is demonstrated by experiments verifying the so-called "placebo effect." In these studies, the doctor administers a pharmacologically inert substance to the patient rather than an active medication. Since the placebo is inert, its beneficial effects derive from the patient's confidence in the doctor's prescription and in the institutions of science and medicine which he represents. There is evidence that placebos can have marked physiological effects. Studies have shown that their use has been accompanied by healing of tissue damage ranging from warts to peptic ulcers. A similar effect is the "hello-goodbye" effect in psychotherapy. Patients who merely had contact with a prestigeful (in their eyes) psychiatrist improved significantly over the individuals in a control group who were placed on a waiting list and did not see a psychiatrist. In fact, these minimal contact patients showed almost as much improvement of certain kinds as a third group who underwent prolonged treatment.[22]

Even in thought-reform prisons, there is some suggestion that interrogators or cellmates with higher education and intelligence as this was perceived by the prisoner, were more likely to be able to influence the prisoner than were those whom he "looked down on."[23] Statistical evidence on American prisoners of war in Korea show the small proportion (about 15%) of the prisoners who were classified as collaborators came primarily from low status positions in American society,[24] and therefore among the group most likely to see their interrogators and discussion leaders as prestigeful persons. In one of the most graphic accounts by a prisoner who successfully resisted influence by his interrogators, Gonzales reports that he never came to think of his interrogators as authorities in any real sense nor in any way superior to himself except that they were more numerous than he.[25] There is, of course, abundant evidence in our own study and elsewhere to refute a claim that any change initiated by a high status person will be successful. The process of change is more complex than that. But prestige and power on the part of the initiator seems to be a necessary, if not sufficient, condition for introducing large-scale change in any system. Where the person planning to initiate change does not already possess prestige and power in the organization, as Loomis has pointed out, it is his first task to develop "social capital" for himself, i.e., to build his reputation and power in the social system he intends to change.[26]

Subprocesses

Now let us turn from the conditions which precede and facilitate change to an examination of the change process itself. The subtleties and interdependencies of the process, of course, are difficult and, in many ways, impossible to represent or describe because the phenomena occur simultaneously and are "of a piece." But as is shown in the diagram, we were able to distinguish four major subprocesses, all of which seemed to proceed simultaneously in those instances where individuals and groups were influenced to change their behavior and where these new behavior patterns persisted. Movement along each of these four streams characterized the Junior Managers and Senior Scientists at Nampa but were either absent or restricted among the other men at the Center whose behavior and attitude changed least.

Movement along each of these streams, where present, appeared to follow a consistent pattern or direction, and while each seemed distinct and separable, movement along all four appeared to occur simultaneously. The first two of these deal with changes in shared objectives and relationships, while the last two concern changes within the individual.

Movement Toward Specific Objectives

The first pattern which consistently seems to characterize successful attempts to bring about behavioral and attitudinal change is a movement from generalized goals toward specific and concrete objectives. As the change progresses, the targets take on greater immediacy and concreteness; one of the clearest signals that a new pattern of behavior will not be established and maintained is the objectives' remaining general and nonspecific. In the Nampa Center the changes outlined for all the groups began at a very general level. The Junior Managers, for example, were told they were to take on more responsibility for the administration of their groups and to "plan the technical work" for their groups. The Senior Managers were told to spend at least half their time doing long-range planning. Soon afterward, the Junior Managers were asked to prepare budget requests for their groups. Later they were given responsibility for performing a specific technical objective and a target date was set for completion, and soon they were working out a week-by-week projected schedule. The assignment given the Senior Managers to do long-range planning, however, remained essentially at that level of generality, with neither the Director nor the Senior Managers working out intermediate or sub-objectives. Fifteen months later, of course, it was the Junior and not the Senior Managers whose attitudes and behavior had changed in the intended direction.

In each of the other studies, whenever someone successfully influenced another person or group of persons to change their behavior or attitudes, movement toward greater specificity of goals was a prominent feature. Sometimes the person initiating the change set the sub-goals, sometimes those being influenced set them; most often it was a joint or alternating arrangement. But the consistent element was that someone set concrete subgoals and the behavior change moved along step-by-step. Guest reported that the new manager at Plant Y began by outlining a "few general goals" such as better planning. He set up meetings for discussion general problems, but attention was steadily brought to focus on improving specific areas, such as accounting methods and inspection procedures.[27] Jaques' report of a three-year period of change in the Glacier Metal Company described how the project team worked successfully with councils and management groups at various levels and departments throughout the organizations. The process followed in their work with each group showed remarkable consistency—beginning with the general goals of "understanding their difficulties," Moving to a goal of understanding their own "here-and-now" relationships and finally heading toward the resolution of specific problems or the writing of a new constitution.[28]

The Plant Manager's initially announced objective at "Banner Corporation" was to introduce "participation management" into the organization. "After several months, four sub-goals were explicitly stated as a way of implementing the overall goal:

(a) increased emphasis on the work group, as a functioning unit,

(b) more supportive behavior from supervisors,

(c) greater employee participation in decision-making, and

(d) increased interaction among and influence among work group members.

A series of meetings with all the supervisors in the experimental department followed in which the objective became more and more operational in the minds of the supervisors. Finally, these intermediate goals were translated into more specific goals, such as bringing the employees into the decisions about a new shift rotation scheme.[29] The changes reported by Blake, *et al.* at the Sigma refinery followed an identical pattern.[30] Beginning with a training program in which the objectives for the participants were the general goals of understanding the concepts and assessing their own present management style. Other meetings followed in which the objectives were to explore ways to transfer the new concepts and personal learning of the Seminars to the operations of their own group. The objective became even more concrete as the men consciously tried to use some of their new problem-solving methods in working out a program for reducing utility costs and in negotiating a difficult union-management contract.

Outside organizational settings, the most carefully conceptualized example of this aspect of the change process is found in the descriptions of the therapeutic process. At the beginning of the relationship between the patient and the therapist, the mutually understood objective is usually relatively general in character: to help the patient to operate more effectively in his environment, to find relief from serious distress, or to achieve an understanding of the patient's problems and their causes. Explorations may begin by looking at the patient's past behavior, his relationships outside therapy, and his feelings about these. But nearly all schools of therapy agree that as the relationship continues, the patient comes to show his feelings and behavior towards the therapist similar to those making trouble for him outside therapy. The examination of these concrete specific events acted out in their own relationship is undertaken as a means of achieving the more general objective.[31] Religious conversion begins with the goals of total repentence and "Casting off the old man for the new," but where the conversion has lasting effects, this general goal moves toward the specific objectives of giving up certain practices, making contributions, or proselyting others. Then as an individual makes small behavioral commitments in a certain direction, he justifies and rationalizes these acts by accepting values and explanations which reduce dissonance between these acts and his self-image. He becomes his own socializing agent. Even in the thought-reform prisons, the early demand of the interrogator for confession of guilt narrows and focuses to the objective of producing a written document confession of specific "criminal acts" which the interrogator will accept.

Altering Old Relationships and Establishing New Social Ties

The second pattern which seemed to characterize successful change was the loosening of old relationships and the establishment of new social ties which support the intended changes in attitude and behavior. Old behavior and attitudes are often deeply imbedded in the relationships which have been built up over the years, and as long as the individuals involved maintain these relationships unaltered, changes are unlikely to occur. By the same token, new behavior patterns are most readily and firmly established when they are conditions of regular membership in a new group, for group members exercise the most powerful tool for shaping behavior, selective reinforcement of responses with immediate rewards.

In other studies this was the dimension of the change process that has been most explicitly recognized: the beliefs, attitudes, and activities of a person are closely related to those of his reference groups. New attitudes and new activity patterns are most likely to be established when an individual becomes associated with a new reference group.[32] Certainly, not all of an individual's former associations will counteract an intended change, nor will new groups formed in a change situation always work in the direction that the influencing agent intends, but in general, any significant changes in activities or attitudes include some movement from old object relationships toward new ones.

Behavioral scientists did not originate the ideas that an alteration of old relationships facilitates change in individuals or groups. Most influencing institutions in our society separate the individual whom they wish to influence from his regular social contacts and routines. Convents, monasteries, and prisons tend to make this a total separation, and educational institutions make the same separation to a lesser degree by their physical distance from home and a demanding work load. Perhaps the best reported study of this is the work done by Newcomb at Bennington College. During their four years at the College, the girls tended to take on the attitudes of the faculty and student leaders, and to relinquish those of their parents.[33] The individuals' greater susceptibility to influence when he is separated from social contacts which support his current beliefs was ingeniously demonstrated by the famous Asch experiments: when subjects were placed in a situation where no other person agreed with the subject's own judgments, a third of the subjects came to doubt their own perceptions to the extent that they reported seeing what the others reported in over half the trials. Yet, if only one person in the group confirmed a subject's own perception, his resistance to social pressure was significantly increased.[34] Rice, in his study of change in a textile weaving mill in India, found some confirmation for his argument that this need for removal from previous contacts applied also to groups where the group was the focus of change. Otherwise the prior social relationships continued to support the behavior patterns and attitudes which the change program was trying to alter.[35]

Breaking up or loosening former social ties may act to unfreeze an individual or group, but this alone provides no assurance that any resulting changes will be in a given direction or that they will have any permanency. Establishing new relationships which reward the desired behaviors and confirm the modified attitudes also seems to be essential. Otherwise, there will be an active seeking to return to former activities and attitudes and to the relationships which supported and reinforced them.

In our study of the Nampa Center, all the men in the experimental sections reported some disruption of their former relationships. Changes in job requirements and work schedules broke up former important interaction patterns in all the groups, but there was a sharp difference among the groups in the extent to which new relationships were established. The men in the groups which eventually changed most were assigned to new decision-making committees with their peers from other parts of the company. When decisions were made in the groups there were strong pressures from the other members of the group to defend these decisions even in dealings with the Senior Managers. The men who eventually changed least, on the other hand, established no new relationships. Their previous ties were attenuated, but they formed no new relationships which might have pulled them more deeply into new patterns of activities and beliefs.

One of the most interesting studies illustrating this phenomenon was the follow-up study of an International Harvester Company training program emphasizing human relations skills which the investigators categorized as "consideration." Tested before and after the two-week training program, the foremen's attitude test scores showed an immediate increase on "consideration," but, over time, the scores shifted until these foremen actually scored lower in consideration than did a control group who had not been trained. Only those foremen whose immediate superiors scored high on consideration continued to score high themselves. The other foremen, whose superiors did not place a high value on consideration, returned to a pattern very close to that of their chief. Daily interaction completely negated the effect of the training program. The formen's ties had been interrupted only during the two week training period. Then they returned to a situation where the most significant relationship was with their own supervisors. No continuing new relationships had been established which would act to confirm and reinforce any attitude changes begun in the training program.[36]

A study which differs in important ways from the International Harvester study, yet confirms its findings, is the Barnes and Greiner investigation of the effects of Blake's organization development program at the Sigma oil refinery. At Sigma the management and staff members at all levels of the plant went through an initial training program during which men were taken out of their regular work groups and placed among relative strangers. They then returned to their old work groups, as in the International Harvester program, but with the difference that their superiors and colleagues had also been through the same training experience. In addition, a second series of meetings was held in which the teams who worked together jointly examined their own operations and made mutual commitments to change. A follow-up study revealed that the program had had an impact on the plant's operations and on the behavior and attitudes of some of the men but, again, not all. In this case, 92% of the supervisors who were rated as most changed by their subordinates, worked in groups where a majority of their colleagues were also rated as "most improved" by their subordinates, while only 26% of the supervisors rated as "least improved" worked in such groups. In fact, it appeared to the investigators that even the presence of only one "least improved" cynic was enough to have a strong dampening effect, since 60% of the "most improved" supervisors worked in settings where there were no "least improved" colleagues whatsoever.[37] As in the Nampa and International Harvester studies, there was no behavioral change unless relationships changed to support the new behavior. The Sigma study, however, differs in one significant way: the major reinforcing relationships in the refinery study were with the same people with whom they had worked before. The parties to the relationship had not changed, but the relationships had. This, of course, has important implications for an administrator who wishes to maintain his work teams intact, but hopes to alter behavior and attitudes in these groups. Still, the major point to be made here is that unless the relationships change, behavioral change is more difficult.

Some of the other studies involved an actual break-up of former associations, while in others the parties did not change, but the relationships between those parties did. Guest, in his study of a successful change, reported a high incidence of personnel shifts breaking up old social ties and established new relationships which supported the new behavior patterns. There were few discharges, but a program of planned and deliberate lateral transfers and promotions was instituted. Only 25% of the plant's supervisors held the same job throughout the period studied. Moreover, the Plant Manager set up a new pattern of interactions through an increased use of meetings.

> The scope and function of the meetings established by the new
> manager stood in marked contrast to those of the earlier period:
> there were more of them, they were regularly scheduled, they
> covered a wider range of activities, more people took part in
> them . . . . .[38]

Relationships in these meetings were established around new attitudes and behaviors, and support and reinforcement for the new behavior patterns came from these ties.

The studies reported by Jaques and by Seashore and Bower, however, focused on changes in the nature of the existing relationships. Jaques found that at Glacier Metals a number of new relationships had been established around the new activities (new worker-management committees, etc.) but the primary thrust of the research team's efforts was to alter the expectations and the reinforcement patterns in the existing relationships. This came primarily through what they termed "role clarification" and "working through." Role clarification consisted of a joint examination of the several roles members were expected to play in the group and in the organization as well as the achievement of a common set of expectations about the new ways in which those roles were to be filled. Jaques described "working through" as a serious attempt to voice the unrecognized difficulties, often socially taboo, which have been preventing the group from going ahead with whatever task it may have had. The research team's focus on "working through" was not to aid in the solution of any one problem but to alter the relationship and the manner of working together. Jaques' underlying thesis was that, "Once a group has developed insight and skill in recognizing forces related to status, prestige, security, . . . (etc.) these forces no longer colour subsequent discussion nor impede progress to the same extent as before."[39]

The most vivid example of new social interactions acting to bring about the intended change itself is in the "struggle sessions" in thought reform prisons. In some reform prisons on the Chinese mainland, western prisoners were placed in cells with a group of "advanced" prisoners, who had already made confessions or were in the process. These prisoners, who themselves were taking on the reformed attitudes, and who were given to know that the progress of the entire cell was dependent on the performance of the least-reformed member, exerted strong pressures (accusations, browbeating) on their new member. The potency of this pressure from fellow prisoners was so pronounced that Schein concluded it was the single most effective device used to influence the prisoners to confess and change attitudes.[40] The Communist prison struggle groups are an extreme form of a group influencing a new member to assume new behaviors and attitudes, but the same process goes on in all groups with lowered intensity. The entering member is required to demonstrate adherence to the norms and values of the group to a greater extent, even, than established members.[41]

The establishment of new social ties for confirmation and reinforcement of changes already begun also has traditionally been a part of evangelistic programs. John Wesley organized his converts into small units of twelve or less. This small group, with a chosen leader met together weekly to tell of their experiences. The leader visited a member each week to collect dues and to verify the sincerity of his conversion. Quarterly, each member was reassigned a ticket of membership admitting him to sacrament meetings. Backsliding was watched carefully and even three or four absences could bring the loss of his ticket and expulsion from the Society.[42]

The importance of the establishment of new social relationships which confirm and support change begun probably is best illustrated by examining change attempts where new ties are not established. Following a Billy Graham crusade in New York City, an informal survey of individuals who came forward and converted during the Crusade found that only those who were subsequently integrated into local churches maintained their faith. For others, the conversion became merely a temporary and lapsed response.[43]

There are those who lay complete stress on group membership and social pressure in explaining the change process. Such explanations seem incomplete, and that is obviously not our position here, but movement along this dimension appears to be a necessary if not sufficient condition for inducing significant and lasting behavioral change.

Heightening Self-Esteem

Changes in self-esteem on the part of the person being influenced also appear to be an integral part of the process. Interestingly, a movement toward greater self-esteem seems to be a facilitating factor not only in the establishment of new patterns of thought and action, but also in the unfreezing of old patterns. The abandonment of previous patterns of behavior and thought is easier when an individual is moving toward an increased sense of his own worth. The movement along this continuum is away from a sense of self-doubt toward a feeling of positive worth—from a feeling of partial inadequacy toward a confirmed sense of personal capacity. The increased sense of one's own potential is evident throughout this continuum, not merely at the end. This may seem a paradox, but the contradiction is more apparent than real.

As noted earlier, one of the preconditions for successful change is the experience of stress within the system. Though stress is usually present even before the intervention of the change agent, the agent himself can play an extremely important role in challenging the individual's sense of adequacy. His means of doing this may be explicit or implicit. The negative diagnosis may be openly stated as when the religious revivalist points to the prospective proselyte's indulgent life and he calls him to repentance. The older members at an A.A. meeting may confront the alcoholic with the fact that he is destroying himself and his family. The Communist prison interrogator may insist on the prisoner's "criminal acts against the people." On the other hand, the negative diagnosis may be communicated implicitly by the agent's acting to introduce change in the object system, such as a psychotherapist embarking on a program of treatment after he has had exploratory talks with the patient.

In organizational change, we also find both patterns. A new executive may himself confront the members of the organization with the inconsistencies and inefficiencies in their operations as he did in the Nampa case. An outside consultant, however, will more often seek a confrontation among the members of the organization. For example, Robert Blake, in working with the management of the Sigma plant, suggested an initial meeting between plant managers and the headquarters staff, at which the problems uncovered "shocked" the plant management. From this meeting came the impetus to design a development program in which each of the members of the supervisory group was likewise confronted by others' perceptions of his behavior.[44] Jaques and the research team at Glacier Metals worked with the staff in their meetings, helped them to "express feelings which they had been suppressing sometimes for years." Many, for the first time, were able to assess the consequences of some of their behavior.[45]

On the other hand the manager of the plant studied by Guest entered into a situation where the men had already had abundant evidence of the unsatisfactory consequences of their behavior. He felt it necessary only to acknowledge this evidence.

> In the first meeting with all supervision he put forward what he called "a few basic goals" for the organization in terms of expected efficiency and quality. He stated candidly to the group that Plant Y had a bad reputation. He said he had heard that many members of the group were not capable of doing their jobs. He said he was "willing to prove that this was not so, and until shown otherwise, I personally have confidence in the group."[46]

In each of these instances, the manager or consultant signalled that the men needed to change; that their former performance was not adequate or appropriate. How, then, does this kind of action foster a heightened sense of worth? The men cannot help feeling they are of some worth, receiving this much attention from someone whom they respect. He is making an investment in them. Even though he is communicating a negative evaluation of their present behavior or attitudes, he is also indicating that he has higher expectations. He is saying, in effect, that he respects their potential. Finally, when he communicates his negative diagnosis he also offers hope implying that there is a better way and that he knows that better way. The effect on self-esteem is negative at this point in that the attention received derives from their past inadequacy—their need to change. But it is positive in that it lays a foundation for a new beginning, and promise of better results in the future.

For instances of successful change, there is a movement toward increased self-regard as the person finds himself capable of making the changes in behavior. He experiences a sense of accomplishment, a relief from tension, and a reintegration around a new pattern of activity and thought. The Junior Managers at Nampa, for example, had the opportunity to assume new roles and take on new tasks. As they accomplished these tasks, which had been previously performed by their superiors, they gained a new confidence rooted in their own achievements.

This gain in self-esteem was evident in each of the studies. Early in each of the organizational studies, managers began listening to their subordinates and responding to them. In each case subordinates began taking on responsibilities and participating in decisions that had been withheld from them in the past. The confidence gained from success in these early attempts led to further steps. In Guest's study, men expressed an increasing feeling of competence ("Just gradually we learned how to do the job.") and confidence in their future ("The foreman knows that he's got the staff, he's going to be recognized and promoted."). Toward the end of the period studied, the "promotion" theme was mentioned often in the interviews, while only three years earlier none had expressed the hope of advancing.[47] At the Sigma Refinery, studied by Barnes and Greiner, a new set of programs for increasing productivity and improving costs was confidently and successfully carried out.[48] At Glacier, Jaques reported that increased confidence and self-esteem was demonstrated in a capacity to tackle formerly taboo problems with considerably less anxiety.

The study of the Banner Company, conducted by Seashore and Bower, is perhaps the most interesting of the four concerning this factor, in that managers and consultants were explicit about the need for increased self-esteem. The consultants set a goal to build "supportive supervisory behavior," which they defined as increasing "the extent to which subordinates (at all levels) experienced positive, ego-sustaining relations with superiors and peers whenever they undertook to act in ways which would promote their common goals."[49] Paradoxically, it was at Banner where increased confidence was most difficult to attain, as the early attempts at supervisory support became the focus of misunderstanding and illwill. The supervisors attempted in good faith to be "supportive" but often found no way to link this up to accomplishment. Undiscriminating support not only failed to build self-esteem, but actually undermined it. This factor, plus a deteriorating economic situation and some formal organizational blocks controlled by higher management, retarded progress to the point where the representative from the Survey Research Center proposed a suspension of the field work. It was only after a reorganization, allowing the plant greater freedom, that the latent gains from the early change efforts began to produce the spiraling achievement and confidence that increased plant productivity.

The best-known study demonstrating that a heightening of self-worth is an integral part of the influence process comes from the Relay Assembly Test

Room Experiments begun in 1924 by the Western Electric Company at their Hawthorne works. The tests, of course, were initially designed to examine the "relation of quality and quantity of illumination to efficiency in industry," but the baffled experimenters found that productivity increased in their "test groups" and "control groups" in almost equal magnitude. They were obtaining greater efficiency, but it apparently was not "illumination that was making the difference!" Further study, this time experimentally varying rest pauses and working hours, again revealed no simple correlation between the experimentally imposed changes and rate of output. Production rose steadily even when the experimental conditions were returned to their original condition. This time, however, the experimenters took careful note of other factors, one of which was the experimenters' influence on the girls to increase productivity. Ostensibly, the experiment had not been an attempt to change behavior, and the experimenters disclaimed any conscious desire to influence the girls toward increased production. The superintendent's notes concerning the first meeting held with the girls indicated that great care was taken to convince them that the purpose of the test was not to boost production:

> The group were assured that the test was not being set up to determine the maximum output, and they were asked to work along at a comfortable pace and particularly not to attempt to see how much they could possibly do.[50]

But in fact the girls received signals which conveyed an exactly opposite message.[51] The superintendent's next words were:

> If increased output resulted from better or more satisfactory working conditions, both parties would be the gainers.[52]

Increased productivity *was* what interested the experimenters! The girls could see that it was the production output which was being recorded so meticulously and subjected to such careful scrutiny.[53]

In retrospect the treatment the girls were given seems almost perfectly designed to increase their sense of self-esteem. A new supervisor who was promoted to department chief became the test observer and he treated them very differently from their previous superior. The observer and the experimenters made every effort to obtain the girls' whole-hearted cooperation for each change, consulting them about each change and even canceling some change which did not meet with their approval. The girls' health, well-being, and opinions were the subject of genuine concern. Investigators spent full time recording and analyzing their output and the Superintendent of the Inspection Branch visited the room frequently, accompanied by an intermittent stream of industrial psychologists and university professors. Each of the girls became a valued member of a cohesive and cooperative group, and as their efficiency increased, so did their sense of confidence.

The experimenters had sought to hold all factors constant except those which were explicitly manipulating in each period. In their attempts to provide an optimal climate for objective research, however, the things which were changed most were the very factors most likely to facilitate change. Each of the conditions and processes so far described was present. (1) The girls, in a new and unfamiliar situation, were initially tense and unsure; (2) persons holding great prestige in the girls' eyes introduced the change; (3) initially the objective which the researchers sought was vague and unclear to the girls, but, judging from the reports, it became increasingly clear to the girls that the search had a specific objective—to find ways to increase productivity; (4) the girls were separated from their former associates and formed a new group built around new activities and attitudes; (5) finally the experimenters created conditions which gave the girls a greater sense of importance and worth. The Relay Assembly Test Room Experiments Series have been cited by many writers to illustrate many things, but whatsoever else it demonstrates, it provides us with a carefully reported instance of influence and induced change with increasing self-esteem—an integral part of that process.

Internalization

Internalization of the motive for change was the fourth part of the influence process. The motivating force toward a particular change originates outside the individuals to be influenced. They may be actively searching for more adequate behavior, but the actual kind or direction of the change originates outside. Someone else introduces the plan, the scheme, the interpretation, the suggestion or the idea. Where the new behavior patterns are to become lasting, however, the individuals involved must internalize or come to "own" the rationale for the change.

Internalization occurs as an individual finds the ideas and the prescribed behavior intrinsically rewarding in helping him to cope with external and internal stresses. He adopts the new behavior because he sees it as useful for the solution of a problem or because it is congenial to his own orientation.[54] In the Nampa Center as well as in the historical and experimental settings mentioned earlier, internalization seemed to consist of three elements:

(1) provision of a new cognitive structure

(2) application and improvisation

(3) verification through experience

Provision of a New Cognitive Structure

To judge from the studies examined, the first step in the internalization process is the influencing agent's introduction of a new conceptual framework. The new framework may be restricted to a way of conceiving of a limited set of phenomena or it may be far-reaching in its attempt to explain the totality of a person's experience. In either case, the individual is given a new means for reordering the information he has about himself and his environment. Implicit in the framework are relationships of acts to outcomes so that certain ends call for certain behavior. The framework also provides a language which not only communicates the cognitive structure, but creates an "associative net"[55] by which the individual can relate the events in his own life to the new scheme. Once an idea has been acquired, it serves as a discriminative stimulus and increases the probability that a wide range of relevant behaviors will occur.[56]

This provision of a new cognitive structure by the person seeking to exert influence was a part of all the organizational change studies examined. The new director in our study spent a considerable amount of time differentiating his views of authority from those which underlay the manner in which the Nampa Center had been administered before. At the banner Corporation, the Plant Manager and the consultants agreed that the first step was to "provide the plant management group of fourteen people with a thorough grounding in the concepts and research basis for participation management." A series of seminars was agreed upon partly "to explore the concepts" and to "outline a conceptual scheme."[57] At the Piedmont Oil Refinery, a training program which emphasized a conceptual scheme developed by Robert Blake called the Management Grid, initiated the change providing the managers at the plant with new ways of conceiving of their experiences and actions.[58] In other instances, such as the automobile assembly plant studied by Guest, the new scheme was not presented so formally. The new manager met with the plant in various meetings and told them "what he believed in." He outlined in writing a long-range program and he set up a series of regular meetings to examine their operations. Gradually, the men were brought to "a greater awareness of how the total organization 'fitted together'."[59]

The introduction of a new conception of experience as a part of the internalization process is even more apparent in non-organizational settings. The religious evangelist presents a world view which explains events in terms of spiritual force and points to the relationships of man's actions to this force. The Communistic prison interrogator advances a world view which interprets events as part of a struggle between "progress" and "reaction." From this world view proceeds a prescription of "progressive" and "reactionary" behavior. Different forms of psychotherapy provide a conception of health and sickness that enables the patient to reconceive of his life and supplies him a consistent way of interpreting his experiences.

Application and Improvisation

Introduction of a new cognitive structure is not sufficient for internalizing to take place, however. The individual must, in some way, "make it his own." Our data suggests that he must actively participate in trying to understand the scheme and apply it to his own problems. Where internalization occurs, typically the guidelines are general enough that the person being influenced is forced to improvise. Thus the new cognitive structure has to be amplified and integrated into the individual's existing thought patterns. King and Janis demonstrated the effectiveness of improvisation for inducing opinion change in an experiment with college students.[60] Three groups of male students were presented a written document concerning the induction of graduating college students into the military service, a topic of personal importance to them. Men in one group were asked only to study the statement. Men in a second group were asked to read it aloud with as much effect as possible so that the statement could be tape-recorded and played to judges. Those in the third group were asked to read the statement, then to role-play the part of an advocate of the views stated in the paper. Results of questionnaires filled out several months before and immediately after the experiment showed that only the group who had had to improvise showed a significant opinion change. Moreover, the experimenters' analysis showed that the difference between the groups could not be attributed to closer attention to the written statement nor higher satisfaction with their performance.

In the studies at Banner, Piedmont, and Guest's auto assembly plant, the supervisors had to improvise to make the suggested ideas operational in their own departments. At Banner, the managers and supervisors had to build on their own ideas in order to implement "participation management" in their own part of the plant. At Piedmont, the men had an idea at the end of the training session about the aims of "9.9" management, but they had to improvise to apply the ideas to their own unique situation. At the auto assembly plant studied by Guest the supervisors were impressed by the way the new manager treated them and by his use of meetings to gather the relevant information and to plan the work. But they had to take his pattern, modify it, and improvise to make the new approach work for them.

Schein and his associates reported that in the Chinese thought reform prisons, the prisoners were kept under extreme pressure to make a confession of their guilt.[61] But they were not told what the content of the confession was to be. The prisoner had to supply the material for the confession himself. He was only told repeatedly to stop holding back and to make a complete confession. Only then would there be any promise that the pressure would cease. His task was to produce a confession which would demonstrate to the satisfaction of his captors his complete and unqualified acceptance of the Communist scheme of things. To do this he had to improvise with material from his own experience. Usually, completely fabricated confessions were condemned and rejected. For an acceptable selection and interpretation of this material he had to look for cues from his interrogator, his fellow prisoners who had successfully confessed, and from the controlled mass media. The prisoner had to try repeatedly to demonstrate he had come to interpret the events in his life in terms of the constructs of his captors. Having had to use these constructs to analyze his own life experiences, the prisoner found the communistic world view less implausible and foreign.

Verification Through Experience

Testing a new scheme through one's own experience is probably the most important of the three elements of internalization, and it is too often overlooked in the rush to examine the irrational aspects of the influence process. The individual adopts the attitude or behavior and gives it meaning independent of the original source only as he finds it valid in working with his own problems. He must test it against the world as he perceives that world.

At Nampa the Junior Managers were told that they would be the contact men for their projects with Research and Sales, and before long they were assigned to committees with important and urgent tasks with these men. In approximately the same manner, the Senior Scientists were given an open-ended assignment: to make themselves more useful to the line projects. Soon afterward they were assigned to committees where the task was to plan and execute line projects. Specific organizational mechanisms were provided by the Director to help both groups achieve their objectives, and thus they consistently found their experience coinciding with their expectations.

For the other two groups the situation was very different. The Senior Managers' assignment to do long-range technical planning was no more open-ended that the assignments given the two groups just discussed, but no mechanisms were established to implement this difficult assignment. Moreover, the Senior Managers could see that the Director was not in the same power position to support them in their role as long-range planners that he was for the Junior Managers and Senior Scientists in their new roles.

Though the situation for the Junior Scientists was different, the net result was the same. The Director did have the power to support his assertion that the changes would give the Junior Scientists more responsibility and autonomy, but he provided no specific organizational mechanisms to help bring this about.

At Banner, experimenters first introduced participative management in an industrial engineering project; efficiency rose and morale remained high. So later they set up an experimental department and again the early results were close enough to those anticipated that the superintendents in the plant chose to extend the new management methods to other departments. At Plant Y the supervisors tried new methods of running their departments and produced better results. Following the new manager's lead in holding regular meetings, they found it possible to coordinate their efforts better. They took chances, made mistakes, and were not fired. In recommending technical changes they found each change gave them "that much more chance to think ahead so we won't get in the hole next time." At Sigma the management at the plant drew heavily on the approaches developed in the Gris Laboratory sessions in deciding how to handle a manpower reduction, and the results were so encouraging that they sought to use the approach on more of their operating problems.

In each of the above instances, the new scheme found confirmation in the individual's experience, but there is also the other side of the coin. One of the striking outcomes of the Chinese thought-reform program among western prisoners is that, among most returned prisoners, it did *not* produce long-range ideological changes independent of the external support provided in the prison setting. Only a very few former prisoners maintained an espousal of the ideological position "taught" in the prison after they had had time to re-evaluate the prison experience and had new sources of information which they could check. What would have happened to these prisoners had they returned to a Communist society is impossible to say, but where the viewpoint of his captors failed to find validation in the prisoner's experience after the prison experience, it was not internalized. Of course, in those areas where the Chinese captors' scheme *did* continue to be congruent with their experience, the change in the ex-prisoners' attitudes and behavior continued to be affected.[62]

In one sense, this part of the internalization process may be termed reality-testing, but this is not to say that uniform views of reality prevail. Indeed, an individual's perception of reality may be distorted, but for an individual to integrate the new construct into his system of beliefs he must validate it through his perception of reality.

Implications

So much for the model itself, what are its implications? For those who have a major interest in organizational change, a model such as this raises three kinds of issues:

(1) technical

(2) moral

(3) social

By the term technical, I refer simply to the issues concerning how someone can do his task more effectively. In this vein, even an elementary paradigm like this shows the utility of such a device to a practitioner. If nothing else, it serves as a check list forcing him to ask himself what he has neglected. For example, the importance of tension and the recognition by those involved that some change is required would seem to be nothing beyond common sense. But how often is it ignored by the managers or by the organizational development staff man who is eager to demonstrate the utility of his methods? It is my hope that better models will keep the organizational development specialist from becoming a victim of the "law of the instrument" (i.e. if you give a boy a hammer, he'll find things to hit) and push him toward an improvement of his diagnostic skills.

The near-necessity that the change be introduced or supported by those with power and respect has been learned many times the hard way by those in management training. Although a chief executive's actual participation may not be necessary or in some cases even desirable, his understanding and support can be vital. A full recognition of this feature of organizational change processes may lead the O.D. staff man to spend more time as a counselor to the line executive and less time in training sessions. The line manager may accomplish more using means available to him than the staff specialist can with many times the effort. But, this will require those engaged in organizational development work to educate themselves not only in training methods but also in the creative design of formal structures, and in the behavioral effects of information and measurement systems.

Movement toward increasingly specific goals, while seeming the most obvious, is, from my observation, probably the dimension on which most change efforts flounder. General goals, often widely and genuinely shared, too frequently die for the lack of the crucial idea as to how the first few concrete steps can be taken. Laboratory training often provides a first useful step, but the steps which can help an individual or a group translate the goal from there into daily job performance arise only from planning and creative collaboration of the parties involved.

The use of laboratory training methods has made a major contribution to organizational change in providing a means, however imperfect, of changing relationships without requiring that work teams be broken up or that change wait upon shifts in personnel. But, more needs to be learned about the use of groups to support and reinforce change and experimentation. Work by Schein [63] and others suggests that there is much to be learned about helping individuals use entrance into and exits from organizational units with greater understanding in order to maximize their own effectiveness and freedom.

At an intuitive level, we all understand the part self-esteem plays in change, but the message from the learning theorists about the superior effectiveness of positive reinforcement as a teaching strategy has yet to be utilized fully. Concerning internalization, it is my opinion that as we improve our models of behavioral change, we will become even more impressed with the importance of the cognitive constructs. The constructs now used more widely by those in industry (such as McGregor's X and Y) benefit from the impact which a dichotomy provides, but they also suffer from the polarization it induces. In my opinion, we need new constructs and have been living on the conceptual capital of a prior decade for some time.

The moral issues raised by the use of some explicit representation of the influence process probably are heightened by citing examples drawn from clearly coercive instances of influence as I have done here. In one sense, this is a semantic issue. "Influence" as a descriptive term may cause concern while "leadership" would have an opposite effect. But, there is more here than semantics. Manipulation does occur. Anyone who deals with others in a responsible position is in danger of becoming manipulative. His only effective means of coping with this danger is an intelligent awareness of his own actions and motives and an openness in his dealings with others. A refusal to examine his aims and the processes in which his actions play a part can do no more than serve as a psychological defense against some guilt he may feel. We are all in the business of influencing others. It is not our understanding or consciousness which presents the real moral issues, but our motives and methods. These can be better scrutinized when made explicit.

The social implications primarily are potential rather than actual. Given the swiftness of technological change, it seems imperative that we understand and learn to manage the social change which must accompany it. From scientific invention until the manufacture of the product, the time lag for photography was 112 years. The telephone took half that time—56 years. That period for the transistor was only 5 years, and the integrated circuit went into production in 3 years. This technological pace is becoming increasingly unforgiving of those who fail to anticipate and remain abreast. Organizations, groups, and individuals which do not change rapidly enough must be shunted aside and, at best, placed under some disguised form of care-taking. Even if (in our abundance) we can afford this economically, there is an increasing intolerance in our society, particularly among the young, with our failure to change our organizations to keep pace with shifts in the environment and our failure to keep all segments of our population in the swift mainstream. They impatiently demand that we plan for and cope with change more effectively and humanely—now. These demands cannot be completely dismissed as naive, for within almost all our organizations are individuals who are aware of the environmental shifts and who have some vision of the required behavioral changes. Management's challenge is to translate that awareness to effective action. The implication for students of organizations, it seems to me, is that mine should be only one of an increasing number of attempts to become explicit about the process by which planned change takes place.

Notes

1. R. A. Guest, *Organizational Change* (Illinois: Richard D. Irwin, Inc.).

2. S. E. Seashore and D. G. Bower, *Changing the Structure and Functioning of an Organization,* Monograph, No. 33 (Ann Arbor, Michigan: University of Michigan, 1963).

3. E. Jaques, *The Changing Culture of a Factory* (London: Tavistock Publications Ltd., 1951).

4. R. R. Blake, J. S. Mouton, L. B. Barnes and L. E. Greiner, "Breakthrough in Organizational Development," *Harvard Business Review* (November-December 1964).

5. K. Lewin, "Group Decision and Social Change," *Readings in Social Psychology,* edited by T. M. Newcomb and E. L. Hartley, 1947.

6. R. H. Guest, *op. cit.,* pp. 17-39.

7. S. E. Seashore, and D. G. Bowers, *op cit.,* p. 11.

8. E. Jaques, *op. cit.,* pp. 45-48.

9. R. R. Blake, J. S. Mouton, L. B. Barnes, and L. E. Greiner, *op. cit.*

10. L. E. Greiner, "Antecedents of Planned Organizational Change," *The Journal of Applied Behavioral Science,* Vol. 3, No. 1 (1967), p. 62.

11. O. H. Mowrer, *The New Group Therapy* (Princeton, New Jersey: Van Nostrand Co., 1964).

12. J. Frank, *Persuasion and Healing* (New York: Schocken Books, 1963).

13. E. H. Schein, *et al., Coercive Persuasion* (New York: W. W. Norton and Co., 1961), p. 167.

14. R. Rosenthall, and L. F. Jacobsen, *Scientific American* (April, 1968).

15. R. H. Guest, *op. cit.,* pp. 42, 108.

16. D. C. Pelz, "Influence: A Key to Effective Leadership in the First-Line Supervisor," *Personnel,* Vol. 29 (1952), pp. 209-217.

17. E. Jaques, *op. cit.,* pp. 1-23.

18. S. E. Seashore, and D. G. Bowers, *op. cit.,* pp. 10-15.

19. R. R. Blake, J. S. Mouton, L. B. Barnes, and L. E. Greiner, *op. cit.,* p. 146.

20. C. J. Hovland, I. L. Janis, and H. Kelley, *Communication and Persuasion: Psychological Studies of Opinion Change* (New Haven: Yale University Press, 1953).

21. C. A. Mace, "Satisfaction in Work," *Occupational Psychology,* Vol. 22 (1948), pp. 5-12.

22. See Note 12.

23. E. H. Schein, *et al., op. cit.*

24. J. Segal, "Correlates of Collaboration and Resistance Behavior Among U.S. Army's POW's in Korea," *Journal of Social Issues,* Vol. 13, pp. 31-40.

25. V. Gonzales, and J. Gorkin, *El Campesino: Life and Death in Soviet Russia* (New York: Putnam, 1952).

26. C. P. Loomis, "Tentative Types of Directed Social Change Involving Systematic Linkage," *Rural Sociology,* Vol. 24, No. 4 (December, 1959).

27. R. H. Guest, *op. cit.*

28. E. Jaques, *op. cit.*

29. S. E. Seashore, and D. G. Bowers, *op. cit.*

30. R. R. Blake, J. S. Mouton, L. B. Barnes, and L. E. Greiner, *op. cit.*

31. J. I. Stein, *Contemporary Psychotherapies* (Glencoe, Illinois: Free Press, 1961).

32. B. Berelson, and G. A. Steiner, *Human Behavior: An Inventory of Scientific Findings* (New York: Harcourt Brace, 1964).

33. T. M. Newcomb, "Attitude Development as a Function of Reference Groups: The Bennington Study," *Readings in Social Psychology,* E. E. Macoby, T. M. Newcomb, and E. L. Hartley, eds. (new York: Holt, Rinehart, and Winston, Inc., 1958). See also E. Schein, *et al., op. cit.,* pp. 270-271.

34. S. E. Asch, "Effects of Group Pressure Upon the Modification and Distortion of Judgments," *Groups, Leadership, and Med,* H. Geutzkow, Ed. (Pittsburgh: Carnegie Press, 1951).

35. A. K. Rice, *Productivity and Social Organization: The Ahmedabad Experiment* (London: Tavistock, 1953).

36. E. A. Fleishman, E. J. Harris, and H. E. Butte, *Leadership and Supervision in Industry* (Columbus, Ohio: Personnel Research Board, Ohio State University, 1945).

37. R. R. Blake, J. S. Mouton, L. B. Barnes, and L. E. Greiner, *op. cit.,* pp. 154, 155.

38. R. H. Guest, *op. cit.,* p. 45.

39. E. Jaques, *op. cit.,* p. 307.

40. E. Schein, *op. cit.,* p. 193.

41. G. C. Homans, *The Human Group* (New York: Harcourt, Brace and Co., 1950).

42. W. Sargent, *Battle for the Mind* (Garden City, New York: Doubleday, 1957).

43. E. Schein, *op. cit.,* p. 282.

44. R. R. Blake, J. S. Mouton, L. B. Barnes, and L. E. Greiner, *op. cit.,* p. 141.

45. E. Jaques, *op. cit.,* p. 306.

46. R. A. Guest, *op. cit.,* p. 42.

47. R. A. Guest, *op. cit.,* p. 60.

48. R. R. Blake, J. S. Mouton, L. B. Barnes, and L. E. Greiner, *op. cit.,* pp. 144-145.

49. Seashore and Bower, *op. cit.*, p. 53.

50. J. F. Roethlisberger, and W. J. Dickson, *Management and the Worker* (Cambridge, Mass.: Harvard University Press, 1939), p. 33.

51. Committee on Work in Industry, National Research Council, *Fatigue of Workers: Its Relation to Industrial Production* (New York: Reinhold Publishing Corporation, 1941), pp. 56-66.

52. F. J. Roethlisberger, and W. J. Dickson, *op. cit.*, p. 33.

53. There seems little doubt that the girls received this message whether the experimenters were consciously trying to convey it or not. Studies have shown that even when one person in a close interpersonal relationship is trying to be "non-directive," the other person's behavior can still be strongly influenced by the subtle signals of approval and disapproval which the first person unintentionally gives.
E. J. Murray, "A Content Analysis Method for Studying Psychotherapy," *Psychological Monographs*, Vol. 70 (1956), p. 420.

54. We are very close here to Kelman's formulation of identification. (See "Processes of Opinion Change," *Public Opinion Quarterly*, Spr. '61. And "Compliance, Identification and Internalization, Thru Processes of Attitude Change," *Journal of Conflict Resolution*, Vol. II, No. 1 (March, 1958).
Kelman, however, argues that internalization is not a necessary part of the influence process. An individual, he reasons, may adopt a new behavior pattern through *compliance,* not because he believes in the content, but in order to gain a specific reward or avoid some anticipated punishment. Or he may, through *identification,* accept influence in order to establish or maintain a relationship with another person or group. This distinction between compliance, identification, and internalization can be made conceptually, but in complex interpersonal relations, in which social influence is being exerted over an extended period of time, neither compliance to external demands nor identification with new reference groups appears to operate successfully without internalization of content on the part of the persons being influenced. Certainly in the Nampa situation, it would be difficult to explain the changes we have noted in terms of compliance or identification alone.

55. D. C. McClelland, "Toward a Theory of Motive Acquisition," *American Psychologist* (May, 1965).

56. A. H. Brayfield, "Human Resources Development," *American Psychologist*, Vol. 23, No. 7 (July, 1968).

57. S. E. Seashore, and D. G. Bower, *op. cit.*, pp. 11-12.

58. R. R. Blake, J. S. Mouton, L. B. Barnes, and L. E. Greiner, *op. cit.*

59. R. A. Guest, *op. cit.*, p. 111.

60.   B. King, and I. Janis, "Comparison of the Effectiveness of Improvised Vs. Non-Improvised Role Playing in Producing Opinion Change," *Human Relations,* Vol. 9, pp. 177-186.

61.   E. Schein, *et al., op. cit.,* p. 136.

62.   E. Schein, *et al., op. cit.,* pp. 157-166.

63.   E. Schein, "Organizational Socialization and the Profession of Management," *Industrial Management Review* (Winter, 1968).

BEYOND BEHAVIORALISM?
ORGANIZATION DEVELOPMENT IN PUBLIC MANAGEMENT*

William B. Eddy

Professional public administrators and their academic cohorts have traditionally gleaned through developments in the field of organization and management in search of approaches to greater effectiveness. This search has encompassed business as well as public management techniques and has reached into the disciplines of social science and various new technologies. Of course, several significant developments have occurred within public management itself. A relatively new approach labeled "organizational development" or "OD" is now available. There is evidence that the new approach holds promise for helping cope with some of the perennial problems of government institutions. However, OD is based on a somewhat different model of organization and a different value system than those under which many agencies presently operate. Thus it would seem to require rather careful examination.

Most of the earlier approaches to organizational effectiveness were related to the bureaucracy and administrative management models. They were based on a legal-rational philosophy and utilized "principles of management." These approaches have as their main focus the regularizing of organizational behaviors and procedures in order to achieve greater reliability. It is assumed that the organization will operate most effectively if all requisite performances are

*Reprinted from *Public Personnel Review,* Vol. 31 (July, 1970) pp. 169-175. Reprinted by permission of the international Personnel Management Association, 1313 East 60th Street, Chicago, Illinois 60637.

planned, organized, and programmed according to an established set of procedures, and enforced by a hierarchy of authority.

This approach has been described by contemporary theorists as being primarily a "command" or "compliance" system. There is no question about the considerable utility of this approach to government institutions as well as other organizations. Other approaches related to administrative management, or at least consonant with it, include the development of the professional administrative function, the search for talented manpower, and the civil service merit system.

New Management Approaches

Two new, or at least newly visible, approaches to organization effectiveness are now becoming available. One of these is the set of technologically based approaches to management control which involve such techniques as systems analysis, operations research, program budgeting, and other methods facilitated by the computer. This collection of methodologies has clearly caught the fancy of many of those in public administration and is beginning to prove its usefulness in a variety of settings.

The other newer approach, which has been utilized to a lesser degree in government, is not as clearly defined. It sometimes goes by the name of "applied behavioral science," sometimes "planned change," and sometimes "organization development" or "OD." It is based on the social sciences and focuses particularly upon utilizing more effectively the human resources of the organization. It involves the kinds of concepts referred to by political scientists as "behavioralism." However OD puts the social scientist in a new role in dealing with organizations.

Social scientists and others with behavioral orientations have previously spent considerable time describing, judging, and frequently upbraiding bureaucracy. The works of Merton and Thompson are examples of this position. Even those who were concerned with application of behavioral science remained somewhat distant from the basic fiber and day-to-day operation. The social science literature on application has tended to fall into the following categories:

1. Training programs in which information and principles regarding human behavior are presented to managers in order to help them understand their peers and subordinates, and practice "better human relations," i.e., to humanize the organization.

2. Attitude and morale surveys in which employee responses are gathered, summarized, and sometimes made available to management as well as incorporated into scholarly articles. (For example, Delbert C. Miller, "Using Behavioral Science to Solve Organization Problems," *Personnel Administration,* Jan.-Feb. 1968, pp. 21-29.)

3. Descriptive research studies which bear generalizations about various aspects of the operation. For example, employee response to change, problems of role conflict, leadership characteristics, etc. (As in Robert Presthus, *Behavioral Approaches to Public Administration*, University of Alabama Press, 1965).

4. The technology of personnel psychology has been applied in such areas as testing, performance appraisal, employee relations, and placement.

Additionally, some consulting firms have utilized social science knowledge in their analyses and recommendations.

Recently a new thrust involving much more direct *intervention* into the ongoing process of the organization has been evolving, and is being applied in some private businesses and a few public agencies.

This new approach is a result of two major developments in the field of organizational behavior. The first is the accumulation of data leading to more sophisticated theories of organizational behavior with major emphasis on developing the human potential of an organization. Antecedents to this current approach include the Hawthorne studies; the work of Lewin, Lippitt, and others on planned change; the adult education movement in the United States; the motivationally oriented management theories of McGregor, Argyris, Likert and others; and the focus on interpersonal process developed by the National Training Laboratories. These approaches tend to deemphasize the aspects of technical competence and substantive knowledge and to pay close attention to the *process* whereby people interact in organizations. They view the organization as a social system and focus upon interpersonal and intergroup relationships.

The second development is a set of skills and techniques involving the application of behavioral science. These skill areas have come out of such sources as management consulting, sensitivity training, the role and techniques of the change agent, action research, and counseling psychology. The organization development approach leads the practitioner considerably beyond the earlier approaches to the utilization of social science. The process is much more than the "expert" analyzing the situation from the point of view of his discipline and providing generalizations about what he sees occurring. OD involves injecting the social science practitioner with his knowledge and skills into the mainstream of the organization. It involves him as a person as well as a storehouse of knowledge in the risks and responsibilities of organizational life.

Although many of the concepts of behavioral science are several decades old, they have not been consolidated into a singel point of view. Their sum and substance however is considerably more than the old position that organizations, and thus organizational behavior, consists of nonrational people who are influenced to deviate from the prescribed organizational procedures by a variety of social and emotional factors. The purpose of this paper is to explore the meaning of some of these developments in applied behavioral science and to examine the possible value of this approach in public administration.

The Organization Development Model

Before doing this however, it may be useful to spell out more clearly what is meant by the current practitioners who use and operate within the concept of organizational development.

Organizational development is an organic, process-oriented approach to organizational change and management effectiveness. It seeks to bring about change and improvement by involving members of the organization in problem analysis and planning. It builds on the Theory Y assumptions of Douglas McGregor, and proposes an alternative normative model for human behavior in organization. It stresses interpersonal competence, collaboration and teamwork, and group dynamics skills. It counts on gaining increased effectiveness and adaptability by helping free employees from the limitations and restrictions of highly structured organizations. It seeks to build more employee participation and more collaborative decisionmaking and problem-solving. It is first cousin to other recently developed approaches such as management by objectives, job enlargement, action research, and the Scanlon profit-sharing and participation plan.

The theoretical basis or organization development is anchored in the contemporary writings of Argyris, Beckhard, Likert, Bennis and Blake, to name a few. Current publications on organization development efforts include those in the Weldon Manufacturing Company (Morrow, et al.), TRW Systems Group (Davis), Esso Standard Oil Company (Foundation for Research on Human Behavior). Behavioral scientists and trainers in universities, companies, and consulting firms have formed an "OD network" for the purpose of sharing ideas and experiences.

A Sample Effort

Although there is no single formalized set of procedures, a typical organization development effort might include the following stages:

1. A problem recognition stage in which the organization recognizes the fact that its productivity is being hampered by ineffective interpersonal relations or other kinds of socially related variables, and calls in outside consultants or addresses its own members to exploring these problems.

2. A data gathering stage in which interviews, observations, meeting analysis techniques, or other approaches are utilized to pinpoint difficulties involved in the organization's operation and provide suggestions for reasons for these difficulties.

3. A data analysis and feedback stage in which members of management are brought together and involved in reviewing the findings, diagnosing problem areas, and planning strategies for improvement and change.

4. The intervention programs which are designed to bring about desired changes may include meetings (on-site or at retreats) at which organizational members are helped to participate in developing new programs or new approaches to existing situations.

5. The responsibility for helping the organization come to grips with change problems and to work its way through the difficulties encountered is often assigned to someone in a "change agent role" who is either a member of the organization or an outside consultant. This individual usually does not play the role of the expert advisor, but rather uses his clinical skills as well as his knowledge to help facilitate the problem-solving process of the group.

6. Members of the organization collaboratively develop procedures, policies, and norms which reinforce and implement the new ways of operating developed in the previous change efforts.

7. Training is an important component of OD. Ongoing programs integrated into the change process are made available to employees. Training methods tend to be participatory and experience-based. The laboratory approach of the National Training Laboratories (T-Groups or sensitivity training) is frequently used to help employees develop interpersonal competence and teamwork skills such as group problem-solving and decision-making.

It is important to emphasize that organization development involves more than simply teaching good human relations and going off on week-end retreats for cathartic purpose. One of the central concepts in the process is that of "confrontation." Emphasis is placed on helping organizational members recognize and come to grips with organizational problems at the human interaction level which are often ignored or swept under the rug under the assumption that conflict is to be avoided at all costs. Structural and procedural change, often the beginning points of the more traditional approaches, may be the end result of involvement in an organizational development program.

Applications in Public Management

Experience indicates that OD has enough promise that professional public administrators might well wish to examine it for possible usefulness in government. Organizational development and the kinds of variables with which it deals may help agencies come to grips with some of the problems that plague them. Long standing problems that do not seem to be amenable to solution by traditional administrative approaches include the following.

Difficulty in attracting, holding, and developing competent, committed employees. A more meaningful and stimulating working environment, with more opportunity for participation in agency planning and decisionmaking, and with greater possibility for personal growth and development, may be required to help government compete with private industry for employees.

Overcoming rigidity and resistance to change. Collaborative models of preparation for and implementation of change are needed to help facilitate change while reducing some of the traditional difficulties and resistances encountered in change programs.

Overemphasis on structure and compliance to the neglect of goal-orientation and innovation. Ways need to be found to enhance rather than restrict the potential contributions of employees.

Another set of difficulties has been complicated by attempts of government to deal with urban life. These include:

Intergroup cooperation. The increasing complexity of the urban society and the developing technologies make it mandatory that units of government as well as subunits within the agency be able to communicate and collaborate effectively as they take on highly related projects. Yet it is very difficult to legislate cooperation. Organizational development approaches focus on clearing away some of the barriers to collaboration and helping people to learn how to work more effectively together.

Operation in arenas in which there is a lack of traditional hierarchical power. Government administrators at a variety of levels find themselves in situations in which it is important to influence others or to bring about collaborative action, but there are no mechanisms for *requiring* that things be done. They are finding that they need greater skills in facilitating cooperative action among volunteers, community groups, etc., utilizing mechanisms other than power.

Temporary systems. Much of the work of problem-solving at the local government level occurs within the context of groups formed outside or at the perimeter of traditional governmental agencies (Model Cities groups, citizens task forces, community action programs, intergovernmental organizations, etc.). It is no secret that these kinds of organizations have often floundered in their attempts to "get organized" and fulfill their missions. Yet knowledge currently available about how to build and maintain temporary social systems should be able to increase the probability of success.

There are beginning to be a few examples of organization development activities in public management. These include Project ACORD in the State Department (reported by Marrow), the work of Golembiewski, and activities with the City of Kansas City (reported by F. Gerald Brown). A few communities and federal agencies are using some of the components of organization development—particularly laboratory training techniques.

Does OD Fit Public Administration?

Several possible reasons for the minimal utilization or organization development in government are suggested below as hypotheses for consideration.

1. The older methods for improving organizational performance (O&M, systems and procedures, etc.) are more consonant with, and supplement, the legal-rational bureaucratic approach in which most government units have been built. Although the traditional approach has been changed in several respects by some of the new methodologies, the basic tenets of the "command system" have usually not been questioned or challenged. The older methodologies have instead been largely ways of shoring up, protecting, and increasing the efficiency of the traditional approach. Utilization of organizational development may require a more drastic change in focus than would other techniques.

2. Applied behavioral science and organization development have "natural enemies" in the fields of political science and public administration. Some political scientists have viewed with suspicion the "behavioral" view of the organization. They have often seen its value, if any, as suggesting difficulties or limitations to the existing system rather than proposing alternative ways of managing. Additionally, it seems to the present writer that some in the field of political science and public administration are somewhat fixated on the Machiavellian concept of authority. They tend to react against any approach which suggests decreasing the amount of direct and unilateral authority held by individuals in top level positions.

3. There is the feeling, shared by some in business, that the behavioral sciences are proposing a "tender-minded approach" to organization which overplays the need to have workers happy and satisfied and underplays the emphasis on productivity (the "human relations" approach of the 1940-50 period).

4. There is a certain degree of misunderstanding and lack of information regarding some of the basic ideas involved in participative management. There is suspicion that this approach courts the disaster of turning the organization over to the employees, abdicating leadership and authority, and establishing management by committee. Supporters contend that an emphasis on the people process does not necessarily require a deemphasis on production and that greater involvement of organizational members in decisionmaking does not decrease the authority of the manager.

5. The basic assumptions and values of organization development may be inappropriate in public organizations. The behavioral science that supports the OD approach is more than a set of techniques or ways of improving the efficiency of the traditional form of organization. It questions some of the basic operational assumptions underlying bureaucracy, and raises possibilities of changing not so much the *structure* as the *process* and *philosophy* of organizations. Some of the assumptions and values about human behavior in contemporary organizations which the OD approach supports are the following:

> *Openness of communication and authenticity of human expression are appropriate behaviors.* They not only help people perform more effec-

tively as individuals but they make for more effective work relations. Individuals should be encouraged to "level" with each other regarding feelings and ideas.

Conflict is an inherent part of organizational operation. It should not be covered up or compromised away, but should be acknowledged and dealt with openly. It is possible to learn how to "manage" conflict and turn it to productive use.

Wider participation in decisionmaking and planning and wider sharing of information are valuable. They not only help motivate employees through greater involvement, but also bring about greater utilization of human resources and more efficient problem-solving.

A climate of mutual trust is an important factor in organizations. It minimizes defensiveness, opens communications, allows people to take more creative risks and thus be more innovative.

Organizations can operate more effectively if there is less reliance on formal structure, rules, regulations, red tape, and procedures. People can be counted on to behave more responsibly rather than less responsibly if they are partially freed from organizational control. Self-direction, rather than external direction, is a distinct possibility, granting acceptance of the organization's goals.

Concepts of power and authority need to be revised. Unilateral authority is not necessary for organizational effectiveness. Managers who delegate and in other ways share a good deal of the decisionmaking will, in the end, build more productive work units.

An important value in organizations involves the development of the employees as people to greater degrees of commitment, responsibility, and personal awareness. Many in the field of OD are committed to the humanistically-oriented psychology of Carl Rogers, Abraham Maslow, and others.

There is an emphasis on change. It is assumed that continual receptivity and adaptability to change are important organizational values.

Public administrators considering the possible utilization of organizational development will have to review these values and decide whether or not they are antithetical to the particular values and needs of their own organizations, and whether they would pose too much difficulty for the existing form. For example, some may assert that political competition and public accountability via the press mitigate against openness of communication and objective problem-solving. Costello has identified several points of contrast between public and private organizations relevant to the question of how change takes place in city government. Some of the unique characteristics of public agencies—such as sudden and drastic leadership changes, high visibility of decision-making and extreme difficulty in cutting existing functions and services—may place conditions upon the application of OD in some situations.

Conclusion

The implementation of the behavioral science approach to organization development is not quick and cheap, nor is it a panacea. More is needed than speeches, policy statements, and short-term training programs. A decision to try organization development must be a decision to commit time and money over a relatively extended period of time to the development of people and of the organization. Development activities cannot be routinized and written into the procedures to be handled by a staff assistant. Indoctrination training must be replaced with training approaches which tie the individual's learning needs and experiences directly into his organizational performance. Risks must be taken and the possibility of feedback which is uncomfortable for those in power has to be anticipated.

TRW Systems, a fast-moving aerospace contracting firm, is a heavy consumer of applied behavioral science and advocate of the OD model. "Based on what we know today," says an executive of another firm, "TRW Systems may turn out to be one of the earliest complete models of the American business-industrial organization of the future." (See John Poppy, "New Era in Industry: It's OK to Cry in the Office," *Look,* July 9, 1968, p. 66.)

Public administrators may or may not be making similar statements in a few years. But it is likely that they will be called upon to make decisions about the potential value of organizational development programs to their organizations.

The author is indebted to Robert Saunders, F. Gerald Brown, and Thomas P. Murphy for their comments and suggestions.

References

Argyris, Chris. *Personality and Organization.* New York: Harper, 1957. *Organization and Innovation.* Homewood, Illinois: Irwin-Dorsey, 1965.

Bennis, Warren. *Changing Organizations.* New York: McGraw-Hill, 1966.

Blake, Robert R., and Jane S. Mouton. *The Managerial Grid.* Houston, Texas: Gulf, 1964.

Brown, F. Gerald. "Applications of Organization Development Concepts in a Large City: The Kansas City Case." Paper presented to the 1969 Annual Conference of the American Society for Public Administration, Miami Beach, Florida, 1969.

Costello, Timothy W. "An Organizational Psychologist Looks at Change in Municipal Government—From the Inside." Address at American Psychological Association Convention, San Francisco, 1968.

Davis, Sheldon A. "An Organic Problem-Solving Method of Organization Change." *Journal of Applied Behavioral Science, III,* Jan.-Mar. 1967, pp. 3-21

Foundation for Research on Human Behavior. *An Action Research Program for Organization Improvement.* Ann Arbor, Michigan: 1960.

Golembiewski, Robert T. "The Laboratory Approach to Organization Change: Schema of a Method." *Public Administration Review, 27,* No. 3, Sept. 1967, pp. 211-21; "Organization Development in Public Agencies: Perspective on Theory and Practice." *Public Administration Review, 29,* No. 4, July-Aug. 1969, pp. 367-77.

Likert, Rensis. *New Patterns in Management.* New York: McGraw-Hill, 1961. *The Human Organization.* New York: McGraw-Hill, 1967.

Lippitt, Ronald, Jeanne Watson, and Bruce Westley. *The Dynamics of Planned Change.* New York: Harcourt, Brace, and World, 1958.

McGregor, Douglas. *The Human Side of Enterprise.* New York: McGraw-Hill, 1960.

Marrow, Alfred J. "Managerial Revolution in the State Department." *Personnel, 43,* Nov.-Dec. 1966, pp. 2-12. With David G. Bowers and Stanley E. Seashore. *Management by Participation: Creating a Climate for Personal and Organizational Development.* New York: Harper, 1967.

Maslow, Abraham H. *Eupsychian Management: A Journal.* Homewood, Illinois: Irwin-Dorsey, 1965.

Merton, Robert K. "Bureaucratic Structure and Personality," *Social Forces, 17,* 1940, pp. 560-68.

Rogers, Carl R. *On Becoming a Person.* Boston: Houghton Mifflin, 1961.

Schein, Edgar H., and Warren Bennis. *Personal and Organizational Change Through Group Methods: The Laboratory Approach.* New York: Wiley, 1965. With Warren Bennis and Richard Beckhard (eds.). *Addison-Wesley Series on Organization Development* (6 volumes). Reading, Massachusetts, 1969.

Thompson, Victor A. *Modern Organization.* New York: Knopf, 1961.

APPLIED BEHAVIORAL SCIENCE
IN URBAN ADMINISTRATIVE/POLITICAL SYSTEMS*

William B. Eddy and Robert J. Saunderst

It is legitimate, if not novel, to assert that local government institutions must find ways to increase their effectiveness if they are to solve the pressing problems of this urban society. One of the aspects of government that needs improving is the administrative system. A variety of avenues to upgrading administration are being proposed and tested. These include accounting and decision-making tools based on computer technology, infusion of professional and technical expertise into problem areas and federal support to create new ancillary organizations such as neighborhood organizations, metropolitan area coordinating groups, and pollution control agencies. The establishment of this latter variety of new organizations is apparently based at least in part on the assumption that existing local government structures cannot be relied on to do the job.

Each critic of local government generates his own description of what is wrong—depending upon his own orientation and the perspective from which he views the community. From the point of view of applied behavioral science the problem looks something like this: Most governmental organizations were built upon and still fit reasonably well the traditional bureaucratic model. This form is characterized by an emphasis on efficiency and rationality, a pyramidal

*Reprinted from *Public Administration Review,* Vol. 32, No. 1 (January/February, 1972) pp. 11-16).
†The authors acknowledge the assistance of F. Gerald Brown, Thomas P. Murphy, and John L. Taylor, who made helpful contributions to this article.

113

authority system (or command system), functional units clearly separated on the basis of mission, and a system of rules and procedures to direct and control the behavior of employees. This kind of system is a rational design for the accomplishment of order, reliability, accountability, and precision as basic outcomes. But for all its rationality and reliability, the bureaucracy has distinct disadvantages in attempting to deal with the dynamic and complex urban scene. Some of the organizational problem areas that require attention include the following: (1) the need for increased flexibility and adaptation to change; (2) the need to shift from major emphasis on control, structure, and compliance to a focus on problem identification, problem solving, and innovation; (3) the need for more effective teamwork and collaboration within and among operating units; (4) the need to develop managerial approaches which utilize the full potential of employees and enhance motivation and commitment; (5) the need to develop more "open" organizational systems which are more in touch with and responsive to external as well as internal factors.

One approach to the resolution of these kinds of problems has been to leave the basic model of the organization intact, but to beef it up by increasing the rationality through the use of control systems, structural redesign, and more qualified professional experts. An alternate, though not incompatible approach to organizational improvement has emerged from the field of behavioral science. There is no one term nor single set of techniques which define this area. The term "applied behavioral science" is broadest and subsumes within it such approaches as planned change, organization renewal, organization development (OD), and grid organization development. The purpose of this article is not to describe nor argue for the application of behavioral science in public organizations. These issues have been discussed in detail elsewhere. The present purpose is to identify and address some issues related to the "fit" between the behavioral science change model and urban agencies where the political/administrative mix may pose problems different from those encountered in private business.

When evaluating the applicability of behavioral science in specific kinds of systems, it is important to review the norms, values, and principles proposed in the new model which may differ in significant ways from those inherent in the traditional approach. Many applied behavioral scientists take a position about appropriateness or inappropriateness of certain kinds of organizational behavior based on a combination of values, insights, and empirical evidence. The following are illustrative.

1. *Openness and authenticity.* Communication about perceptions, ideas, and feelings should be free and open in all directions. People should be encouraged to "level" with each other—to be frank about their reactions. Feelings are viewed as important and appropriate aspects of interpersonal relations and should not be covered up.

2. *Trust.* A necessary component of effective collaborative relations is a level of mutual trust which will support openness, acceptance of others' positions, risk-taking, and mutual support.

3. *Shared influence and participation.* Unilateral authority is not always the best approach to management. Organizations may function more effectively if employees at all levels are allowed a sense of ownership through opportunities to influence decisions and pland that affect them.

4. *Development of people.* The organization has a need and a responsibility to help its members continue to develop themselves as fuller, more competent, and actualizing total persons.

5. *Confrontation.* Traditional norms stressing avoidance of direct confrontation are dysfunctional. Avoiding conflict, "keeping feelings out of it, " and compromising differences may prevent problem solving.

6. *Interpersonal competence.* Substantive technical knowledge is not enough. Organizational members need to gain greater self-understanding and operational skills in such areas as communication, teamwork, and conflict management.

7. *Change and renewal.* Organizations should devote time and resources to the development of mechanisms that assure a continuing review and renewal process. Evaluation and change rather than fixed procedures should become the organization's way of life.

Application of Behavioral Science in Government

Organization development programs utilizing applied behavioral science have been tried extensively in business firms.[1] There is less direct experience in public agencies. Golembiewski[2] and Eddy[3] have discussed some of the problems in applying OD programs in government. Golembiewski's analysis emphasizes the federal government and focuses on organizational characteristics which differentiate it from business. He lists the major differentiating characteristics of government as: (1) multiple access—the system is more open to influence at many levels; (2) greater variety of interests, reward structures, and values at subgroup levels; (3) more competing command loci or influence centers rather than a clear-cut "management group"; and (4) weak linkages between executives and operating managers.

Golembiewski also discusses the unique "habit background" of public agencies. These are patterns within the institutional environment which may inhibit the process of change. Phenomena discussed indlude reluctance to delegate because of the need to maximize information and control at the top—where responsibility is affixed; legal specification of appropriate work behaviors;

greater emphasis on security; stress on procedural regularity and caution; and a less strongly developed concept of professional management.

Eddy identifies several possible reasons for the current minimal utilization of behavioral science in government: (1) alternative change programs such as systems and procedures methods are more consonant with the legal-rational bureaucratic approach and may be perceived as less threatening to the status quo; (2) some political scientists and public administrators are "natural enemies" of behavioral science—particularly in regard to its challenges to traditional notions about the need for "strong" leadership; (3) behavioral science is often seen as "tenderminded" with an undue focus on keeping employees happy; (4) participative approaches are suspected as cover-ups for management by committee or turning the organization over to the subordinates; and (5) the values underlying applied behavioral science (discussed earlier in this article) may be in conflict with values inherent in some agencies.

Other authors have, of course, discussed differences between public and private organizations which affect management behavior. A paper by Costello is particularly relevant because it describes unique characteristics of public agencies which may affect the ways in which change takes place.[4] His list which refers to local government includes: (1) sudden and drastic changes in leadership; (2) goals and outcomes which are less amenable to measurement; (3) more heterogeneous constituency—sub-groups have conflicting interests; (4) decisions and policies are more highly visible and more subject to critique; (5) local governments are subjected to more legal constraints and can make fewer of their own decisions than other institutions; (6) it is much more difficult to "go out of business"—to shut down a facility or withdraw a service; and (7) programs which have immediate visibility and seem to demonstrate progress may receive political priority over slower and less dramatic—though more meaningful—efforts.

Political Issues Related to Behavioral Science in Local Government

Our experiences in carrying out organization development programs in local government agencies have made us aware of several other potential problem areas that need further attention and understanding. Most relate in one way or another to the political environment.

a. There are, of course, the usual problems of interfacing any administrative system and political system. These include public mistrust of bureaucracy and bureaucrats' mistrust of the public, politicians vs. administrators in policy formation, concerns about keeping the technocrats publicly accountable, generalized resistance to change, and political pressures in relation to specific programs. While these certainly are not unique to behavioral science applications, they may well be important factors.

b. There is a potential incompatibility between political systems and the "ideal" organization from a behavioral science point of view. Political systems are by nature *distributive*–or at least are usually operated that way. They function to divide a finite amount of resources among various interest groups. This "cutting of the pie" is a win/lose game in which a variety of tactics are used to increase the rewards to one group–which frequently means they are decreased to others. The well-functioning administrative system aims at being integrative.[5] Emphasis is placed on commonality of purpose, collaboration, and win/win relationships. Ways are sought to minimize win/lose competition among operating units, and to enhance shared problem solving and planning. A highly integrative organization at the local government level may not serve the felt needs of politicians whose own goals require special output from a particular segment within the organization–to the possible detriment of other units.

c. Trust and openness may not be possible (or at least not perceived as possible) in situations with political implications. An official in NASA is quoted as saying ". . . we never punish error. We only punish *concealment* of error."[6] This policy is, of course, intended to reinforce openness and disclosure. Many local government officials may feel they cannot afford this much risk, and may be much more concerned about concealing errors than whether or not errors were made in the first place. In an "Affairs of State" editorial in the *Saturday Evening Post,* Stewart Alsop castigated behavioral scientists for their attempts to "unfreeze" the Foreign Service Office and create more openness and candor. He argued that secretiveness was functional. Instead of this "final humiliation" he urged, "Just let the poor old Foreign Service alone. . . ."[7]

d. Some of the techniques of the application of behavioral science involve recognizing and dealing with the feelings, attitudes, and personal styles of participants–a departure from Weberian "formalistic impersonality." There is considerable misunderstanding and suspicion regarding approaches such as sensitivity training and team building which are designed to promote communication and learning about interpersonal relationships. Many laymen, politicians included, do not have the information to distinguish between legitimate programs for personal learning and growth and various so-called thought control schemes. The protestations of the far right and the "wild" turn-on nudie groups have not helped the image either.[8] One of the authors recently conducted a brief team-development program for members of a city council. The methodology involved confidential interviews with individual councilmen regarding intracouncil and council-management concerns, followed by a retreat at which generalized interview data were fed back and discussed in some depth. There was no sensitivity training involved. One council member refused to participate in the program and was quoted in the press as follows:

> I feel that the presence of a psychologist, regardless of what his title may be, is somewhat insulting to members of the council. I am quite

sure that neither President Nixon nor Governor . . . would suggest such a thing to members of Congress or the Legislature.

The role of the city councilman is to serve the people who elect him. I believe that rather than attending retreats we ought to be out in the districts conferring with the people, not psychoanalyzing one another.

I personally do not believe in the techniques of group therapy, sensitivity training, or any other device which would reduce our individual thinking to the thinking of a group; that is, making the individual feel he is committing a mortal sin to have a thought of his own. . . .

There is no substitute for training a councilman, and that is basically what these retreats purport to do, like conferring and meeting with the people in the districts and then reporting their views on the council. In other words, there is no substitute for "government of the people, by the people, and for the people." The administration needs to look no further for a philosophy nor do we need a psychoanalysis of the job we have been elected to do than to adopt the philosophy of government of, by, and for the people.[9]

e. Conventional wisdom, political thinking included, views "good" leadership, assertive-authoritarian leadership, and masculinity as essentially synonymous. Approaches to leadership which assert that subordinates should have upward influence, that dissident points of view should be listened to, and that solving problems is preferable to discipline are seen as weak and ineffectual. Two articles in the *Buffalo Evening News* illustrate what may happen.[10] Behavioral scientist Warren Bennis resigned his position as executive vice president of the State University of New York at Buffalo in protest against the way in which police were involved in dealing with a student disturbance. He was quoted in the article as follows:

"I have throughout the sequence of disturbances remained firmly convinced that police occupation could do nothing but exacerbate the troubles, that they were and are unnecessary," Dr. Bennis said in an interview.

"I did not approve that decision then and do not approve of it now."

"Hadn't done enough."

Dr. Bennis, who retains his post as vice president for the academic development, also criticized what he termed "a lack of candor" and an unresponsiveness to student concern by the Regan administration since a clash between police and students Feb. 25 set off a student strike and a week-and-a-half of disorders on the Main St. campus.

"I thought we hadn't done enough to demonstrate either sensitivity to the reactions on our campus, to the events on Feb. 25, particularly the police actions in Norton Union, nor did I feel that we had as an administration adequately communicated a responsiveness to the issues facing this campus," he daid.

"If I felt we had done the best we could on these latter issues, and the violence had still continued, I might have then—but only as a last resort—called for police occupation."

In a subsequent meeting of the city council, a councilwoman criticized the university administration. "The campus disorder," she said, "is separating the men from the boys. One of the boys has just resigned, thank goodness."

f. Organization development proposes that work time is legitimately spent working on relationship issues. Terms such as "team building," "working the problem," and "processing" refer to situations in which administrators do not do *work* in the traditional sense, but meet to talk about *how* they might work more effectively together. Politicians and the public may feel that this is wasted time and that people paid to manage local government ought to *know* how to work. The fact that human systems require *maintenance* in much the same way that machines do is not widely understood, and training which is not technical training is not valued. The fact that working on relationships requires getting together in meetings heightens the problem—since meetings are often viewed as a waste of time.

g. Special problems may be caused by a press which maintains a traditional view of organizations and of local government. There is pressure for all "official" meetings to be open, and everything to be on the record. This condition reinforces closed, safe discussions ("you have to watch what you say") and discourages sound problem solving in groups. In order for groups to solve problems effectively, work out relationships, explore ideas, manage conflict, and make good decisions, an atmosphere of nondefensiveness, provisionalism, exploration, and trust must prevail. This cannot be accomplished in a fishbowl. Members of the press need to gain insights which allow them to differentiate between "dealing with policy" and "dealing with each other" meetings. Some newspapers are willing to accept a few closed meetings so that personal issues may be worked, but in doing so imply that secrecy is necessary out of good taste because the administrators are at each other's throats.

h. Laws and policies relating to accountability take a "Theory X" position regarding human motivation—as described by McGregor[11] They grow out of assumptions that people in general are not to be trusted, they are not responsible, they must be closely watched. Applied behavioral science tends to assume different motives—most people want to work, to develop, to assume responsibility and contribute to the system. Shared decision making, less rigid controls, decentralization, and delegation are seen as improving, not damaging, the organization.

i. The reform movement of the early part of this century has left strong tendencies to value local government structures which provide for strong authority figures, centralization, control, and accountability as defenses against potential spoilers. In essence, it may be perceived better to run a highly controlled system whose members care less and accomplish less individually and collectively, but which runs less risk of scandal.

j. The hard sciences have managed to gain the trust of many people. The "soft" sciences of human behavior have not reached that point. They have no easily visible "better things for better living" or men on the moon to win friends. Further, the application of the medical model to the analysis of behavior has tended to associate psychology with the sick and the flawed—not a positive association in political terms.

There are doubtless other issues related to behavioral science in the political/administrative mix. And those listed probably apply differentially according to a variety of factors not presently understood. It is hoped that the listing will alert behavioral scientists and public administrators to avoid snags in the implementation of change programs.

Overcoming Resistance

Although it is risky to propose solutions before the problems are clearly defined, several possibilities for coming to grips with some of the difficulties listed above can be offered.

The authors have been involved in several efforts to utilize organization development in the interface between administrators and politicians. One was the council-manager retreat mentioned earlier. Although it was a very short-term program and was boycotted by one council member, it was deemed useful by most who attended. Another was a longer-term effort to help elected and appointed officials in an urban county government develop better understanding and collaborative skills. The program is described by Murphy.[12] Experience indicates that such efforts are feasible and worthwhile—but one must proceed carefully. Learnings for us that have come from these programs include the need for clear prior acceptance by all parties of the relevance and validity of the problems to be attacked and a commitment to facing and solving them. Also, it is important to clarify norms that can allow trust to develop. For example, that conversations be kept confidential within the training group, that participants attempt to view feedback as an attempt to be helpful and not to be resented later, and that major conflicts and disagreements be acknowledged and worked through—rather than avoided and allowed to fester. This further suggests that some continuing attention should be paid to the "contract" between client and consultant so that expectations and roles of both parties will not stand unnecessarily in the way at some critical point in the change process.

Behavioral scientists and administrators know much more about overcoming resistance to change than they tend to utilize in implementing their own change programs. For example, involvement in planning the program by those likely to be affected by changes—both within and outside the organization—is often helpful. The greater the degree to which those involved are informed, allowed to contribute to the effort, and feel able to exert influence on the process (sometimes in order to increase their own safety), the less they are likely to resist or sabotage the effort. Other strategies for preventing resistance include building a climate of trust between the client and the change agent, not violating important organizational norms, and beginning the change with problems that the client feels are most important and most pressing.

Organizational change efforts may need to be preceded by thorough informational and educational programs conducted both within and outside the organization. The need for change and development, the rationale, and case examples can be usefully pointed out. It is particularly important to help the public understand that ways of viewing and evaluating organizations are changing —along with the rest of the urban scene. Elected officials are not likely to encourage different models of administrative behavior in the organizations they oversee until they feel constituents will accept such approaches.

Costello asserts that the principal coin in the realm of politics is power, and that behavioral scientists have written more about the process of power equalization than about acquisition and effective use of power.[13] The implications of this state of affairs may be that behavioral scientists are either uncomfortable or unknowledgeable in regard to one of the major dimensions of government, and that they may be ineffective in dealing with those who seek and use power. Costello asserts that the behavioral scientist who would bring about change in municipal affairs must build a power backing. He may do this by (1) direct political activity in support of sympathetic candidates, (2) relating to strong community action organizations, or (3) personal cultivation or reaching out to men in power to gain understanding and personal acceptance. Although only (2) is usually acceptable to the scientist, (3) is most promising.

In the long run behavioral scientists and public administrators may have to move from a defensive to an offensive stance. Frequently the political system is accepted as the one which is fixed, and conventional wisdom is presumed to be indisputable. Those who think they know a better way to view the conduct of urban government may have to press for changes, rather than simply study and write about the problems.

Notes

1. See, for example, Sheldon Davis, "An Organic Problem-Solving Method of Organizational Change," *Journal of Applied Behavioral Science,* Vol 3 (January 1967), pp. 3-21, and Warren G. Bennis, *Organization Develop-*

ment: Its Nature, Origins and Prospects, first volume in a six-volume series (Reading, Mass.: Addison-Wesley, 1969).

2. Robert T. Golembiewski, "Organization Development in Public Agencies: Perspectives on Theory and Practice," *Public Administration Review,* Vol. XXIX (July/August 1969), pp. 367-378.

3. William B. Eddy, "Beyond Behavioralism? Organization Development in Public Management," *Public Personnel Review,* Vol. XXXI (July 1970), pp. 169-175.

4. Timothy W. Costello, "Change in Municipal Government," in F. G. Brown and T. P. Murphy (eds.), *Emerging Patterns in Urban Administration* (Lexington, Mass.: D. C. Heath, 1970), pp. 13-32.

5. The distinction between distributive and integrative situations is developed by Richard E. Walton and Robert B. McKersie in *A Behavioral Theory of Labor Negotiations: An Analysis of a Social Interaction System* (New York: McGraw-Hill, 1965).

6. Marvin R. Weisbord, "What, Not Again? Manage People Better, " *Think,* Vol. 36 (January-February 1970), p. 7.

7. *Saturday Evening Post* (March 11, 1967), p. 14.

8. For analyses of the criticisms of sensitivity training, see American Psychiatric Association, *Encounter Groups and Psychiatry,* Report of Task Force on Recent Developments in the Use of Small Groups (Washington, D.C.: American Psychiatric Association, 1970), and W. B. Eddy and B. Lugin, "Laboratory Training and Encounter Groups," *Personnel and Guidance Journal.*

9. *Kansas City Star* (February 7, 1969), p. 1.

10. *Buffalo Evening News* (March 11, 1970).

11. Douglas McGregor, *The Human Side of Enterprise* (New York: McGraw-Hill, 1960), chapters 3 and 4.

12. Thomas P. Murphy, *Metropolitics and the Urban County* (Washington, D.C.: Washington National Press, 1970), pp. 134-135.

13. Costello, *op. cit.,* pp. 22-23.

ORGANIZATION DEVELOPMENT
Public Sector Theory and Practice*

Edward J. Giblin

Contextual Factors: Barriers to Achieving Planned Change

In attempting to develop insights into OD theory and practice in the public sector, it is necessary first to identify those characteristics of government agencies that bear on success. The characteristics and situations of public sector agencies that bear on their success can be conceived mainly as barriers to organization development and effectiveness. In fact, an understanding of these contextual factors in itself provides insight into OD theory and practice in government.

Further, the characteristics of government agencies that bear on their success are most easily defined in terms of the basic differences between most public, as opposed to private sector, organizations. An understanding of these basic differences is essential, because most OD literature deals with the private sector. These salient differences relate to organizational variation, long-range planning, the civil service system, crisis atmosphere, and organization style and effectiveness.

*Reprinted from *Public Personnel Management,* Vol. 5, No. 2 (March/April, 1976) pp. 112-119. Reprinted by permission of the International Personnel Management Association, 1313 East 60th Street, Chicago, Illinois 60637.

1. Organizational Variation

As compared to business organizations, the public sector involves a greater variety of individuals and groups with different and often mutually exclusive sets of interests, reward structures, and values.[1] Role conflicts between legislators and high-level administrators are illustrative of this characteristic. The commitment of career officials to programs may inhibit or even thwart executive direction, rendering the chain of command almost useless.[2] The legislative branch often encourages a weakening in the chain of command, in order to increase its own influence over agencies and programs. In addition, a great number of interest groups wield tremendous power over policy and program directions.

    Certainly, such incongruities also occur in business organizations—the relations between managements and unions being a prime example. However, these problems do appear, by comparison, to be less intense in the private sector. They also appear to take on less complex forms.

2. Long-Range Planning

The roadblocks to long-range planning, faced by all public organizations, represent a serious impediment to an effective organization development process. The problems confronting government agencies, in regard to their ability to do long-range planning, have been noted since the first Hoover Commission. While these agencies can develop long-range plans, the uncertainties of the yearly budget process make it a very tenuous practice. Most agencies, fundamentally, do their planning on a year-by-year basis.

    In terms of an OD process, which is best conceived of as an ongoing (long-range) effort, this inability to plan for long periods necessitates reliance on a series of short-run efforts. The continuity of these efforts is always in doubt, thereby reducing their influence on these organizations and their participants.

3. The Civil Service System

Most civil service systems represent a major barrier to achieving greater organizational effectiveness in public organizations. A substantive discussion of the pathology of the municipal, state, and federal civil service system would represent a major undertaking and go far beyond the scope of this article. However, it is well known that the civil service system does have a multifaceted and very negative impact on public organizations' ability to engender substantive OD programs.

    Essentially, civil service compromises the public administrator's responsibility to manage his organization, by limiting his authority to hire the persons he wants at all but the very highest (i.e., appointed) levels. It limits his authority to discharge staff for poor performance; and, even more seriously, it limits his discretionary power to advance staff for outstanding performance. Drucker summed up the issue by noting that while civil service protects the machinery from politics, it also protects the incumbents in the agencies from the demands of performance.[3]

Civil service tends to be an all-pervasive influence in these agencies. Most often, the entire management team will be civil service employees, with the exception of the top administrator. Thus, in a real sense, the entire organization is "unionized." In actuality, many management persons also belong to public employee unions. Most managers in private organizations say they experience difficulty with the fact that blue-collar workers are unionized. The public administrator, by contrast, must deal with an organization that is virtually 100 percent "unionized."

4. Crisis Atmosphere

A pronounced dissatisfaction with government organizations is a growing phenomenon in U.S. society. Recently, many client groups have taken legal action against "human resource agencies" that fail to serve them effectively. These external attacks have resulted in a crisis atmosphere in many of these normally lethargic agencies.

This crisis atmosphere has a positive side in that it tends to facilitate the initiation and conduct of OD projects. It has been noted in the literature that many OD programs are initiated in response to crises.[4] But crisis atmosphere also has negative implications for OD. OD often tends to engender uncertainty in the short-run, which may add to the agency's tendency to isolate and defend itself. Under such conditions, public agencies may place even greater stress on procedural regularities and caution. This excessive reliance on established practice runs counter to OD goals, which stress management according to relevant objectives, as opposed to reliance on past practices.

5. Organizational "Style" and Effectiveness

The static style, low propensity for program change, and general ineffectiveness of most public organizations render them very poor candidates for the realization of successful OD efforts. To a considerable degree this "style" is a function of patterns of administrative regulations, which are usually spelled out in minute detail in legislation. It is almost axiomatic that the most successful and expedient organizational changes can be made in organizations that are already functioning reasonably effectively. Most public organizations, however, tend to function relatively ineffectively.

The following propositions should be evaluated in the context of these environmental barriers to change in public organizations.

Proposition 1: The low degree of organizational effectiveness in public organizations necessitates that the initial goals set for an OD effort be both modest and operationally oriented. It is best not to institute OD in public sector organizations by attempting to alter the basic values and interactional patterns of the organization and its work groups. Rather, it is more effective to begin by setting realistic goals of a highly operational nature; that is, by improving some aspect, however minor, of day-to-day operations. Such goals tend to be more readily achieved, and change more easily measured. Early and demonstrable success, which can be realized from a careful implementation of planned change, will tend to reinforce commitment to modest social experimentation. Even a modest commitment to such experimentation is some indication of change in the values and behaviors of organizational participants. This, hopefully, will engender broader support, which, in turn, will permit the OD effort to deal with the underlying causes of the organization's problem.

The healthier the climate of the organization becomes, the easier it is to deal effectively with the more salient concerns of organizational development, through an incremental series of interventions aimed at gradually improving the climate of the organization.

Corollary 1.1: A structural-technical approach to organizational change represents a viable alternative for initially conducting OD in public organizations. The consultant can consider beginning with a structural-technical approach to change, rather than starting with an emphasis on interpersonal interventions. In the Employment Service project, the approach involved in collaborative attempt to better integrate the structure and technology of the organization, in order to improve operational (task) performance.

Corollary 1.2: The structural-technical approach should be complemented by an incremental effort to alter the existing climate of the organization. While a major effort to alter the organization's climate is inadvisable in the short run, from the inception of the change program a minimal level of effort must be undertaken to begin to alter the perceptions, values, communications and decisionmaking processes in the organization. The actual extent of this effort will vary with the needs and problems of each organization. Probably, the minimum level of effort should include: ongoing small group meetings to keep participants informed on all aspects of the program; discussion with participants in such meetings as to the problems they are experiencing in the effort, so that steps can be taken to mitigate them; orientation training in the nature and goals of OD, begun early and reinforced during the process; and, to the extent that it is practicable, full involvement of the participants in the diagnostic and decision-making processes as early as possible. The minimum desirable outcome of these initial efforts is to at least prevent unintended, negative reactions toward the OD effort.

Proposition 2: Where a fundamental change in organization climate is not feasible in the short run, the OD effort may initially use existing bureaucratic structure, rules, and accepted customs for achieving the desired (short-run) changes.[5] It could be argued that this proposition does little more than beg the question. If most OD approaches will not succeed in public sector organizations in the short run, then the organizations should continue to function in their usual fashion. To some extent, this is a fair argument.

However, there are several points in support of using the existing bureaucracy to achieve change. First, there is meager evidence to show that the structure, rules, and customs of public sector organizations are the direct cause of, or even the sole cause of, the organization's ineffectiveness. Second, over a period of time, the characteristics of public sector organizations tend to support the needs of their incumbents. In the short run, a sudden change in any one or all of these variables could be destructive to a majority of organizational participants and certainly to the goals of OD. Third, while many behavioral scientists appear to be convinced that bureaucratic structure, rules, and customs must quickly pass from the scene, they offer very few alternatives. Most of the ones they do offer tend not to be practical.

Finally, this proposition is not intended to imply that bureaucratic structure, rules, and customs be left completely intact or fully utilized. As Corollary 1.2 suggests, the OD effort must continually strive to reduce the rigidity and inflexibility of existing structure and conditions. However, certain aspects of the bureaucracy can be used in a manner that will help achieve the initial goals of an OD project.

Corollary 2.1: In the early stages of the OD effort, the consultant can rely on top level bureaucratic (legalistic) endorsement, in order to broaden support and overcome overt resistance. Bureaucratic endorsement should be used only in the initial phases of the effort and only if, in the judgment of the consultant, it will not prove ultimately harmful to the goals of the effort. While such a strategy may overcome overt resistance, it may also engender a greater degree of covert resistance, thereby diluting the overall change effort. Thus, the consultant must proceed with considerable caution.

The key to using legalistic-bureaucratic endorsement is to employ it only in a positive manner. For example, in the Employment Service OD effort, the client system did not want direct responsibility for the effort, but accepted the responsibility when the consultant and federal agency insisted that they become prime contractor. (It should be noted that acceptance of a contractual responsibility did not directly result in commitment to the goals of the effort.) Again, such mandates should not be used in a negative manner (such as proscribing greater limitations on the scope of lower level organizational participants' responsibility for the OD effort). Even in the example cited, continued reliance on this type of support would have been self defeating from an OD viewpoint.

Corollary 2.2: At crucial times, the consultant may have to rely on the unilateral power of top management to bring about necessary (initial) changes. Again, the power of top management should only be used in the initial phases of the effort and at carefully selected times. The use of unilateral power can be applied by the bureaucratic incumbent or the consultant, as it has been informally conferred upon him—the former choice being the lesser of two evils. While the practice may appear incongruous with the accepted values, theories and approaches of OD, Warren G. Bennis, a noted theorist and practitioner, has alluded to its possible utility.[6]

Still, there are undeniable risks in using this approach. Excessive and capricious use of it would only reinforce the lack of initiative among participants in these already inflexible organizations. The key is for the consultant to control it by limiting his approval of its use to those instances when it is deemed essential to the survival of the effort. Over a period of time, he must gradually encourage and facilitate greater sharing of power.

Corollary 2.3: In the early phases of these OD projects, the consultant may have to adopt a posture which is generally congruent with the prevailing leadership style of the organization—in general, a more directive posture than would normally be advisable for an OD consultant. As was true of the previous approaches, this one is highly discretionary and would be self defeating if the consultant were to rely on it exclusively. A more directive posture does not imply that the consultant should act as authoritarian leader. It does imply that in the early stages of the effort, organizational participants, because of years of conditioning, will look to his leadership. This situation cannot be quickly altered without engendering serious resistance. The consultant cannot be nondirective in this situation. In the early stages, he or she must occasionally take a leadership role and provide considerable direction. Gradually, the consultant must reduce direct intervention and develop the skills of leaders in the organization, so they may begin to provide the necessary direction themselves. Certainly, there is nothing radically new or inconsistent with accepted OD practice in this approach, as it has been dealt with in the literature.[7]

A caution is necessary, however. In adopting a more directive posture in the early stages of the effort, the consultant must take steps to assure that he is not perceived simply as an agent of top management. His best defense against this potential dilemma is to make clear to organizational participants that he is only temporarily accepting a more directive posture, that it is contrary to his own values, and that gradually he will expect them to become the leaders in the change effort.

In the Employment Service effort (as is true in almost all OD efforts), the consultants were selected by higher levels of management. Ideally, the choosing of a consultant should be a joint decision by top management and managers at the organizational level at which the consultants will make most of their interventions.

Proposition 2 and its corollaries represent a somewhat unorthodox approach to OD practice. They are not intended to be generalized to apply to OD practice in all organizations. Rather, this proposition and its corollaries are intended to apply to public sector organizations that exhibit a low propensity for change.

Further, the essence of these approaches is that they may prove necessary to the survival of OD efforts operating in very difficult organizational environments. The consultant, however, must always be on guard against allowing the means to take precedence over the desired ends of his interventions. In other words, there are times when the problems in such organizations dictate that the effort be terminated, as opposed to the consultant's making unwarranted use of bureaucratic powers and precepts. Unwarranted use of power could destroy the ultimate goals of any organization development effort.

Proposition 3: Given the complex and generally unfavorable environments for change in public organizations, an OD effort should concentrate on the local operating level, and take steps to assure that its influence penetrates the higher levels of the organization. Working within more favorable environmental constraints, Beer and Huse arrived at a conclusion similar to this proposition.[8] The many political and bureaucratic levels in the system, as well as the other factors mentioned, tend to negate the advantages of starting at the top of the organization and working down. In the ES project, change began at the bottom; and, to a limited degree, started to change behavior at higher levels in the system.

For OD to be successfully implemented at lower levels, two conditions are required.[9] First, someone in a top-level position must perceive the need for significant organizational change; although it does not necessarily follow that the person will fully understand or be fully committed to change. Such a commitment, however, must occur as the effort progresses into making more fundamental changes in structure and process. Second, there must be an initial willingness to experiment on a pilot basis.

The problem of *how* to penetrate the higher levels in the organization is most complex. In actuality, each situation undoubtedly requires a somewhat tailor-made strategy. However, there are certain standard attributes of a lower level change effort which can facilitate the process of permeating the higher levels of the organization. First, the initial goals set for the effort at the lower level should be operational in nature (see Proposition 1) and reasonably easy to measure. Second, the approach used at the lower level should be of such a nature that it is easily replicable throughout the system.

Most top managers tend to be results oriented. Operationally oriented goals that are relatively easy to measure will provide top management with tangible feedback on the progress of an OD effort. If the feedback is indicative of success, it will tend to reinforce top management's initial commitment to experimentation. In contrast to such measurable operational results, a report to

top management, for example, that there has been a significant change in the
interpersonal relations orientation of lower level participants is not likely to
have much effect in strengthening their support of the effort.

Equally important is the potential effect feedback to top management will
have on the commitment of lower level participants. In the ES effort, it tended
to create something of a "Hawthorne Effect." The lower level participants became aware that they were the subjects of special attention, so they too became
involved in the process and concerned for its success.

Finally, as we have noted, the change effort should be easily replicable
elsewhere in the client system: it should not be overly complex; it should not
require the expenditure of vast sums of money; and the client system itself
should be capable of replicating it.

Problems Confronting OD in the Public Sector

It has been suggested that one of the greatest challenges confronting both practitioners and theoreticians is the development of technology and models for
change that can be applied successfully in large-scale "open" systems.[10] This
notion of "open" systems is very similar to the concept of "multiple access" and
alludes to systems characterized by pluralistic power and authority, diverse and
often conflicting goals, and different value systems and norms.

If OD is to realize significant success in public organizations, viable interfaces must be developed between all the groups involved in the formulation and
implementation of policy. *Viable interfaces* refers to developing relations between individuals and groups with different values and interests. This need stems
from a characteristic of the public organization's environment, which Golembiewski describes as "unusual opportunities for multiple access to multiple authoritative decisionmakers."[11] Such decisionmakers include groups both outside and within the organization.

Even in the relatively small and limited OD experience with the ES, various
groups were directly and indirectly involved with the organization, thereby com-
plicating the change effort. The consultants made some attempts at building
interfaces, but the attempts met with only modest success.

There are no simple means for developing these complicated interfaces.
It is especially difficult to deal with interfaces between the executive and legislative branches. Such interfaces may even be unconstitutional, in light of the
concept of separation of powers. The experiences of this study offer no models
for dealing with this situation, but certainly provide additional evidence as to
the need to do so.

As we have shown, there are formidable barriers confronting organization
development in many, if not most, public sector organizations. This situation

leads one to question whether or not existing OD theory and approaches are applicable to public sector organizations. This, in turn, leads one to ask whether or not there is a need for a separate body of OD theory and approaches for public sector organizations.

Obviously, there is no clear-cut answer to the above question. On the one hand, a public organization can be analyzed using the same basic variables used to analyze a private sector organization. On the other hand, the unique constraints imposed on public organizations appear to render them almost immune from conventional OD interventions.

Our experience with and knowledge of OD in the public sector are still very limited. As more OD efforts occur in the public sector, the need for a separate body of OD theory and approach may become more evident, as may additional insight into the constructs of such theory.

Conclusion

The aforementioned propositions and their corollaries fall into the category of "middle-range theory."[12] They appear to "fit" the phenomenon, in the context of the type of organization in which the effort took place, and have implications for the actions of OD consultants operating in similar types of organizations.

Perhaps, in a much more limited way, they have implications for general OD theory and approach. Several of these propositions represent deviations from generally accepted theory and practice. They are presented here not to devalue current theory and approach, but rather to suggest alternatives that may be more applicable in severely ineffectual public organizations. Admittedly, each of these propositions is tenuous and needs to be operationalized and tested in a number of organizations. Hopefully, other practitioners will have an opportunity to explore these middle-range theories, in working with similar organizations. Undoubtedly, they will find themselves faced with a most challenging and potentially rewarding OD experience.

Notes

1. Robert J. Golembiewski, "Organization Development in Public Agencies: Perspectives on Theory and Practice," *The Social Technology of Organization Development*, W. Warner Burke and Harvey A. Hornstein (eds.) (NL Learning Resources Corp., Inc., Fairfax, Virginia, 1972) pp. 16-31.

2. For an excellent discussion of the programmatic commitments of career officials, see John J. Corson and R. Shale Paul, *Men Near the Top* (John Hopkins Press, Baltimore, 1966), pp. 23-51.

3.   Peter F. Drucker, *The Age of Discontinuity* (Harper & Row, New York, 1968), p. 231. This book contains an excellent, if disturbing, discussion of the "sickness" of government, pp. 212-242.

4.   Michael G. Blansfield, "Depth Analysis of Organizational Life," 5, *California Management Review*, 2:29-30 (1962); Gene W. Dalton, Louis B. Barnes and Abraham Zaleznik, *The Distribution of Authority in Formal Organizations* (MIT Press, Cambridge, Mass. 1968), pp. 110-112.

5.   Chris Argyris presents a convincing argument that contradicts this proposition; "Explorations in Consulting-Client Relationships," 20, *Human Organization*, 3:121-133 (1961). However, his position is based primarily on experiences with business organizations.

6.   Warren G. Bennis, "Unsolved Problems Facing Organizational Development," *The Business Quarterly* (Winter, 1969).

7.   John D. Aram and James A. F. Stoner, "Development of an Organizational Change Role," 8, *Journal of Applied Behavioral Science*, 4:438-449 (1972). From the broader perspective of leadership in organizations, Fred E. Fieldler has demonstrated the importance of adapting leadership style to the organizational situation, *A Theory of Leadership Effectiveness* (McGraw-Hill Book Co., New York 1967).

8.   Michael Beer and Edgar F. Huse, "A Systems Approach to Organization Development," 4, *Journal of Applied Behavioral Science*, 2:79-101 (1972).

9.   These conditions are exactly the same as those found to be necessary by Beer and Huse, *Ibid.*

10.   Newton Margulies and Anthony P. Raia (eds.) *Organizational Development: Values, Process, and Technology* (McGraw-Hill Book Co., New York, 1972), pp. 477-478.

11.   Golembiewski, *op. cit.*

12.   The concept of middle-range theory is discussed in Richard E. Walton's "Advantages and Attributes of the Case Study," 8, *Journal of Applied Behavioral Science*, 1:73-78 (1972).

ORGANIZATION DEVELOPMENT IN PUBLIC AGENCIES
Perspectives on Theory and Practice*

Robert T. Golembiewski

The special genius of each age is reflected in distinctive ways of organizing work. If the preceding age stressed stability and consistency, roughly, the emphasis today is on organizing for change and variability. The specific implications are diverse and still obscure, but the general point is overwhelming. John W. Gardner reflects both the certainty and the caution. "What may be most in need of innovation is the corporation itself," he notes. "Perhaps what every corporation (and every other organization) needs is a department of continuous renewal that could view the whole organization as a system in need of continuing innovation."[1]

The major recent response to the need for planned organizational change is the burgeoning emphasis on organization development, or OD. Three themes constitute the core of typical OD concepts. As Winn explains:

> The term "organization development" . . . implies a normative, re-education strategy intended to affect systems of beliefs, values and attitudes within the organization so that it can adapt better to the accelerated rate of change in technology, in our industrial environment and society in general. It also includes formal organizational restructuring which is frequently initiated, facilitated and reinforced by the normative and behavioral changes.[2]

*Reprinted from *Public Administration Review,* Vol. 29, No. 4 (July-August, 1969) pp. 367-77, bimonthly publication of the American Society for Public Administration, 1225 Connecticut Avenue, N.W., Washington, D.C.

Changing attitudes or values, modifying behavior, and inducing change in structure and policies, then, are the three core-objectives of OD programs. In contrast, the reorganization literature in political science is concept-oriented and gives little attention to changes in attitudes and behavior necessary to implement its guiding concept.

This article provides a variety of perspectives on the characteristics of OD programs, and also summarizes experience from a number of OD efforts in public agencies at federal and local levels. Not all these agencies can be identified here, unfortunately, but the data-base consists of seven cases. No attempt will be made to evaluate the effectiveness of any particular OD application; and even less is the purpose here to assess the specific technology of OD programs such as the use of sensitivity training.[3]

The motivation of this piece derives from the following propositions. First, government agencies have begun experimenting with various OD approaches, if less bullishly so than business and service organizations. Second, the public sector has a variety of distinctive features that provide special challenges to achieving typical OD objectives. Third, these distinctive features have received inadequate attention in the literature and in the design of OD programs in public agencies. Fourth, applications of OD programs in public agencies probably will become more common. The need to tailor OD programs in public agencies more closely to the distinctive constraints of their environment should consequently increase sharply. Finally, students of public administration can play useful and distinct roles in such OD programs, providing they develop appropriate competencies.

A Typical OD Program and the Underlying Network of Findings and Hypotheses

Despite their variety, OD programs rest on similar conceptual foundations. These foundations are a mixed bag, including relatively "hard" empirical findings and plausible hypotheses. These foundations of OD programs also prescribe how organizations ought to be so as to be effective, "healthy," or morally acceptable.

Figure 1 simplifies the web of findings/hypotheses/values that underlies the typical OD program. The figure focuses strictly on the "front-load" of OD programs; that is, on how sensitivity training or related techniques can induce greater openness, trust, and shared responsibility. Based on such social and psychological preparation, OD programs can flower diversely. For example, early exposure to sensitivity training might encourage greater openness in an organization, which in turn might highlight critical needs for changes in policies, procedures, structure, or technology. An OD program then would be appropriately expanded to meet such needs, as by additions of training programs, etc.[4]

A Typical OD Program:
Major Objectives

The findings/hypotheses/values underlying OD programs imply several common objectives. Overall, the goal is to release the human potential within an organization. Specifically, a typical OD program emphasizes major objectives such as these:

1. To create an open, problem-solving climate throughout the organization.
2. To supplement the authority associated with role or status with the authority of knowledge and competence.
3. To locate decision-making and problem-solving responsibilities as close to the information sources as possible.
4. To build trust among individuals and groups throughout the organization.
5. To make competition more relevant to work goals and to maximize collaborative efforts.
6. To develop a reward system which recognizes both the achievement of the organization's mission (profits or service) and organization development (growth of people).
7. To increase the sense of "ownership" of organization objectives throughout the work force.
8. To help managers to manage according to relevant objectives rather than according to "past practices" or according to objectives which do not make sense for one's area of responsibility.
9. To increase self-control and self-direction for people within the organization.[5]

Basically, the organization is seen "as a system in need of continuing innovation," and an OD program begins by stressing the development of attitudes, behaviors, and skills that will support such continuing innovation.

The list of OD objectives does double duty here. In addition to providing additional content for the concept "organization development," the list of objectives helps highlight some of the special difficulties facing OD programs in public (and especially federal) agencies. The discussion below focuses on one major question: What specific properties of public agencies make it expecially difficult to approach specific objectives such as those above? Evidence comes primarily from seven OD programs at the federal and local levels in which this author has participated.

Basic Premise: To the degree that individuals can meet their own needs while meeting organizational needs, two simultaneous conditions become increasingly probable:

- satisfaction of organization members will heighten
- output will increase, both in terms of quality and quantity

Individual

Organization

An individual's basic needs center around *self-realization* and *self-actualization*. The former involves a person seeking himself as he is in interaction with others, with the goal of increasing the congruence between his intentions and his impact on others. Self-actualization refers to the processes of growth by which an individual realizes his potential.

An individual whose basic needs are being met experiences corresponding *psychological growth*, the prime conditions for which, and consequences of which, are:

- a growing awareness of the needs and motivations of self and others
- a lessening of the degree to which his relationships and actions are distorted, especially via more actively inducing feedback from others and by more effectively interpreting it
- an increasing ability to modify behavior in response to feedback about its impact on others, to respond appropriately rather than stereotypically
- a growing tendency to seek or develop conditions that promote psychological growth for self and others
- an expanding capacity to determine goals and internal motivations for self

An individual who experiences psychological growth will be correspondingly motivated *to search for work, challenge, and responsibility.*

An efficient organization will develop an appropriately shifting balance between *institutionalization* and *risk-taking.* The former refers to *infusing with value* the activities of the organization, so as to elicit member support, identification, and collaboration. Risk-taking is necessary in *innovating* more effective ways to deal with existing activities and in *adapting* to environmental changes in society, markets, technologies, and so on.

An organization's successful balancing of institutionalization and risk-taking will depend upon:

- the increasingly complete use of *people* as well as nonhuman resources
- the development and maintenance of a viable balance between *central control* and *local initiative*
- fluid lines of *communication*—vertically, horizontally, and diagonally
- *decision-making* processes that solve problems that stay solved without creating other problems
- *infusing the organization with values* that support its existence as a stable institution and that also motivate its developmental change as an adaptive structure

An organization with such a working balance of institutionalization and risk-taking will develop appropriate norms that support efforts of organization members to search for work, challenge, and responsibility.

Satisfaction of both individual and organization needs will be facilitated by, if such satisfaction

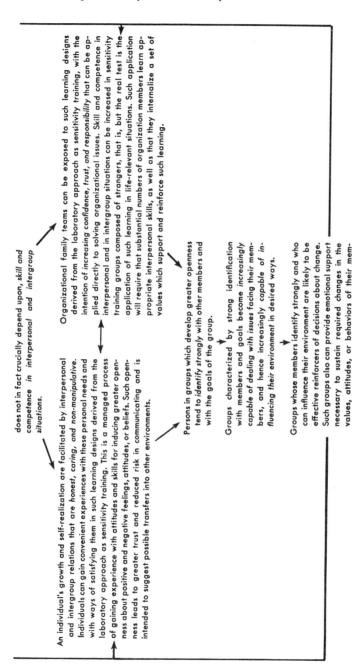

An individual's growth and self-realization are facilitated by interpersonal and intergroup relations that are honest, caring, and non-manipulative. Individuals can gain convenient experiences with these personal needs and with ways of satisfying them in such learning designs derived from the laboratory approach as sensitivity training. This is a managed process of gaining experience with attitudes and skills for inducing greater openness about positive and negative feelings, attitudes, or beliefs. Such openness leads to greater trust and reduced risk in communicating and is intended to suggest possible transfers into other environments.

does not in fact crucially depend upon, skill and competence in interpersonal and intergroup situations.

Organizational family teams can be exposed to such learning designs derived from the laboratory approach as sensitivity training, with the intention of increasing confidence, trust, and responsibility that can be applied directly to solving organizational issues. Skill and competence in interpersonal and in intergroup situations can be increased in sensitivity training groups composed of strangers, that is, but the real test is the application of such learning in life-relevant situations. Such application will require that substantial numbers of organization members learn appropriate interpersonal skills, as well as that they internalize a set of values which support and reinforce such learning.

Persons in groups which develop greater openness tend to identify strongly with other members and with the goals of the group.

Groups characterized by strong identification with members and goals become increasingly capable of dealing with issues facing their members, and hence increasingly capable of influencing their environment in desired ways.

Groups whose members identify strongly and who can influence their environment are likely to be effective reinforcers of decisions about change. Such groups also can provide emotional support necessary to sustain required changes in the values, attitudes, or behaviors of their members.

Figure 1 A simplified model of findings-hypotheses underlying an organization development program based on the laboratory approach. Source: Adapted from Robert T. Golembiewski and Stokes B. Carrigan, "Planned Change in Organization Style Based on Laboratory Approach," *Administrative Science Quarterly*, Vol. 15 (March, 1970), p. 81.

Character of the Institutional Environment:
Constraints on Approaching OD Objectives

Public agencies present some distinctive challenges to OD programs, as compared with business organizations where most experience with OD programs has been accumulated. Four properties of the public institutional environment particularly complicate achieving the common goals of OD programs.

1. Multiple Access

As compared to even the largest of international businesses, the public environment in this country is characterized by what might be called, following David Truman, unusual opportunities for *multiple access to multiple authoritative decision makers.* Multiple access is, in intention if not always in effect, a major way of helping to assure that public business gets looked at from a variety of perspectives. Hence the purpose here is to look at the effects of multiple access rather than to deprecate it. Figure 2 details some major points of multiple access relevant to OD programs in four interacting "systems": the executive, legislative, "special interests," and mass media systems.

Multiple access has its attractive features in beginning OD programs in public agencies. For example, one large OD program was inaugurated in an economical way: a top departmental career official sponsoring an OD program had developed a relation of deep trust with the chairman and the professional staff of a congressional appropriations subcommittee, and that relation quickly, even mercurially, triumphed over lukewarm support or even opposition from the department head, the Bureau of the Budget, and the U.S. Civil Service Commission.

But multiple access can cut two ways. Funds for that very OD program "became unavailable" after its inception, despite strong support from both career and political officers at the top levels. In short, the successful counterattack was launched by agency personnel in the protected/competitive service, an interest group representing these employees, members of a concerned substantive committee of Congress, and the media. The two themes of the counterattack were common to several reactions against OD programs of which I know. First, ordinary decency required allowing the dedicated civil servants affected to complete their careers in peace and in the traditional ways, rather than being subjected to an unwanted program that was seen as having problematic value.[6] Second, the use of sensitivity training in the OD program was disparaged as violating the privacy of organization members, or worse.[7]

Viewed from the perspective of top-level political and career officials in-

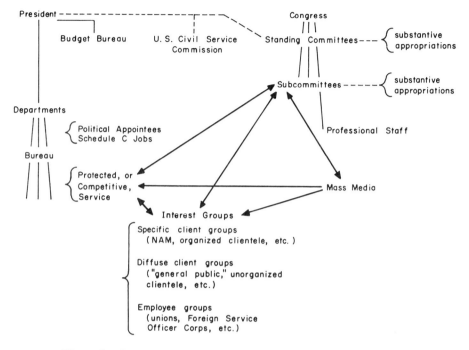

Figure 2 Some critical publics relevant to federal OD programs.

tent on inaugurating a public OD program, the "iron quadrangle" in Figure 2 inspires substantial pessimism about a fair trial, in the general case. Specific conditions may raise or lower the odds, since the several links in the counter-attacking forces above can be variously strong or weak. For example, a public agency may have a very positive constitutional image, which gives its top officials an important edge in presenting their case to congressional committees, the mass media, or the general public. Similarly, top political and career officials can induce—or capitalize on—organized clientele opposition to policies and procedures and use it to force changes at the protected levels. Or political resources and professional skills may provide agency executives with substantial power to control their environment.[8]

Whether the iron quadrangle is more or less integral, the design and implementation of OD programs in public agencies has given that constellation short shift. Perhaps this is because most experience with OD programs has been gained in business organizations, where nothing even remotely like the iron quadrangle exists at managerial levels.

2. Greater Variety

Again as compared to business organizations, the public arena involves in all OD programs a greater variety of individuals and groups with *different and often mutually exclusive sets of interests, reward structures, and values.* In the case outlined above, for example, the appropriations subcommittee was interested in improved operations and reduced costs. But the substantive subcommittee was concerned more with safeguarding program and personnel with which they had developed a strong identification. And never the twain did meet. Role conflicts between legislators and administrators also seem to have been significant. For example, one congressman explained his opposition to an OD program in these terms: "Improvement of efficiency is O.K., but messing with people's attitudes sounds subversive to my constituents." The agency's top administrators felt no such constituency pressure, and their view was that attitudes toward work had to be changed.

Such incongruencies of expectations, rewards, and values also occur in business organizations, of course, as in labor-management issues. In my experience, however, they occur there in less intense and exotic forms.

A conclusion need not be forced. All OD programs have to stress the development of viable "interfaces," that is, relations between individuals or groups with different values and interests. This problem is enormously complicated in public agencies undertaking OD programs, and has received little explicit attention in concept or in practice. For example, in no case that I know of has the development of an explicit interface between legislative and administrative interests been attempted as part of an OD program, apparently in part because of the constitutional separation of powers.

The failure to build such interfaces was a major contributor to the death of a major recent urban OD program. Departmental officers rejected the idea of attempting to build an explicit interface between a substantive subcommittee, an appropriations subcommittee, and the agency as part of an OD program. Tradition, jealousy over prerogatives, and separation of powers were blamed, and with good reason. But it also seemed that departmental officials preferred things as they were. The lack of integration between subcommittees, perhaps, provided alternative routes of access and gave departmental officials some room to operate.

3. Command Linkages

The "line of command" within public agencies, as compared to business and service organizations, is more likely to be characterized by *competing identifications and affiliations.* Again the difference is one of degree, but it approaches one of a kind. Consider only one aspect of the integrity of command linkages common in business organizations. In them, typically, "management" is separated from "labor" only very far down the hierarchy, at or near the level of the first-line supervisor. Moreover, the common identification of all levels of management often is stressed. "Management," moreover, commonly does not enjoy the kind of job security that can come from union contracts. One of the effects of such carrots and sticks, without question, is the more facile implementation of policy changes at all levels of organization.

Hierarchy has its effects in public agencies as well as businesses, but the line of command seems less integral in the former. Thus a unique family of identifications alternative to the hierarchy exists at levels both low and high in public agencies, the apparent underlying motivation being to maximize the probability that evil will not occur, or at least will be found out. That is, the chain of command at the federal level is subject to strong fragmenting forces even up to the highest levels, where political and career strata blend into one another. For example, the ideal of a wall-to-wall civil service is approached closely in practice, and it provides a strong countervailing identification to the executive chain of command. Career officials are "out of politics," but their commitments to programs may be so strong as to inhibit or even thwart executive direction.[9]

That the public institutional environment permits (indeed, encourages) a fragmenting of the management hierarchy at points well up in the higher levels may be illustrated in three ways. First, the "neutrality" of civil servants has been a major defensive issue in at least two federal OD programs in which I have participated, the OD efforts having been painted by many career people as sophisticated but lustful raids on a chaste protected service. Second, Congress is an old hand at creating similar countervailing identifications so as to enhance its control over administration,[10] for which the Constitution and tradition provide a solid rationale. Third, the executive has also played the game, sometimes unwittingly. Consider the presidential-inspired Federal Executive Boards. Basically, these Boards were intended to be a horizontal link between field units of federal agencies and vertically between the presidency and top career field officialdom. The FEB's provide career field managers with a potential way to supplement or even bypass departmental reporting relations, both career employees and political appointees. Indeed, President Kennedy may have intended them as just such a bypass around "the feudal barons of the permanent government" whom he saw as obstacles to change.[11]

A conclusion flows easily. Congress often encourages slack in the executive chain of command to facilitate its oversight of the President and his major appointees; and the executive as well as the protected service itself often uses the same strategy. The integrity of the executive chain of command suffers. Although the consequences are mixed, public executives are limited in initiating[12] (for example) OD programs. Witness the furor over the mere handful of Schedule C jobs removed from the protected service during Eisenhower's first term to permit greater executive leverage. Any corporation president would have an immensely broader field to act upon. The motivation to avoid "spoils politics" is recognized, but managerial rigidity is the other side of the coin. Herbert Kaufman concludes that although extensions of the civil service were intended to provide upper-level political administrators with capable help, the latter have often been driven to "pray for deliverance from their guardians."[13]

4. Weak Linkages

Exacerbating the point above, the *linkages between political and career levels* are weak as a consequence of a variety of features of the public institutional environment.[14] This slippage between managerial levels significantly complicates beginning and implementing OD programs, and severely challenges the linkage of executive management with operating management.

The generalization concerning weak linkages in the managerial chain of command is meant to apply in four distinct senses. First, political and career levels often are weakly linked due to the brief tenure of the former. Second, the job of linking the political leadership and the permanent bureaucracy must be handled by a tiny group of executives—political appointees and occupants of Schedule C jobs—who owe diverse allegiance to the chief executive. Third, there is reason to suspect significant slippage between the top career officialdom and lower levels. For example, what lower-level careerists see as necessary protections of tenure, top career officials perceive as cumbersome limitations on managerial flexibility. Fourth, the executive often weakens its own managerial linkages, as it seeks sometimes-unreconcilable political and administrative goals. Thus the unionization of public employees which has been encouraged by presidential executive order hardly discourages labor unions looking for new fields to conquer. But one of the groups of federal employees to organize were inspectors in the U.S. Civil Service Commission who, if anybody, would be seen as "management" in most business organization.

OD programs consequently must face the issue of somehow interfacing political and career linkages which powerful forces—constitutional, political, and historic—tend to pull apart. Consider only one dilemma facing OD programs. The general rule of thumb is that OD programs should begin "at the top" of organizational hierarchies, or as close to the top as possible. The rationale is obvious: that is where the power usually is in business organizations. Respecting this rule of thumb in public agencies raises a multidimensional dilemma. Basically, "the top" in public agencies is more complex than in most businesses. Initiating an OD program at the level of the political leadership maximizes formal executive support, but it may also raise comples problems. Support of the OD program is problematic because of frequent personnel changes at that level,[15] because of possible well-entrenched resistance from the permanent service, because legislators may fear that any strengthening of the executive chain of command would only mean fewer points of access and sources of information, and because employee associations may resist executive direction. Relying more on support from those in the competitive/protected service maximizes the chances of permanent support, and it may raise congressional and CSC trust in the program. But this approach may encourage executive resistance from such vantage points as the Bureau of the Budget.

The OD specialist faces real dilemmas, then, in choosing the "top" of the hierarchy at which to direct his interventions. I have participated in change programs that have taken both approaches to seeking a power base, and they show only that avoiding Scylla seems to imply meeting Charybdis. The ideal is to appeal to both the political officialdom and to the permanent service, of course, but that is a demanding ideal indeed.

In summary, four properties of the institutional environment of public agencies complicate attaining the objectives of typical OD programs. Consider the objective of building trust among individuals and groups throughout the organization. Technically, viable interfaces should be created between political officials, the permanent bureaucracy, congressional committees and their staffs, and so on and on. Practically, this is a very tall order, especially because the critical publics tend to have mutually exclusive interests, values, and reward systems. Indeed, although it is easy to caricature the point, Congress has a definite interest in cultivating a certain level of distrust within and between government agencies so as to encourage a flow of information. This may seem a primitive approach but, in the absence of valid and reliable measures of performance, it may be a necessary approach. No OD program in a business organization will face such an array of hurdles, that much is certain.

Character of the Habit Background:
Constraints on Approaching OD Objectives

The "habit background" of public agencies also implies serious obstacles to approaching OD objectives. Five aspects of this habit background are considered below by way of illustrating their impact on OD objectives. These five aspects do not comprise an exclusive list, and they are conceived of only as general patterns and behaviors which give a definite flavor to the broad institutional environment sketched above.

Patterns of Delegation

"Habit background" is perhaps better illustrated than defined. First, in my experience, public officials tend to favor patterns of delegation that maximize their sources of information and minimize the control exercised by subordinates. Specifically, the goal is to have decisions brought to their level for action or review. The most common concrete concomitants of the tendency are functional specialization and a narrow span of control, one of whose major consequences is a large number of replicative levels of review.[16]

"Layering" of multiple levels of review is not unique to public administration, indeed it inheres in generally accepted organization theory; but it is supported by forces more or less unique to public agencies that have been powerful enough to substantially curtail innovation of ways to centralize policy and to decentralize operations.[17] The protection of the "public interest" is one such unique factor, for example. The rationale is familiar. Political officials of short tenure often cannot rely on established relations of confidence with personnel at lower levels, nor do they exercise as much control over career rewards and punishments as is common in business organizations or in the military. However, the legislature will hold the political officials responsible. Consequently, political officials seek to maximize information sources and minimize the control exercisable by subordinates. This tendency is reinforced by law and tradition so that it permeates down the hierarchy throughout the permanent bureaucracy. The tendency is often referred to as "keeping short lines of command."

Keeping chains of command short implies constraints on approaching OD objectives in public organizations, based on my experience as well as the logic of the situation. Consider only two of the OD objectives above—three and nine:

> To locate decision-making and problem-solving responsibilities as close to the information sources as possible; and
>
> To increase self-control and self-direction for people within the organization.

To the degree that the rough distinction above is accurate, public agencies will experience difficulties in approaching both objectives. The prevailing habit pattern in public agencies patently constitutes a tide to swim against in these two particulars, although there are outstanding exceptions to this generalization.

Legal Habit

Second, and again only as a description of what exists, legal patterns make approaching OD objectives severely more difficult in public agencies than in business organizations.[18] The point applies in two major senses. Thus patterns of administrative delegation are often specified in minute detail in legislation, basically so as to facilitate oversight by the legislature. To be sure, we are a considerable distance beyond the first Morgan case, which seemed to argue that only administrative actions personally taken by, or under the direct supervision of, a department head were constitutionally defensible. But flexibility in delegation is still a major problem. Perhaps more important, a corpus of law and standard practice exists which also makes it difficult to achieve OD objectives. For example, considering only those employees on the General Schedule, salary and duties are tied to a position classification system whose underlying model emphasizes trans-departmental uniformity and compensation for individual work.[19]

This legal habit background complicates approaching OD values. Thus efforts to achieve OD objective three above may run afoul of the possibility that relocating responsibilities in one agency is considered to have system-wide implications, with consequences that complicate the making of local adjustments. As one official noted of an OD effort in such straits: "I feel like I have to raise the whole civil service by my bootstraps." Relatedly, OD objective two above seeks:

> To supplement the authority associated with role or status with the authority of knowledge and competence

This is hard to do to the degree that a pattern of delegation is specified in law. The same point applies to any rigidities due to the duties classification common in public agencies in the United States, and especially to the concepts for assigning authority and for organizing work underlying the duties classification. Job enlargement begun as part of OD programs has run afoul of such concepts, for example.

At the bread-and-butter level, existing legal patterns also inhibit approaching OD objectives. Consider objective six, which proposes:

> To develop a reward system which recognizes both the achievement of the organization's mission and organization development

Existing law and practice severely limit the search for such a reward system. Thus rewards for exceptional performance—in money payments or in higher-than-normal GS levels for personnel in the civil service—are now possible, but they still are exceptional in practice. Equal pay for equal work, in sum, still practically means that exceptional work is not rewarded exceptionally. Management in business organizations typically has far greater control over reward systems, and especially at managerial levels. More of a problem, neither existing law nor practice promise much in the way of support for various group compensation plans. Experiments in industry with some such plans have yielded attractive results.

Need for Security

Third, the need for security or even secrecy in public agencies as against business organizations is more likely to be strong enough to present obstacles to approaching OD objectives. Military and defense agencies come to mind first, but they hardly exhaust the list. The "need for security" as used here can concern national security, it can be induced by a general anxiety born of a need to make significant decisions whose results will not be manifest for a very long time, or it can derive from felt needs for protection from such outside forces as a congressman with fire in his eye.[20] The need can also be real, exaggerated, or even imagined in various combinations.

Consider one case which seemed to reflect some of all of these components. Agency personnel were exposed to sensitivity training, one of whose major purposes is to increase skills in being open about both positive and negative emotions or reactions. The training staff provided several settings in which these intentions might be approached, one of which was a "park bench." During one week of sensitivity training some time was set aside each evening for a meeting of all participants in a large room which was the locus of the "park bench." But agency personnel seldom used the arena, although there was a good deal of nervous laughter from the periphery of the "park." After some three abortive tries of an hour each, one participant approached me. "I see the point of the thing," he said, "but a park bench is all wrong." Suddenly, the dawn came. "Park benches," were seen as stereotypic sites for sexual assignations and/or for exchanging secrets with enemy agents. Without doubt, some participants thought the "park bench" a silly notion, and hence did not participate. For most participants, however, the symbolism was so compelling that they could not use the "park bench." Moreover, many agency personnel were so closed, distrustful, and fearful of taking a risk that they could not talk about their guiding symbolism, even if they were aware of it.

This greater need for security cannot be established completely, to be sure, and all that may be said definitely is that to the degree this need exists so are OD objectives more difficult to reach. Consider only OD objective one above:

To create an open, problem-solving climate throughout the organization

An open climate and a great need for security or for secrecy do not mix well.

Procedural Regularity and Caution

Fourth, for a variety of reasons, government personnel are rather more likely to stress procedural regularity and caution. Perhaps better said, even if agency personnel are convinced that certain heuristics provide solutions that are "good enough," this conviction may conflict with other (and especially congressional) needs for external control. For example, sample checking of vouchers was widely accepted as an efficient enough administrative approach long before relevant publics in Congress and the General Accounting Office recognized it as appropriate for their control purposes.

Good reasons support this bias toward procedural regularity and caution in public agencies, of course, and so much the worse for OD objectives. For example, the bias patently runs against the grain of OD objective eight above, which seeks:

> To help managers to manage according to relevant objectives rather than according to "past practices" or according to objectives that do not make sense for one's area of responsibility

The underlying rub, of course, is that a "past practice" making little or no sense administratively may seem an utter necessity from the legislative point of view. To be sure, the dictum "where you sit determines what you see" applies to all organizations. But the needs and identifications of administrators and legislators are likely to differ more than is the case for (let us say) the executives and middle managers of a business organization.

"Professional Manager"

Fifth, the concept "professional manager" is less developed in the public versus the business arena, in rough but useful contrast. The relative incidence of business schools and schools of public administration suggests the conclusion,[21] as do the Jacksonian notions deep at the roots of our basic public personnel policies. For example, the "career system" notion has been a difficult one to develop in this country at the federal level. No small part of the difficulty derives from the value we place on an "open service" with lateral entry. Hence the tendency of our public personnel policies to emphasize hiring for a specific position rather than for long-run potential.

Derivations from these taproots have had profound impact. For example, to simplify a little, massive federal attention to training was long delayed by the wrigglesworthian legislative notion that, since the federal service was hiring people who already had the abilities to do the specific job for which they were hired, there was little need to spend money on training.[22] The relative attractiveness of public employment at the federal level at least through World War II provided the proverbial finger in the dike, but conditions changed much faster than did public policy. Instructively, also, the system of regional executive development centers manned by the U.S. Civil Service Commission began as late as 1964, and then only with a miniscule budget and against substantial congressional opposition. Roughly, business has a 10-20 year lead over government in acting on the need for training. Not very long ago, in contrast, the federal government was considered *the* model employer.

The relatively lesser stress on the "public professional manager" implies significant problems for approaching OD objectives. Thus OD objective seven proposes:

To increase the sense of "ownership" of organization objectives throughout the work force

No sharp contrast is appropriate. But a definite bias of public personnel policy limits such a sense of identification with, and commitment to, public agencies. If there is one thing most civil services reformers did not want, it was a public work force who "owned" the objectives of their agency. The only "owner" was the public; the model employee was a politically neutral technician who repressed his own values in return for guaranteed tenure. Only thus could an elite and unresponsive bureaucracy be avoided, goes a major theme shot through our public personnel policies and institutions.

Conclusion

The body of this paper can be summarized tersely. Organization Development programs are appearing with increasing frequency in both business and public agencies. Moreover, applications of OD programs in government agencies face some unique problems. However, these unique problems tend to go unrecognized or underrecognized by OD teams in part because students of public administration have tended to be underrepresented on such teams. Hence this paper.

Some derivative implications seem appropriate, in addition. First, "poaching" in the public sector by OD teams composed basically os psychologists and sociologists will continue to grow, if only because (as William F. Whyte noted in another connection) such poaching is necessary. Second, students of public administration can play a useful and partially distinct role in such OD programs. But, third, students of public administration are likely to play such a role only as substantial numbers of them develop competencies that complement their special interests in public administration. Such competency enlargement for "change-agents" or organization consultants is provided by the NTL Institute of Applied Behavioral Science and by such university-based programs as those at UCLA and Boston University.

Notes

1. John W. Gardner, *Self-Renewal* (New York: Harper & Row, 1965).

2. Alexander Winn, "The Laboratory Approach to Organization Development: A Tentative Model of Planned Change," paper read at the Annual Conference, British Psychological Society, Oxford, September 1968, p. 1. More broadly, see Edgar H. Schein and Warren G. Bennis, *Personal and Organization Change through Group Methods: The Laboratory Method* (New York: Wiley, 1965); and Warren G. Bennis, *Changing Organizations* (New York: McGraw-Hill, 1966).

3. For an overview of the technique, see Robert T. Golembiewski, "The Laboratory Approach to Organization Development: The Schema of A Method," *Public Administration Review,* Vol. 27 (September 1967), pp. 211-220.

4. Sheldon Davis, "An Organic Problem-Solving Method of Organizational Change," *Journal of Applied Behavioral Science,* Vol 3 (January 1967), pp. 3-21.

5. NTL Institute, "What Is OD?" *News and Reports,* Vol. 2 (June 1968, p.1.

6. The theme also appeared in mass-circulation news stories and editorials which argued against Project ACORD in the U.S. Department of State, for example. Steward Alsop, "Let the Poor Old Foreign Service Alone," *Saturday Evening Post,* (June 1966), p. 14.

7. For example, sensitivity training has been criticized as "amateur group therapy." For an incisive distinction between training and therapy, see Chris Argyris, "Conditions for Competence Acquisition and Therapy," *Journal of Applied Behavioral Science,* Vol. 4 (June 1968), pp. 147-178.

8. See, generally, Francis E. Rourke, *Bureaucracy, Politics, and Public Policy* (Boston: Little, Brown, 1969).

9. For a sensitive summary of the programmatic commitments of career personnel, see John J. Corson and R. Shale Paul, *Men Near the Top* (Baltimore, Md.: Johns Hopkins Press, 1966), pp. 23-51.

10. Joseph P. Harris, *Congressional Control of Administration* (Washington, D.C.: The Brookings Institution, 1964).

11. Arthur Schlesinger, *A Thousand Days* (Boston: Houghton Mifflin, 1965), p. 681.

12. President Truman expressed the point directly in contemplating the problems that General Eisenhower would experience as President Eisenhower, without the discipline and definite career patterns and established ways of doing things he knew in the military. "He'll sit here," Truman predicted, "and he'll say, 'Do this!' 'Do that!' *And nothing will happen.* Poor Ike— it won't be a bit like the Army. He'll find it very frustrating." Richard E. Neustadt, *Presidential Power* (New York: Wiley, 1960), p. 9. His emphases.

13. Herbert Kaufman, "The Rise of a New Politics," p. 58, in Wallace S. Sayre (ed.), *The Federal Government Service* (Englewood Cliffs, N.J.: Prentice-Hall, 1965).

14. Dean E. Mann, "The Selection of Federal Political Executives," *American Political Science Review,* Vol. 58 (March 1964), pp. 81-99.

15. One ambitious OD program, for example, was unable to overcome the rumor that several political appointees were negotiating terms of private employment. Agency personnel were encouraged to inaction, since these officials would "soon be riding their OD hobbyhorse" someplace else. These officials did leave, but all claim that the stories were seeded by career

personnel who opposed the OD program, and that it was only the intensity of such "dirty fighting" that encouraged the political appointees to seek private employ after the rumors began.

16. Before a reorganization inspired by an OD program in the Department of State, some review layers were so numerous that "it could take as long as six months for an important problem to reach the Deputy Under Secretary. Now it takes an average of two days." Alfred J. Marrow, "Managerial Revolution in the State Department," *Personnel,* Vol. 43 (December 1966), p. 13.

17. Such innovation has been the major trend in large businesses over the last three or four decades. See Robert T. Golembiewski, *Men, Management, and Morality* (New York: McGraw-Hill, 1965); and *Organizing Men and Power* (Chicago: Rand McNally, 1967). Strong pressures for just such innovation are now being widely felt in public administration. Aaron Wildavsky provides a case in point in his "Black Rebellion and White Reaction," *The Public Interest,* No. 11 (Spring 1968), especially pp. 9-12.

18. A very useful discussion of the antimanagerial thrust of much legislation is provided by Harris, *Congressional Oversight of Administration.*

19. Robert T. Golembiewski, "Civil Service and Managing Work," *American Political Science Review,* Vol. 56 (December 1962), pp. 961-974.

20. Great needs for "security" as here broadly defined can rigidify an organization and curb the effectiveness of its members. To the point, see Chris Argyris, "Some Causes of Organizational Ineffectiveness within the Department of State," Center for International System Research, *Occasional Papers,* No. 2 (1967).

21. Revealingly, it was not until 1946 that Cornell developed the first two-year master of public administration program comparable to the MBA long given by schools of commerce or business administration.

22. Paul P. Van Riper, *History of the United States Civil Service* (Evanston, Ill.: Row, Peterson, 1958), pp. 429-434.

THE ORGANIZATIONAL IMPERATIVE*

David K. Hart and William G. Scott

American values have undergone a massive change. The pluralistic forces that shaped our national character have withered away and the collective strivings of our society have been consolidated into a single social invention: modern organizations. They are *vast, complex, technologically based administrative systems which synthesize clusters of resources into rationally functioning wholes.* In contemporary America, the needs of organization overwhelm all other considerations, whether those of family, religion, art, science, law, or the individual. This has had a shattering impact on us, for it has caused us to become a different people than we thought we would be. However, that value change is by now a fait accompli, and the dominant force behind that change has been "the organizational imperative." Why has this happened?

Basically, it has been because modern organizations have been so immensely successful. They seemed to advance the material welfare of both individuals and the nation quite automatically. Such organizations, under the guidance of administrative elites, turned our enormous potentials—physical and human—into an unprecedented material abundance. This job was done so well and so unobtrusively that the automatism of material progress became an article of faith for Americans. We accepted what we had gained neither gratefully nor ungratefully, but as a simple and just inevitability.

*"The Organizational Imperative," by David K. Hart and William G. Scott is reprinted from *Administration & Society,* Vol. 7, No. 3 (Nov. 1975), pp. 259-284 by permission of the Publisher, Sage Publications, Inc.

However, in order to accomplish such material miracles, we had to become a different people from what we had historically hoped and dreamed for ourselves. The abundance created by modern organizations required a shift away from the values of the American tradition, even though we have continued to profess a pathetic loyalty to the lost values of our national youth. Thus, no small part of our present national malaise is the result of an increasingly obvious disparity between what we had idealized and what we have become. When we look closely at what we made for ourselves, we recoil, for we see American values that are suitable for the efficient performance of organizations, but painfully inadequate for man himself.

However, the situation is even more complicated. There is a dawning realization that the earth cannot sustain our automatic progress into that good future. Even worse, we are beginning to comprehend that affluence has not brought a marked increase in personal happiness. The question now being asked is how we have managed to drift into this appalling situation. We have written this essay in partial response to that question. Our main contention is that a new value *paradigm* (Kuhn, 1970) has displaced the old paradigm, and that the organizational imperative is both the cause and the center of the new order.

The Organizational Imperative

The organizational imperative consists of two a priori propositions and three rules for behavior. The imperative is founded on a primary proposition, which is absolute: *whatever is good for man can only be achieved through modern organization.* The question of what is "good" for man is left open; what must be beyond question is the conviction that the only way to achieve that good is through modern organization. The secondary proposition derives from the first: *therefore, all behavior must enhance the health of such modern organizations.*

From the primary and secondary propositions come three rules for organizationally healthy behavior, which define, guide, and evaluate all administrative performance. They apply to every administrator in every organization in modern society. The behavioral rules require that the administrator be rational, a good steward, and pragmatic. Since the concepts of rationality, stewardship, and pragmatism carry heavy burdens of numerous interpretations, it is necessary to specify their exact meaning as part of the organizational imperative.

Rationality. The rule of rationality provides the common denominator for all scientifically conditioned, technologically oriented organizations in advanced industrial nations: administrators must be rational. This does not refer to the philosophic tradition of rationalism, but to that form of rationality central to scientific method, which requires the economizing of means to achieve ends.

Drawing on its heritage of science, engineering, and economics, administration has made rationality indistinguishable from efficiency—the ratio of $E = O/I$. The task of administration, guided by this operational formula, is to increase the value of E by adjusting the relative values of outputs over inputs. While we may argue over definitional refinements, this formulation must be accepted, along with its behavioral implications, because there is no other way to account for what managers do in modern organizations.

Stewardship. The organizational imperative requires stewardship behavior from administrators. Ultimately, an administrator is a steward of the a priori propositions, but practically he must manage the more immediate affairs of the organization in the interest of "others." It does not make a particle of difference who the others are: the public at large, stockholders of corporations, members of consumer cooperatives, members of labor unions, and the like. The rule of stewardship applies with equal force in all cases. For one thing, it legitimizes a necessary hierarchy. If the administrator as a steward is to fulfill this behavioral commitment, those who work for him must be obedient to his commands and he becomes steward for the combined destinies of his subordinates.

Additionally, stewardship requires the administrator to husband organizational resources. Thus administrators are socially and legally responsible to their clients outside the organization for their behavior as stewards; if the stewardship rule is successfully executed, the health and wealth of the organization is protected and increased, the welfare of the people dependent on the organization is improved, and the fortunes of its administrators are advanced. Just as with rationality, contrary ideas about the nature of stewardship are unthinkable within the framework of administrative theory and practice that has developed during the last 75 years.

Pragmatism. Pragmatic behavior enables the organization to survive in good health in changing environments, since practical circumstances continually impose different necessities on administrators. The rule of administrative pragmatism simply requires expedient behavior, guided by the a priori propositions. Beyond this, the rule for pragmatic behavior has *no other moral content.*

The organizational world of administration is one where complex problems of short-term duration must be dealt with expediently. Pragmatism demands that administrators direct their energies and talents to finding solutions for practical, existing problems within an immediate time frame. The language, reward systems, and activities of administration demonstrate this concern for the present and indicate the devotion that administrators have to securing an orderly, purposeful world composed of endlessly fascinating, narrow puzzles to be solved. This pragmatic puzzle world unburdens administrators of the need for moralistic reflection. Successful, expedient solutions to administrative puzzles are rewarded, and little honor goes to those whose efforts do not have immediate payoffs in terms of organizational performance (Scott and Hart, 1973).

Each of these behavioral rules entails the others. They exist in a web of interrelationships within the imperative, with the primary purpose of strenthening the a priori propositions of the imperative.

Thus, the organizational imperative is the sine qua non of administrative theory and practice. It cuts across all jurisdictional boundaries and applies to all organizations: public, private, educational, religious, or whatever. It changes slowly, if at all. It is not affected tangibly by political and social turmoil, or even war—in fact, the imperative might even be strengthened by them. The imperative is, so to speak, the metaphysic of administration: absolute, immutable, and unchanging. It is *persuasive* (it alters values in order to alter behavior), it is *universal* (it governs through the a priori propositions all collective efforts for achieving major social and individual objectives), and it is *durable* (it is the one source of stability and continuity in a turbulent world). For these and other reasons, the organizational imperative has become the dominant moral force in our society.

Administrative Norms

Administration does the vital job of linking organizations (which are the most elaborate of abstractions) with the institutional infrastructure of society at large. Organizations are run by administrators who must make decisions about goals, policies, and strategies of action that influence human values and behaviors, both within and outside the organizations. Administrators respond with varying sensitivity and accuracy to the needs and interests of the different groups affected by their decisions. But their loyalties are seldom given to those they touch most profoundly, and certainly they are neither trained nor encouraged to speculate about the moral worth and moral impact of their decisions.

Conventional wisdom has it that an administrator's primary loyalty should be to those who own his organization: the stockholders (if it is a private company) or the citizens (if it is a public organization). While this wisdom may have been correct once, it is certainly not now. The overriding concern of the administrator is to keep the organization healthy. This mission of organizational health is best accomplished by the administrator's total allegiance to the organizational imperative. To advance this mission, the values of *all* people who influence the organization—whether from within or from without—must be modified so that they are supportive of the organizational imperative. The administrator, therefore, must discipline himself, his subordinates, and his relevant clients to arrange their values, expectations, and practical affairs so that the organizational imperative is served.

The result of such modification has been the conversion of almost all social values into administrative norms. Administrative norms serve as the guidelines for organizationally useful behavior and are the links between the organizational imperative and social values—partaking of both, but with the advantage going to the organizational imperative. It is important to understand why these norms came to be in this central location, and how they influence the direction of value change.

Traditional American values have always been rooted in the dream that a good life was available to everyone, and no small part of that dream has been the possibility of a relatively high degree of material well-being. Americans believed that this dream could be realized through individual efforts, working directly on the natural environment. Historically optimistic, blessed by the natural advantages of a geographically and geologically favored land, and fired by a work ethic, Americans saw material affluence as a realizable goal—if not for themselves, then at least for their children.

Out of this dream grew the belief that material *growth* was absolutely essential to the vitality of national life and that the material *abundance* obtained from such growth was limitless. These were the necessary preconditions for the good life. Whatever else Americans sought could be found by them, as individuals, in the consumption of products and services. Material well-being was, to an appreciable extent, the basis of a major consensus in the social order.

There has not been much difference between how Americans defined their individual aims and what administrators tried to accomplish within organizations. *Administrative norms generally have been consistent with the expectations of Americans at large, since successful administrative practices were thought to be translatable into individual welfare.* As technology was carried by modern organization into nearly every corner of society, a new—and extremely important— premise was added to the concept for a good life. This premise did not eradicate customary assumptions about individual happiness. Rather, it converted them into organizational terms. The most important change it wrought was to create popular acceptance of the thesis that the dream of individual welfare could be realized *only* by the preeminence of modern organization and its administrative apparatus.

The traditional social values survived, but their connotation changed. Thus, growth was a good, but the most important growth was organizational. Abundance was a good, but it was an organizationally produced abundance. Consensus was a good, but the crucial consensus was among potentially conflicting interest groups within organizations. For the most part these organizationally derived goods did benefit individuals. By managing organizational resources efficiently, growth resulted in material abundance that, when distributed in a reasonably equitable way, promoted positive attitudes about the utility of organization, the legitimacy of administration, and the general community of interest in expanding productivity. Thus the norms of growth, abundance, and consensus were the "guidelines of administrative practice"—administrative norms that resulted from the reconciliation of the organizational imperative with extant social values.

But, as we said in the introduction, we have had to become a different

people from what we idealized for ourselves in order to accomplish the great
achievements made possible by the modern organization. Traditional American
values had been significantly battered about in the process of our industrial maturation, creating major social and psychological displacements—value lags separating what we thought we were from what we were forced to be as citizens
within an organizational society. As technology, organization, and administration penetrated the social order, collisions of increasing severity could hardly be
avoided between the values of our past and the new value requirements of the
organizational imperative.

The major American value change, nearly completed at present, was largely
unanticipated even a decade ago. However, warnings were sounded by perceptive
observers such as William H. Whyte, Jr. His book *The Organization Man* enjoyed
great success in the 1950s because it was a sensitive, accurate, and timely appraisal of some extraordinarily important events. Whyte argued that America was
shifting from an individualistic ethic to a social ethic—but that the latter was not
then articulated. His contention was that organizations, through their administrative systems, had imposed their imperative on all they contacted, in nearly
every human situation imaginable.

> People grow restive with a mythology that is too distant from the way
> things actually are, and as more and more lives have been encompassed
> by the organization way of life, the pressures for an accompanying
> ideological shift have been mounting. The pressures of the group,
> the frustrations of individual creativity, the anonymity of achieve-
> ment: are these defects to struggle against—or are they virtues in
> disguise? The organization man seeks a redefinition of his place on
> earth—a faith that will satisfy him that what he must endure has a
> deeper meaning than appears on the surface. He needs, in short, some-
> thing that will do for him what the Protestant Ethic did once. And
> slowly, almost imperceptibly, a body of thought has been coalescing
> that does that [Whyte, 1956: 6].

Unfortunately, most people misunderstood that message and read the book
simply as a nonfiction version of the popular novel *The Man in the Gray Flannel
Suit*, which had appeared a year earlier in 1955. The theme of conformity was
blown all out of proportion, and the essential meaning of Whyte's book, pertain-
ing to the organizational imperative behind the value change, was almost completely overlooked.

Somewhere in the turmoil of the last decade, Whyte's warnings were for-
gotten. But in spite of campus riots, civil rights demonstrations, militant peace
movements, and all of the other distractions of that era, the organizational imperative continued to work, and to work well indeed. As America drifted inexorably into an organization-dominated society, the contemptible organization
man of the 1950s turned into a laudable model of administrative obedience.
Further, in order to bring coherence and security into his life, he constantly ex-

erted pressures to bring social values into a harmonious and reinforcing relationship with the organizational imperative, to which he had given total allegiance.

So, contrary to popular assumptions, the "ideal" man of the 1960s was *not* the "with-it" hippie, the peace activist, the committed and articulate university student, or the humanist psychologist. Rather, he was the superbly trained, functionally amoral administrator—the "best and the brightest" among us. They were we, and most of us became they—if not in actuality, then at least in spirit. The irony of it all was that we presumed we were following another path: John F. Kennedy set a style and proclaimed the doctrine of an accelerated national performance in 1960. But we did not become like him—we became like those he hired. Whyte's prophecy was fulfilled with barely the slightest public acknowledgement of what was happening.

The new faith of which Whyte wrote emerged as a public acceptance of the organizational imperative—that large-scale, technologically based administrative systems are the optimal mode of social organization. From commitment to this belief, all else follows, including the fact that the organizational imperative must go on unremittingly even if American values change. Administrators can serve the imperative regardless of whether society is faced with scarcity or an abundance of resources; whether the economy is expanding or contracting; or whether conservation or exploitation of the environment is the order of the day. The point is that through the intermediating process of administration, social values have become either actually or potentially reinforcing to the organizational imperative. In defense of this contention, in the next few pages we compare some of the displaced values of our past with some of the present, organizationally determined values that serve as administrative norms.

Cultural Values and Administrative Norms

The new order of organizational dominion fired by the human instrumentality of administration requires specific cultural value commitments if it is survive. To illustrate, we discuss five sets of paired values: the first indicating a value of our tradition, and the second indicating the value now dominant. The pairings are: from individuality to obedience; from indispensability to dispensability; from community to specialization; from spontaneity to planning; from voluntarism to paternalism. The pairings are not exhaustive—they do not describe "either-or" situations, nor are they complete. However, they do delineate the major changes in the fundamental American value paradigm.

From Individuality to Obedience

De Tocqueville, among others, correctly observed that Americans have ranged, with marvelous inconsistence, from individuality to conformity. Nevertheless, individuality held a unique and dominant place in our tradition, no matter how badly we abused it. It has been interpreted many ways, but central to them all was the confidence the individual knew (or could know) what was best for himself. As Mill (1950: 178) wrote: "with respect to his own feelings and circumstances, the ordinary man or woman has means of knowledge immeasurable surpassing those that can be possessed by any one else." Thus, legitimacy was conferred on social, economic, and political values to the extent that they conformed with the individual's perception of the right. Granted, this was an ideal, but nonetheless it was an ideal we tried to practice. The most significant justifications for action came from the individual, and the satisfactions derived from such personal actions were infinitely superior to those that came from obedience to collectivities. All of that has now changed.

Poignantly, we still proclaim the importance of individuality on public occasions—knowing all along that very little of importance gets done without modern organization. Given that reality, we have shifted our allegiance from individuality to obedience to the organizational imperative and that obedience must be total. The belief is now that superior satisfactions are to be obtained from such obedience. In short, it is good to be obedient.

There are many things that should be said about obedience, for it is the cornerstone of the organizational edifice. However, it would take a book to develop these and related ideas in the detail they deserve (Milgram, 1974; Janis, 1972). We will limit the discussion herein to some observations about two features of obedience that are particularly important.

First, we have become an obedient people, as distinguished from a conformist people. Milgram (1974: 113) distinguishes between the two as follows:

> *Conformity* . . . [is] . . . the action of a subject when he goes along with his peers, people of his own status, who have no special right to direct his behavior. *Obedience* . . . [is] the action of the subject who complies with authority.

To say that Americans have become an obedient people is to say that we have accepted the premise of the organizational imperative. In that way, we have become all the same, not because we are conformists—looking to significant others in search of security—but because we have *individually* committed ourselves to a single ultimate value. By all accepting (most often implicitly) the organizational imperative and by agreeing to abide by the administrative norms derived therefrom, we become, de facto, homogenous. This is different from conformity— we have not become a herd. The traditional value of individuality was NOT abolished—rather it was converted into an individual commitment to obedience to the demands of the organizational imperative. This makes us homogenous.

Second, a widely accepted administrative truism for modern organizations is the disruptiveness of individual goals that are not congruent with organizations' goals. Obviously, individual idiosyncrasies cannot be allowed to impede the effective functioning of the organization. Hence, the desired moral stance for individuals vis-à-vis the organization is functional amorality—the willingness to substitute organizational valuations for personal valuations. In order to be maximally useful to a modern organization, an individual must be personally amoral and organizationally moral. That is, he must willingly internalize the goals of the organization as his goals, without qualm. Notice, we do not say that the individual must be immoral—just that he must be ethically malleable. If the goals of his organization are socially approved, then he will be adjudged a worthy man by his society. The reverse is also true. However, the comparative goodness or badness of organizational goals, in and of themselves, is not the central issue. The key issue is the nearly unanimous acceptance, in administrative theory and practice, of the ethical superiority of the organizational imperative over individual ethical commitments. The reader may argue that he is not required to do such things, not would he, even if management insisted. Perhaps. But obedience to authority is so deeply ingrained by now that it takes a formidable personality to be disobedient.

We are not talking about a new phenomenon altogether. Human history is filled with accounts of "true believers"—individuals who obtained meaning for their lives by committing themselves totally to mass movements. What is new is that the organizational imperative does not require the fanaticism so common to mass movements. Indeed, the organizational way of life is scarcely a mass movement at all. But the central feature of mass movements is present: the substitution of the collective absolute for personal values.

Certainly, this is *not* the age of the individual; heroes are in short supply, the individual moral virtue, while often extolled, is seldom separated from organizational needs. Thus, individual values are usually implicit, not clearly understood and, hence, weakly defended. When confronted with the clarity and force of the organizational imperative, conflicting individual values are easily converted into organizationally relevant values. By adopting the organizational imperative as the foundation of personal values, the individual articulating his moral commitments removes his agonies, and purpose is returned to private lives.

This situation is strongly reinforced by the fact that the conversion is usually painless, materially rewarding, and brings with it the distinction of being "a professional." The hallmark of professional administrative education is the emphasis it places on loyalty to the organizational imperative and the resultant administrative norms. The moral rule that emerges from this—which is nearly universal throughout our institutions—is that efficiency in the service of organizational goals equals morality. Thus, we condition ourselves for functional amorality.

To summarize, because of the successes of modern organizations, organizational values are given precedence over individual values. The individual is invariably rewarded for such value substitution. This necessitates a belief in man's moral malleability—that he can make value substitutions whenever and as often as required. Once that malleability is accepted, there is no "reason" why people should hold values other than those that are organizationally useful (Scott and Hart, 1971; Hart and Scott, 1972). Thus the burden of individual responsibility for identifying a personal value system is removed. The organizational imperative is now sufficient.

From Indispensability to Dispensability

An important value in the American tradition has been the right of individuals to feel indispensable to the groups, organizations, and communities of which they are a part. An honorable man could feel confident that his loss would have a profound effect on those who surrounded him. For beyond sorrow was the fact that their world would be less without him. The reader may protest, arguing that throughout history—including our own—men have dispensed with one another in callous and brutal ways. It is also safe to assume that most people have never really felt indispensable. Be that as it may, the *ideal* of personal indispensability has been central to our tradition as one of the important rewards earned through good effort. Simply, it was the sense of being necessary to one's world.

Presently, the organizational imperative demands that nothing be indispensable and that, indeed, dispensability is a prized commodity. The modern American economy is built on the dispensability of things. Obsolescence serves the major purpose in enriching organizations. Our lives are spent in surroundings of constant material replacement, because our technology and our economy have made it more efficient to dispose of things rather than to reuse them.

All of this is well known. What is less well understood is how an individual within a society that exalts dispensability might eventually come to view himself. Alternatively, how does a society which demands that nothing be indispensable come to value the individual? The answer is obvious. The organizational imperative requires that each person understand he is dispensable and, further, that this is a good thing.

Modern organizations cannot allow individuals to become indispensable. If they did, the organization then would become dependent on those individuals. That prospect is anathema to administrative theory and practice. Allow us to illustrate with the metaphor of the organization as machine. It assumes that in the organization, as in the machine, each part is linked as efficiently as possible with all other parts. Each performs its specific tasks in a productive rhythm with all of the others. If there is an ample supply of spares, any part of the machine is dispensable, even though some parts are more expensive to replace than others. The primary mission of the engineer is not only to keep the machine running, but also to ensure an adequate supply of spare parts.

So it is with the people in an organization, *at all levels and in all capacities.* Personnel must be instantly replaceable by others with similar abilities, with a minimal loss of efficiency during the substitution. If there are enough human spares, then there need never be any major upheavals with the turnover of personnel. Like the engineer, one of the primary responsibilities of the administrator is to ensure that an adequate supply of spare parts is immediately available, including his own. Indeed, how often do we hear the incantation, "Train your own replacement!"? The difficulty, of course, is that while no machine part needs to be convinced of its dispensability, a human being does.

This educational task is central to all schools of administration. Books, articles, and teachers hammer away at the theme that the individual has no *right* to expect to become indispensable, not should he attempt to. It is stressed (as a "fact of life" in the "real world") that the dream of personal indispensability is childish and, even worse, organizationally bad. The point was well made by one of our graduate students, who observed that he was like a sausage being prepared for consumption by a large organization. He argued that nothing should be stuffed into him that would give his prospective organization "indigestion". This may be a bit blunt, but some variant of this evaluation is drilled into our students as an essential part of the administrative "attitude" they will take with them onto the job.

But the process does not stop at the boundaries of the employing organization. As the organizational imperative has touched more and more social values, this attitude has been extended into all areas of our lives. Thus, there is a pervasive belief in our society that indispensability is an illusion, nowhere to be found. As a final defense, the reader might argue that he is indispensible to his family. Perhaps. But, given the condition of the American family, the unfortunate truth is that the economic role played by the father could be more efficiently performed by an organization. Certainly this theme is constantly stressed by the advertising of our large financial institutions. Thus, a lethal blow is thrown at the last area where personal indispensability might be found. If man has an innate need to be necessary in his world, then this particular value transition is quite destructive. People convinced of their personal dispensability suffer many consequences, from alienation to existential fear. To avoid these conditions, most of us flee more deeply into the organization, searching for security. Ironically, we find there that we are the most dispensable commodity of all.

From Community to Specialization

Part of the American's magnificent inconsistency has been a stubborn commitment to the seemingly contradictory values of individuality and community

(Nisbet, 1969; McWilliams, 1973; Stein, 1972). However, the values of community and indispensability went hand in hand, for one who was valued for his personal qualities contributed something unique to the warm, supporting, and persisting nature of the community. When he was gone, the quality of the communal relationships could never be reexperienced in quite the same manner.

The organizational imperative has diminished and transformed the value of community. In this instance, the organizational imperative requires that the individual's dedication be primarily to a specialty that is harmonious with and contributory to the ultimate success of an organization. Clearly, specialization does not exist for its own sake. For specialization to have any meaning, it must have *utility* for the organization, whether one is a vice-president or a foreman. The stewardship of one's responsibility is measured by its contribution to the total organization. Loyalty must not be given, therefore, to the work group, to the place, or to some abstract ideals of honor, hospitality, or obligation; rather loyalty must be to the specialized function the successful performance of which adds to the whole organizational effort. In short, the organization has evolved as an inadequate surrogate for community.

It is important to note that the criteria on which individual worth is evaluated in a community are quite different from the criteria by which individual utility is assessed in an organization. An individual's worth, in organizational terms, is not measured affectively in the quality of his relationships with others. When has friendship ever been considered as a standard in wage and salary administration? Worth is measured quantitatively, wherever possible, by the level of one's specialized performance relative to the achievement of organizational goals.

Finally, specialization and dispensability are comfortable—even necessary—partners. Specialty has always been treated as depersonalized in administrative theory and practice. The most efficient way to meet the obligations of stewardship is to objectify, as far as possible, what people do in organizations and to assign quantitative standards in order to judge performance. These standards allow little room for affective considerations, other than those that might have organizational utility. There is no room for community, in the best sense of the word, within modern organizations, since in order to thrive it must have stability and continuity of human relationships. The loss of meaning in one's life because of the absence of community cannot be replaced easily by the rewards that come from specialization.

From Spontaneity to Planning

Another value central to the American tradition has been spontaneity. It was interpreted in a number of ways. In its more dramatic form, it was believed that people should be willing to abandon the security of the known in order to venture into the unknown, taking risks for the sake of personal gain. But in its most significant form, it was believed that the really urgent problems most often would be solved by individuals through spontaneous, creative action. While such spontaneity was unanticipatable in detail, it was assumed that it would somehow occur, in mysterious ways and at appropriate times, to the benefit of society in general or to specific organizations in particular. The spontaneous, creative, enterprising individual would work wonders in all areas, from farming to industry, and even to the political system. The results of such actions would be more efficacious ways of doing things, producing more jobs, goods, and services.

Thus, spontaneity became an integral part of the American entrepreneurial ethic, defined as ingenuity or "Yankee know-how." The moral lesson in the Horatio Alger and Frank Meriwell stories was simply that a young man with "pluck and luck" could move inexorably ahead in business, finance, or whatever. The essence of the American value of spontaneity is found in this pluck-and-luck theme. Pluck meant the motivation to act creatively (even impulsively), in unforeseen circumstances, to solve problems. Luck pertained to the element of risk that a plucky person had to assume if he was to make his way successfully through life. The interesting twist in these stories was that if a person took action from an instinctive knowledge of what was right, Lady Luck would bend in his favor. So individual, spontaneous action was prized because it was believed that it brought favorable outcomes for all concerned, especially when guided by a sense of moral rectitude. This gave Americans an additional reason to be optimistic about the future. The uncertainties of the future were not to be feared, for they were the breeding ground of opportunity.

However, this has been changed by the administrative needs of modern organization. As we have said, the world of administration is concerned with complex, short-term problems. Nevertheless, the future must obviously be taken into account in order to set goals, to map strategies, to make budgets, to establish policies, to allocate resources, and so on. Administrators must plan, and there is no way they can plan for spontaneity. Thus, the organizational imperative not only reduces the premium formerly placed on spontaneity, the imperative makes spontaneity dysfunctional. Planning has replaced spontaneity as the primary means of handling the uncertainties of the future. It requires speculation about events that are anticipated but as yet unrealized. So planning is, in some ways, incompatible with the rule of pragmatism. But the needs of modern organizations have forced a reconciliation between the two, and this reconciliation has caused the change in the way spontaneity is perceived and valued.

As more investment capital is committed to plant and equipment, as the time span between the beginning and end of tasks or projects lengthens, as more specialized manpower is hired, and as the flexibility of an organization diminishes in relation to its increased fixed resources, long-range planning activities expand dramatically. The problem is how to adjust the planning function to the rule of pragmatism. Certain planning practices have evolved to this end. First, guess-work must be eliminated. This necessitates the development and application of a technology of forecasting. Second, as many external "variables" as possible must be controlled. They influence the future direction of the organization in uncertain ways. By controlling these variables, today's forecasts are made into tomorrow's self-fulfilling prophecies. Third, the possibilities that aberrant individual behavior will unpredictably alter the course of planned future events must be eradicated. This practice has two subconditions. Behavior in the planning *process* itself must be controlled. This means that planning ideally should be a collective process, because group performance is more visible and predictable than individual performance. Then, the implementation of plans must be controlled by means that are visible and understandable to all involved.

Control, therefore, is the way that planning and pragmatism are reconciled. That control and planning are conceptual counterparts is a frequently cited, but poorly understood, administrative adage. However, it is a certainty that as planning grows, controlling also grows, if for no other reason than to prevent random or aberrant events from confounding plans. This explains why spontaneity is by now a less valued, even dangerous behavior. It is unpredictable, and therefore uncontrollable. So, while the organization may lose some advantage from spontaneously creative acts, this loss is offset by the more easily controlled behavior that arises from collective planning processes.

From Voluntarism to Paternalism

In the past, when individuals desired concerted action to achieve common aims, it was assumed that they would combine in voluntary interest groups and that their resultant efforts would be sufficient to accomplish their goals. Associations of freely participating individuals were so much a part of the American way of doing things that the traditional political theory of pluralism and the economic theory of countervailing power rested in substantial degree on the efficacy of voluntarism. This principle molded the familiar American ideals of industrial democracy, collective self-determination, federalism, decentralization, government by consent, and so on.

We have traditionally believed that social phenomena are the result of deliberate decisions traceable to individual acts. This belief implied autonomy, free will, individual responsibility and accountability, and generalized social norms that guided the conduct of individuals in making choices. However, it is also true that we believed in the usefulness of collective action, especially when the leverage of power was required to advance one's own interests in the face of opposing collective interests. So voluntarism allowed a person to retain the rights and obligations of individualism, but it also permitted him to take advantage of the power of concerted action, within a self-governing organizational framework. The principle of voluntarism was accepted through American society. Laborers, farmers, accountants, consumers, doctors, professors, engineers, businessmen, lawyers, and many others have formed voluntary associations at different times in our history, with varying degrees of success. The point is that voluntarism reflected a compromise between individualism and collectivism, presenting us with an ingenious amalgamation of these polarities.

Voluntarism was an effective but fragile compromise. It was always under assault—both from the side of individualism and from the side of collectivism. For example, even the most conservative—craft unions still are damned in some quarters because they allegedly curtail individual autonomy. Political lobbyists are portrayed as greedy power merchants whose interests are opposed to those of individual citizens. The argument used against the unionization of university professors is that individual freedom, for many the sine qua non of scholarly excellent, will be destroyed. Yet, at present, the most devastating attacks on voluntarism are not coming from those who advocate individualism. Rather, the strongest assault is coming from those who advocate collectivism, and it has taken form as organizational paternalism.

It is not as if paternalism—the benevolent concern of management for the welfare of their employee "children"—is something new on the organizational scene. The spirit of business welfarism has been prevalent in Great Britain and in the United States for a long time. This spirit initially grew out of the social doctrines of Calvinism, which imposed on the "elect" the responsibility for the collective spiritual welfare of their charges. Following the industrial revolution in England such responsibilities were reflected in the rules of work and worship that were widely circulated and applied in factory towns. Regardless of how primitive, convoluted, and cynical this early paternalistic thinking may seem to us now, it was justified as following Christian teachings.

As social change swept through Great Britain and America, it produced major transformations in paternalistic doctrines. First, society became secularized, so that the religious justification for paternalism became irrelevant. Second, organizational economic benefits became the dominant rationale. As Carnegie (1902: V) put it: "The employer who helps his workmen through education, recreation, and social uplift, helps himself." Third, responding to the challenge of unionism in the 1920s, management adopted the paternalistic "American plan" as a counterstrategy.

Paternalism was used by management for the practical purposes of either fighting unions or raising worker productivity. While the focus of paternalism shifted from the spiritual to the temporal, it remained basically a collective undertaking, ideologically justified as the means of promoting general employee welfare. In any event, there was nothing in paternalism that allowed for any tolerance of the voluntaristic principle of self-determination.

With the rise of sophisticated professional management in the 1930s another shift occurred in the doctrine of paternalism that can be traced directly to the rule of stewardship. This new aspect of the doctrine is, in some respects, the most effective attack on voluntarism yet mounted. It is the result of some fundamental value changes, directly attributable to the growing dominance of organizations in our society and to a concomitant influence of the behavioral sciences over social policy-making. While the first assault of paternalism on voluntarism was spiritual in origin and the second was clearly secular, the third and most recent assault is therapeutic.

As we explained earlier, professional administration from its inception has been guided by the rule of stewardship. The separation of corporate ownership from control gave managers virtual sovereign power to dispose of the resources of the organization in ways that would most satisfy the interests of its clientele. When stewardship and the separation of ownership and control were being examined analytically for the first time (Berle and Means, 1933), emphasis was on the management of material resources, particularly financial resources. However, it did not take long for the grasp of managerial stewardship to extend to the human resources of an organization as well. How were they to deal with them?

Managers of modern organizations quickly succumbed to the utility of behavioral science therapy values. The lessons of the various humanistic movements were learned and put into practice by administrators. These lessons contain the following premises. First, "normal" people behave dysfunctionally in organizations if they do not accept the imperatives of obedient behavior. Second, the administrative elite of the organization has sovereign power to impress the norms of the organization on the people in it, for their own welfare. Third, organizationally "deviant" behavior (and values) should be "cured" by applying behavioral science techniques rather than punishment.

Paternalism has traveled the entire route, starting with spiritual welfare, moving through physical welfare, and ending with the mental welfare of employees. The last is the most insidious, since in our age the best way to ensure obedience is to create a state of psychological dependency. This is exactly what the new form of paternalism does—it defines self-determination, autonomy, and the other conditions of individualism as illness. Clearly, voluntarism as well is a principle that therapeutic paternalism cannot abide. Thus we have completed the circle, returning to where we began this discussion of changing values—to Milgram's analysis of "obedience to authority." There is no more despotic authority than the "father" righteously legislating the terms of mental health for his children, and equipped with the means for enforcing these terms.

Conclusion

The organizational imperative is the core of our well-entrenched value paradigm, which has displaced the values of our tradition. The period of transition was marked by feelings of alienation and dislocation among large numbers of people as those traditional values were found inappropriate to the demands of the present. Regardless, the organizational imperative prevailed and has assumed its final shape. Not all people are committed to the organizational imperative. There are still some few who live in the ignored corners of our society who have little to do with it. Nonetheless, the organizational imperative is the dominant article of faith for all administrators of the innumerable, overlapping, and inescapable organizations that make up contemporary society. Theirs is the significant involvement. But this is also true of workers who must conform to the rules of modern organization and those others whose lives are inextricably involved as clients of modern organizations. In short, *all* must embrace the values of the organizational imperative if they want to obtain the great rewards promised by modern organization.

This promise seemed about to be fulfilled in the decade of the 1950s. The unanticipated turmoil of the 1960s seemed but a temporary setback. During this time the deep-rooted sense of American optimism persisted. We believed that our leaders, public and private, would somehow assert themselves and get us successfully through the heavy weather. Our optimism has not been justified.

The 1970s have brought considerable national peril, exacerbated by the war in Vietnam, festering domestic inequalities, government venality, incivility in our major cities, shortages of basic commodities, serious economic inflation, and a major recession. The dreary list could be multiplied, but, what is even worse, we know that the future will be filled with even greater perils. Somehow, the promise of the leadership of the best and the brightest has turned sour, and the people are increasingly aware of it.

There is evidence of growing public doubt that our expectations for continuous growth and affluence are realizable. Conditions point toward a nongrowth, stable-state economy. Yet politicians, public administrators, and business executives resist policies of economic stabilization, reduction of agency services, or the leveling of sales volume and corporate earnings. Even more, schools of administration will have nothing to do with such topics. Who, for instance, has ever taken a course in an administrative curriculum on "How to Shrink a Business"? Articles and books are seldom found in the professional literature of administration advocating models of nongrowth, although there are some notable exceptions. Such things do not happen, because they are *seemingly* foreign to the organizational imperative, and hence to the norms of administrative theory and practice.

But modern organizations can exist in such an environment. Further, public attitudes about these matters can be conveniently changed and with little disruption (Ellul, 1965). The organizational imperative will *easily* survive. It has the power and the flexibility to ride out these crises without having to change its essential features. In fact, the a priori propositions and their rules will be strengthened in the process of responding to those crises. The major casualty will be the individual. Is there any doubt that modern organizations, public or private, will arrive in that unprecedented future in much better shape than the individual?

Thus, we can anticipate the strengthening of the organizational imperative as large-scale organizations restructure themselves to meet the future challenges. This will require, of course, an intensification of mass loyalty to the organizational imperative. However, that can be accomplished once those in the significant positions in society understand what is needed.

Given this situation, we cannot just sit tight and "muddle through," on the anticipation that everything will turn out well. We are confronted with the problems right now, and administrators have begun to solve those problems. Now if this new paradigm is not harmful to man qua man, then these "soft" normative issues can be dismissed and we can get down to the "hard" work of making organizations more effective. But, if one believes that the paradigm is destructive to man, then corrections must be made immediately.

Thus, the most fundamental task of our time is to provide an answer to the ancient and persistent question, *What is man that these things should or should not be done to him?* Is there anything innate in man that is offended, and perhaps even destroyed, by the values of the new paradigm? Unless that question is answered first, there is really no reason to resist the organizational imperative. In fact, resistance is counterproductive, for it just slows down the fight for organizational survival in times of great peril.

Further, the question cannot be resolved by empirical means, for by its very nature, it transcends empiricism. It will require moral discourse of a high order and a *deliberate* selection of new values that enhance that which is morally innate in man, if indeed there is such a thing. To choose values deliberately is unprecedented in human history, but it must be done (Gorney, 1972: 8-9).

References

Berle, A. A., Jr., and G. S. Means (1933) *The Modern Corporation and Private Property.* New York: Macmillan.

Carnegie, A. (1902) *The Empire of Business.* New York: Doubleday, Page.

Ellul, J. (1965) *Propaganda.* New York: Alfred A. Knops.

Gorney, R. (1972) *The Human Agenda.* New York: Simon & Schuster.

Hart, D. K. and W. G. Scott (1972) "The optimal image of man for systems theory." *Academy of Management J.* 15 (December): 531-540.

Janis, I. L. (1972) *Victims of Groupthink.* Boston: Houghton Mifflin.

Kuhn, T. S. (1970) *The Structure of Scientific Revolutions.* Chicago: Univ. of Chicago Press.

McWilliams, W. C. (1973) *The Idea of Fraternity in America.* Berkeley: Univ. of California Press.

Milgram, S. (1974) *Obedience to Authority.* New York: Harper & Row.

Mill, J. S. (1950) *Utilitarianism, Liberty, and Representative Government.* New York: Dutton.

Nisbet, R. A. (1969) *The Quest for Community.* New York: Oxford Univ. Press.

Scott, W. G. and D. K. Hart (1971) "The moral nature of man in organizations," *Academy of Management J.* 14 (June): 241-255.

Scott, W. G. and D. K. Hart (1973) "Administrative crisis: the neglect of metaphysical speculation." *Public Administration Rev.* 33 (September/October): 415-422.

Stein, M. R. (1972) *The Eclipse of Community.* Princeton: Princeton Univ. Press.

Whyte, W. H., Jr. (1956) *The Organization Man.* Garden City, N.Y.: Anchor.

NEUROTIC ORGANIZATIONS
Symptoms, Causes, and Treatment*

Jerry B. Harvey and D. Richard Albertson

Organizations, like individuals develop neuroses. The toll on an organization's behavior, measured in terms of production, efficiency, absenteeism, turnover, overhead and morale, is tremendous. And since each of these organization variables have personal antecedents, the price paid by individual organization members, measured in terms of misery and loss of self-esteem and confidence, is inestimable. But organizations, like people, can be cured of neurotic behavior and returned to a state of healthy functioning. The purpose of this paper is to describe the symptoms of organization neurosis, to identify some of its causes, and to define a course of treatment for restoring neurotic organizations to health. Implicit throughout the paper are descriptions of the role and function of an organization consultant in the process of diagnosis and treatment.

Symptoms of Organization Neurosis

Perhaps the most effective way to get a feel for the symptoms of organization neurosis is to read summaries of interviews [1] with several employees including the boss of a neurotic organization.

*Reprinted from W. Warner Burke (Ed.), *New Technologies in Organization Development: 1* (Originally *Contemporary Organization Development: Conceptual Orientations and Interventions.* Arlington, Va.: NTL Institute for Applied Behavioral Science, 1972). La Jolla, Calif.: University Associates, 1975, pp. 16-34. Used with permission.

Interview I

Consultant: How are things going on the job?

Employee A: Terrible. I hate to come to work. And once I'm here, I don't get anything done. We just sit around and bitch. The only thing I look forward to is vacation.

Consultant: What's the problem? What's causing the trouble?

Employee A: We have a couple of problems. First, we have a lousy boss. He never holds up our end with the higher ups. He simply can't carry the flag when he deals with his boss. And second, at least two of the five units making up this division should not be reporting to him. Putting Sales and Research under the same man is absurd. In a lot of ways they are competitive. There is no reason for them to work together. They never have and never will.

Consultant: Have you ever confronted your boss with his failure to "carry the flag?"

Employee A: Hell, no. Do you think I'm crazy or something?

Consultant: What about the problem with Sales and Research? What are you doing to solve that?

Employee A: Just last week we met and agreed to operate under a combined budget.

Interview II

Consultant: How are things going on the job?

Employee B: Pretty bad. This is a frustrating place to work. Right now I'm looking for another job. I take as much vacation and sick leave as I can. And I don't get anything done when I'm here. Really, I'm just marking time, hoping things will get better.

Consultant: What's causing all the frustration?

Employee B: Well, for one thing our organization set-up doesn't make sense. Whoever designed it must have been drunk. Having Sales and Research report to the same man is unworkable. We spend half of our time fighting one another. In addition, our boss doesn't represent our viewpoint to the top.

Consultant: Are you taking any steps to deal with the problems you just described?

Employee B: Yes, just last week the president instructed my boss to get us together to solve the morale problem. It's beginning to cut into everyone's production. The last quarter was very poor from a profit standpoint. And two of our best researchers took jobs with another company.

Consultant: What did you do?

Employee B: We had an all day meeting and agreed to operate under a combined budget. That should force us to work together more effectively.

Consultant: One other question. What about your boss? Has he ever asked whether he is doing an adequate job of carrying the division's viewpoint to the top?

Employee B: Yes, just the other day, he said he had heard by the grapevine that we thought he wasn't giving us good representation with the president and his staff.

Consultant: What did you say?

Employee B: I said I thought he was doing a good job.

Interview III

Consultant: What problems and issues are facing your division at the present time?

Boss: Well, morale is at an all time low. We have had a couple of good people quit and go to other companies. And production is down. The heat is on me and everyone else. I've about given up.

Consultant: What's the cause of it?

Boss: One big problem is the way we are organized. My boss gave me several units that don't have any reason to work together. In fact, two of the units are actually competitive in a functional sense. With that kind of arrangement, it's impossible to build teamwork among the staff.

Consultant: What have you done about it?

Boss: Well, last week I gave a pep talk to the staff at our weekly meeting and said we had to work together more effectively. And to insure that we do, we developed a unit budget that ties each subgroup's performance into the overall performance of the division.

Consultant: Have you ever thought about telling your boss that the way you are organized does not make sense?

Boss: I've tried, but I can't seem to make him understand.

Consultant: Have you really pushed him hard?

Boss: I'm not about to do that. He might think I am not an effective manager.

As can be seen by the interviews, the neurotic organization exhibits a number of specific symptoms which are collectively expressed by its members.

Pain and Frustration

Its members complain of frustration, worry, backbiting, loss of self-esteem and a general sense of impotence. They do not feel their skills are being adequately used. As a result, they become less efficient and look for ways to avoid the job, such as taking vacation, taking sick leave, and "giving up" or "opting out" of trying to solve the problems they see as causing the pain.

Blaming Others for the Problems

Its members attempt to place much of the blame for the dilemma on others, particularly the boss. In "backroom" conversations among subordinates, he is termed as incompetent, ineffective, "out of touch" or as a candidate for transfer or early retirement. To his face nothing is said, or at best, oblique or misleading information is given concerning his impact on the organization.

Subgroup Formation

As pain and frustration becomes more intense, its members form into identifiable subgroups. These subgroups may develop on the basis of friendship ties, with trusted acquaintances meeting during coffee or over lunch to share rumors, complaints, fantasies, or strategies for dealing with the problems at hand. The most important effect of such meetings is to heighten the overall anxiety level in the organization rather than to assist in realistically coping with its problems.

Agreement as to Problems

Its members generally agree as to the character of problems causing the pain. For example, in the interviews related above, organization members agree that the organization has two basic problems: 1) The composition of the units reporting to the same superior is inappropriate, and 2) There is a failure to communicate the urgency of the composition issue to upper levels of management. The first problem reflects an important *task* issue (Benne & Muntyan, 1951), i.e., how to organize effectively. The second reflects as equally important *maintenance* concern (Benne & Muntyan, 1951), i.e., how to work together in such a way that the organization functions effectively. That agreement as to task and maintenance issues bridges both hierarchical and functional lines. Stated differently, the boss and his subordinates see the problems in the same way as do employees from Sales and Research. Although organization members may be unaware of the degree to which they agree with one another, the reality is they do agree.

Members Act Contrary to Data and Information They Possess

Perhaps the most unique characteristic of neurotic organizations is that its members act in ways contrary to data and information they possess. In analogous terms, it would be as if an outside observer viewed the following vignette involving twenty people from a neurotic organization:

> Observer: (Approaching a group sitting around a camp fire.) How are things going?

Organization Members: (Who are holding their hands over an open fire.) Awful. It's too hot. We are burning up. The pain is excruciating. Our hands are too close to the coals.

Observer: What do you intend to do about it?

Organization Members: Move our hands closer to the fire, what else?

Although the analogy may sound absurd on the surface, it is certainly no more absurd than the following conversation which occurred in an actual organization.

Consultant: You say there is no possible functional relationship among the groups reporting to your boss and it is impossible to build one.

Organization Members: Yes, that's right.

Consultant: What do you propose to do about it?

Organization Members: Meet more often so we will have more opportunities to learn to work together.

It is this characteristic which really defines neurotic organization behavior the same way it defines neurotic individual behavior. The individual who consistently acts contrary to his best "internal signals" becomes neurotic, and if he acts in concert with a variety of others, the organization as an entity develops neurotic symptoms. Stated conversely, any human system must act congruently with reality if it is to function effectively.

Members Behave Differently Outside the Organization

Finally, key to the diagnosis of organization neurosis is the fact that outside the organization context members do not either suffer the pain nor demonstrate the irrational behavior (such as behaving contrary to their own views of reality) they demonstrate in their day-to-day work. Outside the organization, individual members get along better, are happier, and perform more effectively than they do within it, a fact which heightens their discomfort when living and working within the organization.

Summary

In summary, a neurotic organization is one in which:

1. Organization members feel pain, frustration, and loss of self-esteem.
2. Organization members agree among themselves as to the problems causing the pain.

3. Organization members take collective action essentially contrary to the data, information, and feelings they possess for solving the problems. That action, in turn, increases the pain, frustration, and loss of self-esteem and leads to the emergence of other symptoms.
4. Organization members do not suffer similar pain or demonstrate similar irrational behavior outside the organization.

Causes of Neurotic Organization Behavior

Given a description of organization neurosis, the question is then, "Why do organization members engage in behavior which is both individually and organizationally destructive?" Basically, there are two reasons.

Lack of Awareness

First, organization members are unaware of their behavior and the consequences it has for them as individuals and for the organization as an entity. Such lack of awareness may involve any of three levels. At the most superficial level, an organization member may be unaware of the degree to which the information and feelings he possesses are shared by others in the organization. Thus, a member of the organization may feel as if he is alone in his diagnosis of the organization's problems. Or, he may feel that, at most, the subgroup to which he belongs agrees as to the character of the organization's problems. He seldom realizes that his understandings and beliefs are widely shared across functional and hierarchical lines and that he is not an isolate.

> Consultant: Do you think people other than yourself believe that the unit needs to be reorganized?
>
> Employee: Well, several guys that work with me agree on that issue, but I doubt if any others do.
>
> Consultant: What would you say if I told you that virtually everyone in the division feels the same as you do about that issue.
>
> Employee: I'd say you must be kidding.

Since that lack of agreement reflects a simple information gap, it is the simplest form of unawareness to correct.

At a second level, organization members may be unaware of the dysfunctional group norms and standards which inhibit or prevent their coping with the problems at hand. It is at the normative level that the difference between individual and organization neurosis is most clearly articulated. Individual neurosis stems from *personal* dynamics unique to the individual. Organization neurosis stems from *collective* dynamics unique to the organization. Thus, organizations develop social norms and standards, neurotic in character, the breaking of which by individual members results in the application of social pressure to conform. For example, some organizations develop dysfunctional norms mitigating against open discussion of important organization issues.

> Organization Member A: I think we ought to confront the issue of whether we are appropriately organized. I personally don't think these units belong together.
>
> Organization Member B: Oh, knock it off! Let's not get involved in something like that.
>
> Organization Member D: What are you trying to do? We don't need things stirred up any more than they already are.
>
> Organization Member C: Yes, the problems aren't as bad as you crack them up to be. We really work together rather well. I move we change the subject.

As one consultant put it, "fish are the last to know that they are in water." So it is with organization members. They are frequently the last to know of the dysfunctional norms which govern and occasionally consume them. However, as Lewin (1947) has demonstrated, behavior rooted in group standards and norms is easier to change than behavior rooted in individual character structure. Because of this principle, organization neurosis is potentially more amenable to change than the individual variety.

Finally, a third level relates to the degree to which organization members are unaware of the manner in which they contribute to maintaining the problems. For example, some members may see the part others, particularly the boss, play in maintaining destructive norms and standards; but few sense their own roles in the process.

> Consultant: You say your boss is at fault; that he should demand to his superior that the situation be changed.
>
> Employee A: Absolutely. He is doing a lousy job.
>
> Employee B: You can say that again.
>
> Consultant: Have you or any other members of your division ever demanded of your boss that he do a better job of representing your group to the President?
>
> Employee A: No. That's not what I'm around here for.
>
> Employee B: Me neither.
>
> Employee C: I think it would be foolish and disrespectful to do something like that.
>
> Consultant: It seems to me as if you may be doing exactly the same thing you don't want your boss to do.
>
> Employee C: (lamely) We are?

It is as if the identification with superiors, other peers, or the organization itself is so great that they lose their capacities to understand either their individual or collective contributions to the dysfunctional organization processes. Since the dynamics supporting such lack of awareness tend to be so deep within the individual and group psyche (Freud, 1951) they are the hardest to identify, make explicit, and change.

Fantasies About Consequences of Alternative Actions

Even when organization members are aware of the degree to which they agree as to the substance of the problems, are knowledgeable about the group norms and standards which prevent their coping effectively with those problems and are cognizant of their own unique ways of maintaining those dysfunctional norms and standards, they still may be unable to take effective problem-solving action. Again, the question is "Why?"

In most cases, the inaction relates to rich and varied fantasies organization members have about possible negative consequences which may befall them if they do act. The fantasies have a mythlike quality (Bradford & Harvey, 1970) which are frequently unrelated to reality.

> Consultant: Each of you seems to agree this division needs to be reorganized and that the present format is unworkable. Why don't you suggest to your boss that you reorganize?
>
> Employee A: He might fire us for treading on his territory. He's supposed to think of that, not us.
>
> Employee B: The new organization might be worse than the present one. It's not worth taking the chance.
>
> Employee C: I'm sure things will get better if we just wait it out. Life isn't as bad as we make it out to be.
>
> Employee D: I've got a mortgage payment on the house. I can't afford to do anything that rocks the boat.
>
> Consultant: Is there any possibility that things might get better if you do something other than wait?
>
> Various Employees: We doubt it.

The fantasy-like quality comes from the fact that the projected outcomes are seldom if ever tested for reality. In general, such fantasies reflect a tremendous amount of underlying anxiety and concern that has to be taken into account in any process designed to treat the "neurosis."

Treatment of Organization Neurosis

Like individual neurosis, organization nuerosis can be treated, and like the individual variety, the treatment is complex.

Basically, the treatment requires the following elements.

Data Collection from Organization Members

The first step is to collect data from a representative sample of organization members. It is particularly important that more than one level of the organization be represented in the data collection, since issues of hierarchy and authority are generally central to the kinds of problems identified. On the basis of their experiences with a variety of organizations, the authors have found that open-ended interviews conducted around three basic questions produces the data required. These questions are:

1. What issues and problems are facing the organization at the present time?
2. What is causing these problems?
3. What strengths are available in the organization to solve the problems?

Interviews last 45 minutes to an hour. Basic to the success of the interviews is that they be conducted by someone who can view the organization from an essentially objective standpoint. Although it is possible that an inside consultant with enough functional autonomy can achieve and maintain the kind of objective detachment required, an outside consultant is generally preferred. An outsider is less likely to be caught up in the dysfunctional processes underlying the neurosis and, therefore, is less likely to have distorted perspectives of the organization and its problems.

Essentially, verbatim notes are taken by the consultant. When all interviews are completed, the data from interviewees are sorted into themes[2] which are identified with non-evaluative titles. Actual statements of organization members are grouped under each theme. A typical set of themes and supporting statements are shown in Exhibit I.

It should be stressed that the data must be verbatim accounts of what the organization members said relative to each theme. The data must not be a summary of what the consultant would like organization members to say or believe. Throughout the process of consultation, the actual data contributed by organization members, not the consultant's biases and prejudices, must be the topic of exploration.

Data Feedback to Organization Members

After data are collected and sorted into themes, the consultant presents both the themes and supporting statements to the interviewees in a modified version of a confrontation session (Beckhard, 1967). During this session, which usually requires several hours, organization members are encouraged to discuss, clarify and, modify both the themes and the supporting statements. Whenever organization members are satisfied that the themes and the supporting data are accurate reflections of their own feelings and knowledge, they are asked to develop a single summary statement which adequately summarizes the data contributed under each theme. Examples of summary statements are also contained in Exhibit I.

After each theme has been discussed and a summary statement developed, organization members are asked to vote publicly as to whether they agree or disagree with the content of the summary statement.

Votes are counted and if a clear majority do not agree with a summary statement, the consultant works with the group to clarify the reasons for the disagreement. Discussion continues until the statement is modified so that most organization members can agree with it, or until the statement is eliminated because it does not actually reflect their feelings and attitudes.

Taking a public vote is important because it transfers ownership of the themes and the supporting data from the consultant to the organization members themselves. Stated differently, the vote forces the organization members to accept responsibility for the validity or lack of validity of the data they contributed.

Once the data are identified as belonging to organization members rather than the consultants, the next step is to ask each member to "own up" (Argyris, 1962) to his individual contribution to each issue represented by the various themes.

Thus, each organization member is asked to produce a series of written statements according to the following directions:

> For each of the summary statements, write a few sentences describing the way in which you contribute to the issue which is summarized. Your descriptions will belong to you. Although you may want to share your thoughts with others later on, there will be no requirement to do so.

Here, the purpose is to help each organization member focus on his possible contribution to maintaining the processes causing the problems. It also helps to set a norm of examining one's own contribution to the organization's problems rather than blaming others.

Theme 1: Division Composition

1. The composition of this division does not make sense.
2. This division is a group of independent units operating under an umbrella.
3. It is not a group. It is a collection of units just thrown together.
4. Research does not belong in the division.
5. The way the division is constituted is inappropriate.
6. The division needs to be subdivided.
7. It is a mixture of apples and oranges.
8. The division is made up of remnants of an earlier era. There is not much logic to it.
9. What we have is a variety of sub-groups.
10. Units do not have much in common.
11. It is not a group in any sense.

Summary Statement

The present composition and/or structure of the division is inappropriate, out of step with the opportunity to accomplish our purposes, and should be changed.

Theme 2: Collaboration within the Division

1. Some staff members do not communicate with anyone.
2. No communication within division.
3. Staff share few common goals—the exception is survival.
4. There's no relationship between some units, like Sales and Research.
5. There's too much time talking as a group. The subjects talked about are not perceived as making much difference.
6. There is no support. I occasionally feel close to harassment. We frequently talk to other staff members rather than confronting the person we should talk to.
7. Within the division some are more willing to jump unit lines than others.
8. Other units in the division fight each other for stature.
9. Some units in the division are pro-active while others sit around waiting to be told what to do.
10. Each unit is a kingdom unto itself.

Summary Statement

In general, units within the division do not work together.

Theme 3: Top Leadership

1. The boss is too nice and that causes people to take advantage of him.
2. His style keeps us from confronting problems even when conflict is there.
3. The boss is unable to carry the "flag." I don't know why.
4. He has not been able to change or get the attention of top management.

(Exhibit I continued)

Theme 3 (continued)

5. He spends a lot ot time telling the group that everything is okay—all is right with the world—but that is not true.
6. His style is not congruent with the confrontation style that works in the organization today.
7. He sometimes has to support positions that he does not believe in and that makes him ineffective in dealing with top management.
8. His inability to be defensive and hostile get him in trouble.

Summary Statement

The boss's style is not of a confronting nature.

Theme 4: Pain

1. We are suffering from . . .
2. I feel no support and occasionally feel close to harassment.
3. People who are committed are frustrated as well.
4. Nothing feeds failure like failure.
5. Creativity is squelched.
6. Joe Smith is being stiffled.
7. We want to contribute in a positive way, but can't.
8. There is a lot of insecurity and morale is very low.
9. The division is not conducive to good mental health and working conditions.

Summary Statement

Most division personnel are frustrated, worried, and feel insecure; morale is low.

Exhibit I   Examples of themes, supporting data and summary statements.

Sharing the Theory

One of the most important steps in the treatment process involves the sharing of the consultant's theory with organization members. Again, organization members' own views or reality, which they have affirmed through a public vote, is central to the presentation process. The rationale for presenting the model is that theory itself is a powerful intervention. In brief, it helps organization members to diagnose and understand organization problems and to plan action steps which do not foster the continuation of these problems.

Basically, the theory is presented by the consultant as follows:
When organization members:

1. Experience pain and frustration,

2. Agree with one another as to the problems and causes, and

3. Act in ways contrary to their own thoughts, feelings, and information;

the following assumptions should be tested:

1. Organization members are implicitly or explicitly collaborating with one another to maintain the status quo,

2. Organization members have fantasies about the disastrous consequences of confronting those issues and concerns they know and agree cause the pain and frustration.

At this point, the consultant helps organization members apply the model to their own lives by "walking them through" an actual case involving their own organization.

Consultant: In this organization you agree that you are unhappy and frustrated (Theme 4), that the organization is inappropriately constituted (Theme 1), and that units do not work well together (Theme 2). Yet, when asked by top management to make a proposal for solving the problems of the organization, what happened?

Organization Member: We made a proposal.

Consultant: What did you say in the proposal?

Organization Member: That we develop a matrix organization and operate under a combined budget.

Consultant: What will that decision require?

Organization Member: Well, for one thing, a lot more teamwork.

Consultant: Is that decision congruent with the reality that everyone feels the organization is inappropriately constituted and that the various sub parts do not work well together?

Organization Member: Oh, hell! We've done it again, haven't we?

Using members' own data forces them to become aware of the discrepancy between their own views of reality (We don't work well together) and the actions they take which, in effect, deny that reality (making decisions which require working more closely together). This new awareness confronts them with the necessity of making a conscious choice to explore alternatives based on their views of reality (for example, dissolving the division and reorganizing, a solution which may require painful shifts in job, status, and location) or continuing to act on the basis of irrational fantasies which are individually and organizationally destructive (organizing in a way that denies their beliefs that the composition of the division is inappropriate).

If the consultant is to be effective in helping the organization alter its destructive patterns, he must continue to help members confront the basic discrepancy which exists between their views of reality and the decisions they make. The ways in which he assists in this confrontation process are discussed in the following sections.

Consultant Functions in Change Process

Throughout the data feedback session, and in other encounters within the organization, events occur which mirror the problems organization members have in working during their day-to-day activities. In these encounters, the consultant has a variety of functions all of which require his being sensitive to underlying emotional and process issues. Examples of the consultant's functions include:

Building Awareness of Dysfunctional Group Standards and Norms

The process of presenting data to the persons who contribute it helps organization members become aware of the degree to which they agree with one another about the character of the organization's problems. In effect, the sharing of data assists in solving problems stemming from an "information gap." However, the consultant must also help organization members become aware of dysfunctional norms and group standards which inhibit their capacity to cope with problems identified in the data sharing stage.

> Organization Member: (to consultant) I did not like being forced by you to fill out the questionnaire regarding my contribution to maintaining the problems. When you asked me to do that, I felt very manipulated. I didn't think the process would lead to anything and still don't. I just filled it out to suit you. It sure as hell didn't suit any need of mine.
>
> Consultant: I wonder how many others felt that way.
>
> Various Members: I did.
>
> Consultant: In some ways, that is similar to the tendency of members of this organization to act contrary to their own best views of reality.
>
> Organization Member: I don't understand that either. We just did as we were told. What's wrong with that?
>
> Consultant: Well, it looks as if most of you did not want to respond to the questionnaire because you didn't think it was relevant. Yet everyone responded and nothing was said at the time. That's very similar to not confronting the problem of reorganization even though there is uniform agreement that reorganization is needed.
>
> Organization Member: Damn it. You got us again.
>
> Consultant: I didn't get you.

Organization Member: Yeah. We got ourselves. We contributed to the problem again.

Previous Member: Yes, but he still makes me mad, catching us.

Coping with Feelings

As the previous vignette indicates, the members of a neurotic organization, like neurotic individuals, demonstrate extreme difficulty in the area of learning new behavior. They find it difficult to appraise the past in the light of the present. As a consequence, they find it hard to assimilate and utilize new knowledge although it may be all around them and clearly apparent to an outsider. They seem to be restricted to coping responses rooted in history. Although these responses may be inadequate and dysfunctional, organization members persist in using them and even exert a tremendous amount of collective energy in trying to maintain them.

Much of that energy in a change process may be directed against the consultant in the form of anger and resentment or lavish praise.

Organization Member: He makes me mad, catching us that way.

Organization Member: He doesn't make me mad. He sees things none of the rest of us see. He's doing a great job.

The feelings of ambivalence are understandable for the consultant, in ways similar to the individual therapist, represents both a threat and a promise to organization members.

It is important for the change process that the consultant understand this and be prepared to cope with such feelings when they arise, because in any organization change process, as in an individual therapeutic process, there is an initial period of disorganization, pain and anxiety before new, more functional norms and standards are developed.

The coping can take two forms. One is to help members learn from their feelings.

Consultant: Both comments may reflect some reality and some fantasy. For example, I don't think I "caught" anyone. And I also doubt that I'm the only one who sees what I reported. I would like to check that out with others here.

The other form of coping is more pragmatic. The authors suspect that it is around this issue that many organization change processes are terminated. Thus, organization members must be informed in advance of the possible turmoil they may feel and of the potential positive consequences. Otherwise, a change process may be stopped at the very time constructive change takes place. In short, just as it is with a neurotic individual, the neurotic organization is its own worst enemy.

Encouraging Fantasy and Reality Testing

One of the basic reasons for acting contrary to one's own view of reality are fantasies about the consequences for alternative actions. Again, underlying these fantasies is a great deal of emotionality and concern that must be dealt with if organization members are to clearly differentiate fantasy and reality. One way to facilitate the process of clarification is to encourage the process of fantasizing.

Consultant: One of the reasons people sometimes act contrary to what they really know is that they have notions about what will happen if they really do what needs to be done.

Organization Member: What do you mean?

Consultant: Well, one of the reasons people may not want to question whether Jim (the boss) is confronting enough in upholding the viewpoint of this organization to top management is that they don't know what he might do to those who question his actions.

Organization Member: Damn right. He might fire me. (nervous laughter)

Another Member: Or send me back to the production line.

Another Member: Or get back at me when annual reviews come along.

Interviewer: Has anyone in this group ever questioned Jim's actions before?

Organization Member: I have.

Consultant: What did he say?

Organization Member: He said "thanks" and that he was unaware of what he was doing.

Another Member: Same thing happened to me.

Consultant: I wonder if all of the worries you have voiced are justified? Do they have any reality?

Organization Member: It doesn't sound like they do.

Coaching

Although organization members may (a) have full access to information, (b) be aware of dysfunctional norms and standards, (c) understand the way they contribute to maintaining those norms, and (d) be able to distinguish between fantasized consequences and reality, they still may not be able to develop new ways of coping. Therefore, a third function of a consultant in a change process is to "coach" organization members in new behaviors. Such coaching can take place in group meetings, in private conversations, and in various sub group configurations.

Organization Member: Okay, I want to tell Jim (the boss) that I don't think he is holding up our end with the President. What do I say? Do I say "Jim, you are a lousy manager." That doesn't seem to make much sense.

Consultant: One alternative would be to admit your own feelings about Jim and what he is doing.

Organization Member: What do you mean?

Consultant: Well, you might say, "When I don't feel you represent us at the top it makes it a lot harder for me to do my job in addition to making me downright angry." That way you're not saying that Jim is personally incompetent. You're saying what his actions do to you.

Organization Member: Hmm. I've never thought of that approach before.

Other Functions

Obviously, organizations cannot be "cured" of neurotic behavior in a single session. About all that can be expected in a brief meeting is that organization members may develop some awareness of the degree to which they agree with one another on important issues and of the manner to which they contribute to maintaining dysfunctional organization processes. They may also become aware of the degree of discomfort they feel with the situation and of their motivation and readiness to change it. In addition, in one meeting organization members may decide whether the consultant and his approach might be helpful to them in coping with their problems.

Assuming that the decision is affirmative, there are several additional roles that the consultant may play in continuing the treatment process, all of which involve building awareness, coping with feelings, encouraging fantasy, and coaching in new behavior. These roles include:

1. Attending regular work meetings of various organization units to serve as an observer, confronter, reality tester.

2. Individual coaching sessions with key organization members concerning their roles in the process. Since the role of the superior of the unit is always central to the underlying problems of an organization (Crockett, 1970), coaching sessions with him can have an unequal impact on the organization's operations.

3. Working with the organization to develop acceptable measures of progress and improvement. Sometimes individually tailored measures are developed and sometimes "packaged" research materials such as Likert scales (1967) are employed. Whatever measures are used, they must be acceptable and agreed upon collaboratively by both the organization members and the consultant. If such agreement is reached, it

is far more likely that organization members will accept measures of progress or regression as valid and as reflecting reality. Collaborating in the development of such measures also helps members to learn to act on the basis of their own view of reality. Thus, such measures do not contribute to maintaining the very norms and standards which are the targets of change.

4. Helping develop reasonable expectations about speed of change. As can be understood from the preceding discussions, the processes supporting organization neurosis are complex, and the skills needed to change those processes cannot be learned quickly. As a consequence, the "do-it-tomorrow" perspective, frequently characteristic of organization members, is unrealistic. However, to the extent that there are ways of measuring progress which are agreeable to organization members and the consultant, periodic assessment of results can be made. Time, thus, becomes less important as an absolute variable in the evaluation process, since it may be viewed in the light of whatever positive or negative results are achieved.

Summary

Organizations, like people develop self-defeating neuroses. Such organization neuroses produce a variety of symptoms which are easily identifiable. The treatment of organization neurosis involves the use of consultants who help members (a) collect reality centered information about the organization, (b) gain understanding of the dysfunctional norms and standards which keep them from using whatever information which is available, (c) help them in differentiating reality from fantasy when assessing alternative solutions to the problems which are identified, and (d) assist them in developing the skills necessary to implement realistic alternatives. Although organization neurosis involves complex long-term treatment, change is possible and well worth the effort in terms of both economic and humanistic savings.

Notes

1. All interviews and dialogues reported in the paper are annotated versions of actual interviews and discussions conducted by the authors in the course of working with neurotic organizations.

2. A theme is arbitrarily defined as an issue or concern which is spontaneously mentioned by at least 50% of the organization members interviewed.

References

Argyris, C. *Organizations and innovation,* Richard Irwin, Homewood, Illinois, 1965.

Beckhard, R. The confrontation meeting. *Harvard Business Review,* Harvard University, March-April 1967, Vol. 45, No. 2, pp. 149-154.

Benne, K. and Mantyan, B. *Human relations in curriculum change,* Dryden Press, 1951.

Bradford, L. P. and Harvey, J. B. Dealing with dysfunctional organization myths, *Training and Development Journal,* Vol. 24, No. 9, 2-6, 1970.

Crockett, W. J. Team building—one approach to organization development. *Journal of Applied Behavioral Science,* Vol. 6, No. 3, 1970, 291-306.

Freud, S. *Group psychology and the analysis of the ego.* Liveright Publishing Corporation, New York, 1951.

Lewin, K. *Field theory in social science.* Harper and Co., New York, 1951.

Likert, R. *The human organization.* McGraw Hill, New York, 1967.

TRANSITION MANAGEMENT—COPING*

Gordon L. Lippitt

Many administrators are wondering if they and their institutions can meet the demands of increased and improved delivery of product and services in a changing society.

The turbulence faced by government and other organizations today is caused both by the increased complexity of their socio-technological functions and by multiple revolutions in contemporary society. In addition, predictable strains are being exerted by similar and more dynamic interrelationships and increased interdependence among government agencies (at all levels), industry, communities, and educational institutions. These multiple forces must be met with a process of organizational renewal, adaptation, and planning for change. Organizational leaders are caught in the stress caused by managing during the transition from the industrial to the post-industrial society.

Trends That Will Influence Change

To examine the trends affecting organizational purpose, structure, process, and management, it is necessary to examine the forces that will be affecting such changes. Some of the larger forces will be: the greatly increased standard of

*Reprinted from *National Training & Development Service, The Dallas Connection: A National Focus on Creating Responsive Organizations* NTDS Press (NTL: Washington, D.C., 1974), pp. 15-37.

living throughout the world; an increasing gap between the powerful and rich, and the powerless and poor; continued changes in value systems; the greater expectation of people for services; the increased influence of governments; an increasing desire for power by minority groups. a continued increase in the influence of mass media; the extensive development of education as it applies to continued growth and development at all ages; a shift from a production to a service economy; a continued increase in technology; an increased confrontation by citizens; the development of new avocations and vocations in society; an increased international interdependence; a continuation of ecological concerns; an increased mobility of people with a lessening of commitment to an organization or community; an increased size of the social systems of mankind so that there will be a greater feeling of powerlessness on the part of members of such systems; a continued explosion of knowledge; and a desire for quality, not just quantity, as a goal in life.

These trends are accelerating at an uneven rate, but at a speed that is challenging all the institutions of man, as well as the individual who works within them. This total picture can be described as a transition from the industrial to the post-industrial society, and involves massive changes that are not under control. The dilemma created by these changes is well stated by Eric Trist:

> . . . the contemporary environment . . . is taking on the quality of a turbulent field . . . This turbulence grossly increases the area of relative uncertainty for individuals and organizations alike. It raises far-reaching problems concerning the limits of human adaptation. Forms of adaptation, both personal and organizational, developed to meet a simpler type of environment, no longer suffice to meet the higher levels of complexity now coming into existence . . . The planner's dilemma . . . may be summarized as follows: the greater the degree of change, the greater the need for planning—otherwise precedents of the past could guide the future; but the greater the degree of uncertainty, the greater the likelihood that plans right today will be wrong tomorrow.[1]

Industrial vs. Post-Industrial Era

Managers of all institutions are coping with this transition more slowly than it is occurring. They are still managing with the values, organizational structures and leadership styles that characterized the industrial era. That era adhered strongly to the values and beliefs of the Christian work ethic, economic efficiency, and a dedication to nationalism. The contrasts cited in Figure 1 reveal some of the differences between industrial and post-industrial society.

These transitions are now taking place in advanced industrial and urbanized societies. Change is always difficult but these shifts are particularly painful, com-

Type of Change	From	Toward
Cultural values	Achievement	Self-actualization
	Self-control	Self-expression
	Independence	Interdependence
	Endurance of distress	Capacity for joy
Organizational Philosophies	Mechanistic forms	Organic forms
	Competitive relations	Collaborative relations
	Separate objectives	Linked objectives
	Own resources regarded as owned absolutely	Own resources regarded also as society's
Organizational Practices	Responsive to crisis	Anticipative of crisis
	Specific measures	Comprehensive measures
	Requiring consent	Requiring participation
	Short planning horizon	Long planning horizon
	Damping conflict	Confronting conflict
	Detailed central control	Generalized central control
	Small local units	Enlarged local units
	Standardized administration	Innovative administration
	Separate services	Coordinated services

Figure 1   Changes in emphasis in the transition to post-industrialism.[2]

plex, and frustrating. Margaret Mead has described this generation as "immigrants in time," as members of the first generation to live in an era when it is not obvious or even plausible that "experience is the best teacher," since the circumstances of today are unlike anything faced by those of middle age. Organizations and their leaders will be living in this transitional period throughout the 70s and 80s.

The task, then, amounts to reorienting institutions so that, amoeba-like, they are capable of continuously and consciously undergoing change and renewal. It is no longer sufficient to depend upon remedial splinting of institutional fractures caused by excessive rigidity.

But recognizing a requirement for organization renewal and change is not equivalent to being able to initiate change. The problem for managers today is whether or not they have the resources and skills to bring about sufficiently timely renewal in their organizations to meet the challenges of the only partially known future.

Organizations have grown in size, but have they matured? Maturation requires adaptability, flexibility, health, and identity, particularly in this era of technological and sociological innovations. Toward what end are institutions growing? This question is brought into focus by changes wrought not just in human and managerial technology but in philosophy. These changes include:

A new concept of MAN, based on increased knowledge of his complex and shifting needs, which replaces an oversimplified, innocent, push-button idea of man;

A new concept of POWER, based on collaboration and reason, which replaces a model of power based on coercion and threat;

A new concept of ORGANIZATION VALUES, based on humanistic/ democratic ideals, which replaces the depersonalized mechanistic value system of bureaucracy.[3]

Organization Models

These potential changes in philosophy are reflected in the ways organizations are structured and managed. In the past century many models of organizations evolved from managerial philosophies, and thereafter were used, although not always successfully, as a guide for specific managerial practices. An attempt to sort out these models may be helpful.

Seven organizational models, distributed along a continuum from autocracy to democracy, have been identified: autocracy (machine model), bureaucracy, systems, decentralization, collegialism, federations, and egalitarianism.[4] (See Figure 2.)

The trend in management tends to be from the autocratic to the democratic side of the continuum in order to meet the changing needs of the post-industrial society. In this context, the models reflect the idea that the practice in organizations is toward greater participation and democracy. It would seem, then, that many of the efforts to change would conform to the described trend; but management practices are not as clear as might be communicated by such listings or terminology. Furthermore, in large organizations, some segments of the system may be operating on one basis and other segments on another.

While these multiple approaches to organization management imply that greater value is placed upon participation, it is important to recognize that the organic and growth concepts of organizations imply that at different stages of growth, different kinds of structure and managerial leadership might be appropriate. In the early stages of an organization some degree of autocracy may be appropriate, while it might be inappropriate at the later stages of uniqueness and

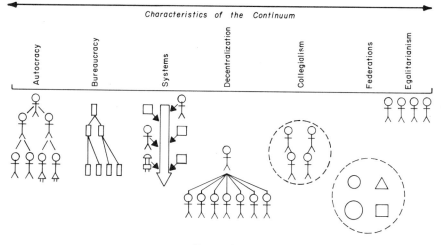

Figure 2

maturity. It is also relevant to point out that as different crises emerge in an organization and the organization is confronted with a recession, competition, or waning interest in its service, it may need to revert to different styles of management to "see it through" a particular period of its life.

Most attempts to examine organizational dynamics tend to ignore the interplay between environmental forces and organizational responses. Every organization is embedded in a total environment that conditions its forms, its decision-making process, and the way it utilizes its resources. In appropriately responding to situations, organizational managers should manifest an awareness of its responsibility and compulsion to conform to its larger environment.

Situational Management

As managers face this confusing transitional era, no *one* thing or style of the leadership is adequate. The demands of the *situation* will be the key factor influencing the manager's response. Kurt Lewin presented the well known formula:

Behavior $= f$ ($Situation + Personality$).

I would like to amend this slightly to the managerial situation by using the following formula:

A.M.B. $= f (S + P)^5$

In this context a manager must be an existential pragmatist to deal appropriately with multiple situations.

In using the word "situations" as the focal point in transition management, it is intended that the multiple and complex nature of such words as "problem-solving," "confrontation," "crisis," and "everyday decision" be included. There will be differences in the various degrees of situational intensity, but let it suffice for us to recognize that "situations" may refer to such things as the death of the leader of the organization, inadequate cash flow to maintain financial stability, an embarrassing error in an annual report, or the pickets posted at the main gate when a strike is in progress.

Decisions are made with respect to situations, rather than situations creating decisions. A situation is not always a problem, but problems are always caused by situations. Situations will test whether individuals and groups are really able to meet many kinds of needs. It is through working on situations and examining the subsequent failures and successes that organizational systems discover the worth of their selection procedure, interfacing process, training program, communication efforts, and development activities.

It is relatively foolish, even in theory, to believe that all responses to situations can be based on predetermined plans, conscious strategy, or objective action. There are occasions when a situation calls for and effectively produces unplanned response. While a great deal of the recent writing on behavioral science and organizational theory has focused on planned change, there is a place for spontaneous action, the seemingly instinctive response, or emotional reaction. It would seem that some of the experts in organizational management wish that all situations could be approached with the kind of rational and unemotional behavior once advocated by a founder of organizational theory—Max Weber.

In referring to such existential pragmatism as an "E Concept," I am purposefully building upon the clarity with which Douglas McGregor challenged the field of management with his two contrasting theories. The concept represented in his Theory "X" was the traditional way in which management or managers "controlled" the human resources of an organization, based upon the assumptions that man is inherently lazy, unwilling to assume responsibility, and resistant to change. Here, the values underlying the bureaucratic organizational model imply that man is not fully utilized, growth is inhibited, and his motivations not fully released. In his Theory "Y" he bases his concept on assumptions about the humanistic values deeply rooted in the nature of man. Here we see the application of those values and beliefs that indicate that man does wish to grow, to influence and control his own destiny, and to maximize the human worth of himself and other people. While McGregor did not intend to dichotomize the field, it frequently has this effect on those who argue for one position or the other.

In advancing an "E Concept" for transition management, it is not my intention solely to compromise or integrate McGregor's two managerial theories. It is my belief that as we complete the twentieth and enter the twenty-first century, the character of few men will fit exclusively either Theory "X" or Theory "Y", as later pointed out by McGregor himself in his book, *The Professional Manager.*

A modern organization is not bound by rituals or taboos; it makes use of professional and technical capabilities as each situation demands, and this invites the moving of individuals from one organization to another. Lastly, organizations are interested only in a limited claim on the life of an individual. Its power over the lives of its personnel is relative. People have additional loyalties and responsibilities; all of their activities cannot be wrapped up in the organization by which they are employed.

This brings into focus the suitability of the existential or pragmatic manager. He concerns himself with actually working out a problem or an idea. He is interested in tackling situations confronted by the organization and in what will change them; he sees organizational life as a set of problems rather than as a mystery, or a set of absolutes, or a systematic ideology. He sees the organization as a resource which should be equipped to respond appropriately to the task or problem confronting it. He encourages and lives with provisional solutions. His existential approach sees the potency and capability of the system to solve problems, even though he recognizes no simple, all-encompassing approach. There is a confidence inherent in this pragmatic and existential approach.

> . . .the fact that we approach life today without feeling the need for
> a big key that fits everything together as one great whole, and are
> able to concentrate instead of isolating particular issues and dealing
> with them as they come up, shows that we have a basic confidence
> that the world is held together, is strong, is self-consistent, has regu-
> larity in it, and can be put to the test without everything in life going
> to pieces.[6]

Use of the expression "existential pragmatism" as a response pattern by managers is not intended to imply that just any response which works is adequate. On the contrary, it implies a professional response based upon effective diagnosis by the manager of the situational forces and persons in the situation. The situation will encompass environmental forces, including the nature of the problem, organizational requirements, and the interrelationships of multiple forces.

The manager will need to take into account the needs of the persons in the situation, and what they can best contribute to the situation as he releases their potential.

Leadership Continuum

In the context of situational or "E" leadership concept, I would like to further develop the concept of a leadership continuum that has been produced by the work of Tannenbaum[7] and Schmidt[8], who point out that forces in the leader, forces in the group members, and forces in the situation apparently combine to make it necessary for a leader to respond at any given moment with a style of leadership appropriate to that particular situation.

This concept is in keeping with my contention that a manager in an organization should respond to situations as a professional existential pragmatist. In a very real sense, I feel that it is not appropriate to classify leaders by the stereotypes of autocratic, benevolently autocratic, democratic, and laissez-faire. In similar fashion I feel that classifying organizations as authoritative or participative may do a disservice to the reality of situational needs and demands.

In whatever manner a leader or management responds, there will always be a degree of participation as indicated in Figure 3. The amount of appropriate participation, involvement, and delegation is not only related to the skills of the leader and the ability of the group members, but also to the nature of the existential situation as it is influenced by organizational needs, response to the environment, and the interfacing process in the human sub-systems of the organization. It may very well be appropriate in the case of a company policy, safety regulation, or the announcement of a budget cut for a manager to permit only a "tell or persuade degree of participation." The survival of the organization or the safety of employees may be the key element in the situation. In determining a new product or service, the manager may want to consult his research scientists, product engineers, marketing people, accountant, and his patent lawyer before making a decision. In another case, the manager may find that a group problem-solving process is the best way to decide on how the company will solve a bottleneck on shipping out orders.

A professional manager-leader will recognize, however, that his leadership response will depend on a sophisticated diagnosis of the complex forces in the existential situation that will guide him in taking the appropriate leadership stance. Leadership is the effective meeting of the situation—whatever the situation is. And this effective meeting comes through confrontation, search, and coping.

Some of the key organizational forces to be confronted for organizational effectiveness are, looking at the organization's potential, developing open communications, developing human resources, coping with planned and unplanned change, and utilizing systems approach to management in transition.

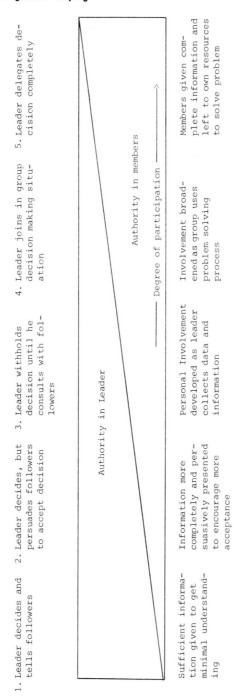

Figure 3 Degrees of participation related to leadership response. Gordon L. Lippitt, *Organizational Renewal*, Prentice-Hall, New York, 1961.

Understanding the Future Potential of the Organization

If organization effectiveness is to become a reality, organization leaders must confront their present stage of functioning. It is essential that they analyze the stages of growth through which their organizations hage passed and that they relate these six stages to fundamental management functions.[9] We find it essential that a community or organizational manager examine with others in the organization the potential and future of their organization in the next five years to set the goals and expectations for management planning and action.

Implementing organization renewal requires the development of skills in confrontation by those *inside* an organization. Organization change can best be brought about by internal confrontation of situations by those in the organization, rather than awaiting external confrontation by those who may have little concern for the long range development of the community or organization. This is where open communication is important to see whether this aspect of situational improvement is present.

Developing Open Communications for Improved Organizational Effectiveness

This second key element of the process of organization renewal requires three phases: (1) confrontation, (2) search, and (3) coping. One hears a great deal today about confrontation. Consumers are confronting manufacturers; civil rights leaders are confronting local communities. But housewives also confront the lack of a stop light near a school. People confront the chopping down of precious trees in parks. Confrontation today is part and parcel of our way of life. Organization leaders should not expect these confrontations to go away. They probably will increase.

Nevertheless, confrontation can be a very valuable thing. A manager cannot change his organization or his way of doing his job unless he confronts the present inadequacy of the organization and his own personal need to improve.

The process of renewal requires awareness, self-development, and organizational change. Each of these, in turn, requires confrontation. Leaders must confront the fact that they are not always aware of the needs of employees, operating situations, youth, clients, environments, and external forces.

Coping with transition management will not occur unless the manager also confronts his own need to improve as a leader of others. Confrontation means facing up to reality. It means "saying it as it is." It means looking at things through clear glasses rather than either rose-tinted or dark-tinted glasses. But confrontation is not enough to bring about action, self-development, or change. It is only a beginning.

Many leaders, however, feel that if they have *confronted,* their problem is solved—and that they have *coped.* This is not necessarily true. It usually is necessary for people to *search* for ways to work on the process of understanding each other, communicating with each other, solving problems, making decisions, planning new activities and new programs, and new ways to get people appropriately involved. Confrontation must lead to the search for unique and innovative ways to solve organizational problems. Search is the key to whether or not coping will take place, because coping means something more than just decision-making or problem-solving. Coping means confronting a problem and searching for ways of working on it—and from working upon it, learning how to solve similar problems, more problems, and new problems. Thus, the essential need for open communications which help make transition management understandable and realistic.

Developing Organizational Human Resources

Transition management requires the process of confrontation, search, and coping. But with whom do we start? One way to start is by building a network of effectively functioning groups in the organization. One group that will need to demonstrate teamwork is the executive group at the top of the organization. By diagnosing factors affecting their teamwork on a weekend or at an extended meeting, the management group can assess strengths and weaknesses, while taking a look at communications, utilization of financial resources, utilization of manpower resources, creativity, and social responsibility. These things need to be confronted openly to find out where the organization is *now.*

Managers may be surprised to find that in some areas they are more advanced than they thought. They may also be startled to find that their organization is only in the early stages of growth—and not, as they think, achieving success and maturity. Through such conferences, leading executives of many organizations are beginning the process of confronting the need to become more effective and relevant to society through improvement in their own teamwork.

In addition to the top executive group, it is desirable to build the kind of teamwork that will make it possible for all functional groups to work effectively together, for project groups to relate effectively, and for professional specialists to build a cohesive work unit that will contribute to the growth and goals of the organization.

Coping With Change in Transition Management

The fourth important area for implementation of the organization renewal process during transition, is the skill and courage of persons in the organization to analyze and cope with change. In less than two decades, modern technology has leaped from conventional power to nuclear power, from the piston age to the jet age, from "earth men" to "space men."

As we examine the needs of organizations to cope with change, it is evident that there are two basic categories. One type is *unplanned change* which will happen to and in all organizations. A tornado that plows down a warehouse, a new interest rate on bank loans, a power failure—these are situations to which the organization *must react.*

A second category of change is *planned change*—the type of change which is involved in the process of organization renewal. It can be defined as a conscious, deliberate, and collaborative effort to improve the operations of a system —whether it be self-system, social system, or community system—through the utilization of action skills. It usually involves both a leader and the elements of an organization, which are brought together to solve a problem or to plan and attain an improved state of functioning by being *pro-active.*

The manager, consultant, or social scientist engaged in planned or inventive change has some social "goals" (objectives) and he has a well-structured "design" (means) for achieving these ends. Planned change, therefore, involves inventing a future, and creating conditions and resources for realizing that future.

Suppose you are a responsible member in a municipality or an organization where renewal involving change occurs or is contemplated. What might you do? How could you start?

In developing plans for change it is important that any organization leader know how to *diagnose* the forces in the planned change effort as a first step to initiate action.

A useful concept, theory, and method for thinking about change, was developed by social scientist Kurt Lewin. He looked upon a level or phase of behavior within an institutional setting not as a static habit or custom, but as a dynamic balance between forces working in opposite directions within the social-psychological space of the institution. He indicated that we should think diagnostically about any change situation, in terms of the factors encouraging and facilitating change (driving forces) and the factors against change (restraining forces). These forces may originate inside the organization, in the environment, or in the behavior of the person or persons who are trying to bring about change.

We can think of the present state of affairs in an organization as an equilibrium which is being maintained by a variety of factors that "keep things the way they are" or "keep us behaving in our customary ways." Those who seek change must assess the potential for and resistance to change, and try to modify the balance of these forces so there will be movement toward improved processes that focus on the themes that help cope with transition management.

Every organizational system has within it the potentiality for either bringing about its own death, maintaining the status quo, or growing into maturity.

The leadership of its management or the concern of its employees—as expressed in action—will be the key factors. The challenge for today's organization leaders is whether or not they have the capability, the resources and the skills to bring about the renewal in their organizations that will be required if they are going to meet the challenge of the 70s. As John Gardner suggests:

> What may be most in need of innovation is the corporation itself. Perhaps what every corporation (and every other organization) needs is a department of continuous renewal that could view the whole organization as a system in need of continuing innovation.[10]

Normally an apparently appropriate action will solve a problem by eliminating or altering a situation. But not always. It can happen that insufficient information has caused misjudgment of the situation. And sometimes—perhaps just to prove the case for human inconsistency—apparently inappropriate action surprises us by somehow dealing with a situation satisfactorily, although it may not contribute to organizational growth.

Organizational Adaptation Requires a General Systems Approach

At the beginning of this article it was suggested that one way to measure the appropriateness of an action is to assess the way it relates to the external environment within which the organization exists. Most attempts to examine organizational dynamics tend to ignore the interrelationship between environmental forces and organizational responses. Every organization is embedded in a total environment that conditions its form, decision-making process, and the way it utilizes its resources. In appropriately responding to situations, an organization should manifest an awareness of its responsibility to the larger external environment and of the multiple social and non-social systems impacting on the community or organization. Transition management will find that coping with the organizations of the future will require utilizing the general systems approach to the organization.

The concept of socio-technical systems is based on the reality that any production or service system requires both a technology and a work-relationship structure that relates human resources to technological resources. In this context, an organization's total system requires looking at the human activities together with interrelationships to the techno-physical-financial resources and the process to make and deliver services. To think about an organization as a socio-technical system helps make viable the man-machine relationships of the future.

All organization systems and subsystems, from the smallest group (a dyad) to the most complex multi-group structure of an international organization, include in their makeup elements and processes. Without attention to these ele-

Dimensions	Characteristics	
	Static Organizations	Future-oriented Organizations
Structure	Rigid: permanent committees; reverence for constitution and bylaws, tradition Hierarchical: chain of command Role definitions: narrow Property: bound and restricted	Flexible: temporary task force; readiness for change constitution and bylaws, depart from tradition Linking: functional collaboration Role definitions: broad Property: mobile and regional
Atmosphere	Internally competitive Task-centered: reserved Cold, formal: aloof	Goal-oriented: People-centered: caring Warm, informal: intimate
Management and Philosophy	Controlling: coercive power Cautious: low risk Errors: to be prevented Emphasis on personnel selection Self-sufficient: closed system re: resources Emphasis on conserving resources Low tolerance for ambiguity	Releasing: supportive power Experimental: high risk Errors: to be learned from Emphasis on personnel development Interdependent: open system re: resources Emphasis on developing and using resources High tolerance for ambiguity
Decision Making and Policy Making	High participation at top, low at bottom Clear distinction between policy making and execution	Relevant participation by all those affected Collaborative policy making and execution
Communication	Restricted flow: constipated One-way: downward Feelings: repressed or hidden	Open flow: easy access Two-way: upward and downward Feelings: expressed

Figure 4   Characteristics of static vs. future-oriented organizations.[11]

ments and processes the system cannot function effectively. Attention has been given to improved financial systems, information systems, decision-making systems, and communication processes. All of these approaches are essential to administrators of the future.

Summary

This list of ways of coping with transition management is incomplete and selective. However, a model of the future potential of man's organizations must be developed to elicit action that will be on the frontier of this transitional generation. Figure 4 represents characteristics of a future-oriented organization.[11]

The proper approach to transition management no longer considers personnel or management technology apart from the human element within either the organization or the larger environment. As a result of an historic trend away from the purely mechanistic, the directed development of organizations in the future is now flexibly oriented to specific tasks and values in a known organizational climate.

"Future shock" is neither a disease nor a disaster, it is a dilemma created by too many problems coming too fast from too many directions for traditional problem-solving tools and techniques to handle. It seems that groups of Argus-eyed men, aided by both cybernetics (systems and analysis) and electronic computation—as well as by behavioral scientists—are capable of integrating multi-man skills and disciplines into antidotal, discrete problem-solving organiz entities of the future. There is an urgent need to develop and perfect this morphology, a new science of man/machine/organization dynamics—this is the requirement of managers in coping with the transition from the industrial to the post-industrial society.

Notes

1. Eric Trist, "Between Cultures: The Current Crisis of Transition," *Organizational Frontiers and Human Values,* ed. W. Schmidt; Wadsworth Publishing Co., Belmont, Calif., 1970, p. 29.

2. Warren Bennis, "Organizations of the Future," *Management of Organization Development;* Univ. of Bradford, United Kingdom, 1971, p. 32 (with minor adaptations).

3. Ibid., p. 16.

4. George Rice and Dean Bishoprick, *Conceptual Models of Organization,* Appleton-Century-Crofts, New York City, 1971.

5. Formula explanation: A.M.B. stands for Appropriate Managerial Behavior; f stands for "the function of"; S stands for Situation; P stands for persons in that situation.

6. Harry O. Morton, "The Mastery of Technological Civilization," *The Student World*, First Quarter, 1963, p. 48.

7. Robert Tannenbaum, Irving R. Weschler, and Fred Massarik, *Leaderhsip and Organization: A Behavioral Science Approach;* McGraw-Hill Book Co., Inc., New York, 1961.

8. Warren H. Schmidt, The Leader Looks at the Styles of Leadership, *Looking Into Leadership Monograph;* Leadership Resources, Inc., Washington, D.C., 1961.

9. Ibid.

10. John W. Gardner, *Self Renewal;* New York, McGraw-Hill Book Co., Inc., 1966, p. 48.

11. Adapted from an unpublished paper written by Malcolm Knowles, Ph.D., Boston University.

AN INTRODUCTION TO ORGANIZATION DEVELOPMENT*

John J. Sherwood

Organization development is an educational process by which human resources are continuously identified, allocated, and expanded in ways that make these resources more available to the organization, and therefore, improve the organization's problem-solving capabilities.

The most general objective of organizational development—OD—is to develop self-renewing, self-correcting systems of people who learn to organize themselves in a variety of ways according to the nature of their tasks, and who continue to expand the choices available to the organization as it copes with the changing demands of a changing environment. OD stands for a new way of looking at the human side of organizational life.

What is OD?

a) A long-range effort to introduce planned change based on a diagnosis which is shared by the members of an organization.

b) An OD program involves an entire organization, or a coherent "system" or part thereof.

c) Its goal is to increase organizational effectiveness and enhance organizational choice and self-renewal.

*Reprinted with permission from the American Psychological Association, Inc. Washington, D.C. The Experimental Publication System. Issue No. 11. Copyright © 1971 by the American Psychological Association. Reprinted by permission.

d) The major strategy of OD is to intervene in the ongoing activities of the organization to facilitate learning and to make choices about alternative ways to proceed.

Objectives of Typical OD Programs

Although the specific objectives of an OD effort vary according to the diagnosis of organizational problems, a number of objectives typically emerge. These objectives reflect problems which are common in organizations and which prevent the creative release of human potential within organizations:

1. To build trust among individuals and groups throughout the organization, and up-and-down the hierarchy.

2. To create an open, problem-solving climate throughout the organization—where problems are confronted and differences are clarified, both within groups and between groups, in contrast to "sweeping problems under the rug" or "smoothing things over."

3. To locate decision-making and problem-solving responsibilities as close to the information sources and the relevant resources as possible, rather than in a particular role or level of the hierarchy.

4. To increase the sense of "ownership" of organizational goals and objectives throughout the membership of the organization.

5. To move toward more collaboration between interdependent persons and interdependent groups within the organization. Where relationships are clearly competitive, e.g., limited resources, then it is important that competition be open and be managed so the organization might benefit from the advantages of open competition and avoid suffering from the destructive consequences of subversive rivalry.

6. To increase awareness of group "process" and its consequences for performance—that is, to help persons become aware of what is happening between and to group members while the group is working on the task, e.g., communication, influence, feelings, leadership styles and struggles, relationships between groups, how conflict is managed, etc.

The objectives of organizational development efforts are achieved through planned interventions based on research findings and theoretical hypotheses of the behavioral sciences. The organization is helped to examine its present ways of work, its norms and values, and to generate and evaluate alternative ways of working, or relating, or rewarding members of the system.

Some Assumptions Underlying the Concept of OD

Using knowledge and techniques from the behavioral sciences, organization development attempts to integrate organizational goals with the needs for growth of individual members in order to design a more effective and fully functioning organization, in which the potential of members is more fully realized. Some of the basic assumptions underlying the concept of OD are as follows:

1. The attitudes most members of organizations hold toward work and their resultant work habits are usually more *reactions* to their work environment and how they are treated by the organization, than they are intrinsic characteristics of an individual's personality. Therefore, efforts to change attitudes toward work and toward the organization should be directed more toward changing how the person is treated than toward attempting to change the person.

2. Work which is organized to meet people's needs as well as to achieve organizational requirements tends to produce the highest productivity and quality of production.

3. Most members of organizations are not motivated primarily by an avoidance of work for which tight controls and threats of punishment are necessary—but rather, most individuals seek challenging work and desire responsibility for accomplishing organizational objectives to which they are committed.

4. The basic building blocks of organizations are groups of people; therefore, the basic units of change are also groups, not simply individuals.

5. The culture of most organizations tends to suppress the open expression of feelings which people have about each other and about where they and their organization are heading. The difficulty is that the suppression of feelings adversely affects problem-solving, personal growth, and satisfaction with one's work. The expression of feelings is an important part of becoming committed to a decision or a task.

6. Groups which learn to work in a constructively open way by providing feedback for members become more able to profit from their own experience and become more able to fully utilize their resources on the task. Furthermore, the growth of individual members is facilitated by relationships which are open, supportive, and trusting.

7. There is an important difference between *agreement* and *commitment*. People are committed to and care about that which they help create. Where change is introduced, it will be most effectively implemented if the groups and individuals involved have a sense of ownership in the process. Commitment is most assuredly attained where there is active participation in the planning and conduct of the change. Agreement is simpler to achieve and results in a simpler outcome—people do what they are told, or something sufficient or similar.

8. The basic value underlying all OD theory and practice is that of *choice*. Through the collection and feedback of relevant data—made available by trust, openness, and risk—more choice becomes available to the organization, and to the individual, and hence better decisions can be made.

Organization Development Technology

Basic to all OD efforts is an attempt to make the human resources of the organization optimally available. Outside consultants often share the responsibility for this process, but they also work toward increasing the organization's own capacity to understand and manage its own growth.

In contrast to management development which is oriented toward the individual manager, OD focuses on groups and changing relations between people. The system—be it a unit of the organization, or the entire organization—is the object of an OD effort.

A frequent strategy in OD programs is the use of an *action-research* model of intervention. There are three processes in an action-research approach, all of which involve extensive collaboration between a consultant and the organization: data gathering from individuals and groups; feedback to key client or client group in the organization; and joint action planning based on the feedback. Action-research is designed to make data available from the entire system and then to use that information to make plans about the future of that system.

Some OD interventions or building blocks of an OD program are the following:

1. *Team Building:* focus is on early identification and solution of the work group's problems, particularly interpersonal and organizational roadblocks which stand in the way of the team's collaborative, cooperative, creative, competent functioning.

   A group's work procedures can be made more effective by using different decision-making procedures for different tasks and learning to treat leadership as a function to be performed by members of the group, not just as a role or as a characteristic of an individual's personality.

   The interpersonal relationships within a team can be improved by working on communication skills and patterns; skills in openness and expression of what one thinks and feels; the degree of understanding and acceptance among team members; authority and hierarchical problems; trust and respect; and skills in conflict management.

2. *Intergroup Problem Solving:* groups are brought together for the purpose of reducing unhealthy competitiveness between the groups or to resolve intergroup conflicts over such things as overlapping responsibilities or confused lines of authority, and to enhance interdependence when it appropriately exists.

   Intergroup problems sometimes exist between different functional groups which must work together, e.g., sales and engineering; or between line and staff; or labor and management; or between separate organizations involved in a merger.

3. *Confrontation meeting* is a problem-solving mechanism when problems are known to exist. An action-research format is used. The entire management group of an organization is brought together, problems and attitudes are collected and shared, priorities are established, commitments to action are made through setting targets and assigning task forces.

4. *Goal-setting and planning:* supervisor-subordinate pairs and teams throughout the organization engage in systematic performance improvement and target-setting with mutual commitment and review. Goal setting becomes a way of life for the organization.

5. *Third party facilitation* involves the use of a skilled third person to help in the diagnosis, understanding, and resolution of difficult human problems—e.g., difficult one-to-one relationships between two persons or two groups.

6. *Consulting pairs:* often a manager can benefit from a close and continuing relationship with someone outside his own organization (a consultant, either internal or external to the organization), with whom he can share problems early.

In an effective OD effort each member of the organization begins to see himself as a resource to others and becomes willing to provide help to others when asked to do so. Such attitudes become norms or shared expectations. Once such a norm is established, members of the organization become potential consultants for one another, and the dependence of the organization on outside resources becomes less and less.

A major characteristic of organization development is that it relies heavily on an educational strategy emphasizing *experience-based learning* and on the skills such a procedure develops. Thus, the data feedback of the action-research model and the confrontation meeting are examples of how the experiences people have with each other and with the organization are shared and become the basis upon which learning occurs and upon which planning and action proceed. To be sure, OD is not simply human relations training (nor is it sensitivity training) however, openness about one's own experiences—including feelings, reactions, and perceptions—represents a cornerstone of many organizational development efforts. Furthermore, laboratory training experiences are often used to help members of the organization develop more interpersonal competence, including communication skills, ability to better manage conflict, and insights into oneself and into groups and how they form and function. Laboratory training programs are, therefore, a good preliminary step to an organization development effort.

VALUES, MAN, AND ORGANIZATIONS*

Robert Tannenbaum and Sheldon Davis

Values in Transition

Deeply impressed with the managerial and organizational implications of the increasing accumulation of knowledge about human behavior, Professor Douglas McGregor formulated his assumptions of Theory Y.[1] According to him, these assumptions were essentially his interpretations, based upon the newer knowledge and on his extensive experience, of the nature of man and of man's motivation. In our view, McGregor was overly cautious and tentative in calling the Theory Y tenets "assumptions" and in limiting them to being his "interpretations." In trying to be "scientific," he seemed reluctant in his writing to assert explicitly as *values* those elements (including the Theory Y assumptions) which so much affected his organizational theory and practice. He was not alone in his reluctance. Perhaps the most pervasive common characteristic among people in laboratory training and in organizational development work is their values, and yet, while organizational development academicians and practitioners are generally aware of their shared values and while these values implicitly guide much of what they do, they too have usually been reluctant to make them explicit.

*This paper was prepared for the McGregor Conference on Organizational Development, sponsored by the Organizational Studies Group, Sloan School of Management, MIT, October, 1967. Reprinted from *Industrial Management Review,* (Winter 1969), pp. 67-86. Footnotes have been renumbered.

210

We want here not only to own our values but also to state them openly. These values are consistent with McGregor's assumptions and in some instances go beyond his. They are not scientifically derived nor are they new, but they are compatible with relevant "findings" emerging in the behavioral sciences. They are deeply rooted in the nature of man and are therefore basically humanistic. As previously suggested, many of the values underlying the bureaucratic model and its typical implementation have been inconsistent with the nature of man, with the result that he has not been fully utilized, his motivation has been reduced, his growth as a person stunted, and his spirit deadened. These outcomes sorely trouble us, for we believe organizations can in the fullest sense serve man as well as themselves.

Growing evidence strongly suggests that humanistic values not only resonate with an increasing number of people in today's world, but also are highly consistent with the effective functioning of organizations built on the newer organic model.[2] As we discuss a number of these values below, we will provide some face validity for their viability by illustrating them with cases or experiences taken from our involvements with or knowledge of a number of organizations which recently have been experimenting with the interface between the organizational and humanistic frontiers described above. The illustrations come primarily from TRW Systems, with which we have had a continuing collaboration for more than four years. Other organizations with which one or both of us have been involved include Aluminum Company of Canada, Ltd., U. S. Department of State, and the Organizational Behavior Group of Case Institute of Technology.

We clearly recognize that the values to which we hold are not absolutes, that they represent directions rather than final goals. We also recognize that the degree of their short-run application often depends upon the people and other variables involved. We feel that we are now in a period of transition, sometimes slow and sometimes rapid, involving a movement away from older, less personally meaningful and organizationally relevant values toward these newer values.[3]

Away from a View of Man as Essentially Bad
Toward a View of Him as Basically Good

At his core, man is not inherently evil, lazy, destructive, hurtful, irresponsible, narrowly self-centered, and the like. The life experiences which he has including his relationships with other people and the impact on him of the organizations with which he associates, can and often do move him in these directions. On the other hand, his more central inclination toward the good is reflected in his behavior as an infant, in his centuries-long evolution of ethical and religious precepts and in the directions of his strivings and growth as a result of experiences, such as those in psychotherapy and sensitivity training. Essentially man is internally motivated toward positive personal and social ends; the extent to which he is not motivated results from a process of demotivation generated by his relationships and/or environment.

We have been impressed with the degree to which the fairly pervasive cultural assumption of man's badness has led to organizational forms and practices designed to control, limit, push, check upon, inhibit, and punish. We are also increasingly challenged by the changes in behavior resulting from a growing number of experiments with organizational forms and practices rooted in the view of man as basically good.

Within an organization it is readily apparent to both members and perceptive visitors whether or not there is, in general, an atmosphere of respect for the individual as a person. Are people treated arbitrarily? Are there sinister coups taking place? How much of the time and energy of the members of the organization is devoted to constructive problem solving rather than to playing games with each other, back-biting politicking, destructive competition, and other dysfunctional behavior? How does management handle problems such as the keeping of time records? (Some organizations do not have time clocks and yet report that employees generally do not abuse this kind of a system.) One of the authors can remember a chain of retail stores which fired a stock clerk because he had shifty eyes, although he was one of the best stock boys in that chain. There are all kinds of negative assumptions about man behind such an incredible action.

For a long period of time, two senior engineers, Taylor and Durant, had real difficulty in working together. Each had a negative view of the other; mutual respect was lacking. Such attitudes resulted in their avoiding each other even though their technical disciplines were closely related. A point in time was reached when Taylor sorely needed help from Durant. Caught up in his own negative feelings, however, he clearly was not about to ask Durant for help. Fortunately, two of Taylor's colleagues who did not share his feelings prodded him into asking Durant to work with him on the problem. Durant responded most positively, and brought along two of his colleagues the next day to study the problem in detail. He then continued to remain involved with Taylor until the latter's problem was solved. Only a stereotype had kept these men apart. Taylor's eventual willingness to approach Durant opened the door to constructive problem solving.

Away from Avoidance or Negative Evaluation of Individuals Toward Confirming Them as Human Beings

One desire frequently expressed by people with whom we consult is "I wish I knew where I stand with my boss [with this organization] [with my colleagues] [with my subordinates]. I'd really like to know what they think of me person-ally." We are not referring to the excessively neurotic needs of some persons for attention and response, but rather to the much more pervasive and basic need to know that one's existence makes a difference to others.

Feedback that is given is generally negative in character and often destruc-tive of the individual instead of being focused on the perceived short-comings of a given performance. It seems to be exceedingly difficult for most of us to give positive feedback to others—and, more specifically, to express genuine feelings of affection and caring.

When people are seen as bad, they need to be disciplined and corrected on the issue only; when they are seen as good, they need to be confirmed. Avoid-ance and negative evaluation can lead individuals to be cautious, guarded, defen-sive. Confirmation can lead to personal release, confidence, and enhancement.

A senior executive reported to one of us that he did not get nearly as much feedback as he wanted about how people thought about him as a person and whether or not they cared for him. He reported that one of the most meaningful things that had happened to him in this regard occurred when the person he re-ported to put his arm around him briefly at the end of a working session, patted him on the shoulder, and said, "Keep up the good work," communicating a great deal of warmth and positive feelings towards the person through this behavior. This event had taken place two years ago and lasted about five seconds, yet it was still fresh in the senior executive's memory and obviously has had a great deal of personal meaning for him. In our culture, most of us are grossly under-nourished and have strong need for the personal caring of others.

Away from a View of Individuals as Fixed
Toward Seeing Them as Being in Process

The traditional view of individuals is that they can be defined in terms of given interests, knowledge, skills, and personality characteristics: they can gain new knowledge, acquire additional skills, and even at times change their interests, but it is rare that people really change. This view, when buttressed by related organ-izational attitudes and modes, insures a relative fixity of individuals, with crip-pling effects. The value to which we hold is that people can constantly be in flux, groping, questing, testing, experimenting, and growing. We are struck by the tremendous untapped potential in most individuals yearning for discovery and release. Individuals may rarely change in core attributes, but the range of alterna-tives for choice can be widened, and the ability to learn how to learn more about self can be enhanced.

Organizations at times question whether it is their responsibility to foster individual growth. Whether or not it is, we believe that for most organizations, especially those desiring long-term survival through adaptability, innovation, and change, it is an increasing necessity. Further, evidence suggests that to have people in process requires a growth-enhancing environment. Personal growth requires healthy organizations. This value, then, carries with it great implications for work in organizational development. In organizations, people continuously experience interpersonal difficulties in relating to the other people with whom they must work. Some reasons for the difficulties are that people listen very badly to each other, attribute things of a negative nature to another person, and make all kinds of paranoid assumptions, with the result that communication breaks down rather severely.

There have been many instances within TRW Systems of people, who, in the eyes of others around them, produce some fairly significant changes in their own behavior. Most of these changes have been reported quite positively. In some cases there have been rather dramatic changes with respect to how a person faces certain kinds of problems: how he handles conflicts, how he conducts staff meetings, etc. In those cases, an individual who is perceived as having changed quite often reports that these changes are personally rewarding, that he feels better about himself and more optimistic and expansive about life.

TRW Systems is committed to a continuation and improvement of its Career Development program, which places considerable emphasis on the personal and professional growth of its members. Although the original commitment was perhaps largely based on faith, experience gained in recent years strongly suggests that one of the most productive investments the organization can make is in the continuing growth of its members and in the health of the environment in which they work.

Away From Resisting and Fearing Individual Differences
Toward Accepting and Utilizing Them

The pervasive and long-standing view of man as bad takes on even more serious implications when individual differences among men appear—differences in race, religion, personality (including personal style), specialties, and personal perceptions (definitions of truth or reality). A bad man poses sufficient problems but a strange bad man often becomes impossible.

Organizations and individuals are frequently threatened by what they consider questioning of or challenge to their existing values and modes, represented by the presence of alternative possibilities. And they choose to avoid the challenge and the related and expected conflicts, discomforts, and the like which might follow. As a result, they achieve drabness, a lack of creativity, and a false sense of peace and security. We firmly believe that the existence of differences can be highly functional. There is no single truth, no one right way, no chosen people. It is at the interface of differences that ferment occurs and that the potential for creativity exists. Furthermore, for an organization to deny to itself (in the name of harmony or some similar shibboleth) the availability of productive resources simply because they do not conform to an irrelevant criterion is nothing short of madness. To utilize differences creatively is rarely easy, but our experience tells us that the gains typically far outweigh the costs.

In the play "Right You Are," Pirandello makes the point that truth in a particular human situation is a collection of what each individual in the situation sees. Each person will see different facets of the same event. In a positive sense, this would lead us to value seeing all the various facets of an issue or problem as they unfold in the eyes of all the beholders and to place a positive value on our interdependence with others, particularly in situations where each of us can have only part of the answer or see part of the reality.

An organization recently faced the problem of filling a key position. The man whose responsibility it was to fill the position sat down with five or six people who, due to their various functional roles, would have a great deal of interaction with the person in that position and with his organization. The man asked them to help him identify logical candidates. The group very quickly identified a number of people who ought to be considered and the two or three who were the most logical candidates. Then the group went beyond the stated agenda and came up with a rather creative new organizational notion, which was subsequently implemented and proved to be very desirable. After this took place, the executive who had called the meeting in order to get the help for the decision he had to make, reported that it was very clear to him that doing the job became much easier by getting everyone together to share their varying perceptions. This meant that he had more relevant data available to him in making his decision. Furthermore, the creative organizational concept only came about as a result of the meeting's having taken place.

In most organizations persons and groups with markedly different training, experience, points of view, and modes of operating frequently bump into each other. Project managers face functional performers, mechanical engineers face electrical engineers, designers face hardware specialists, basic researchers face action-oriented engineers, financial specialists face starry-eyed innovators. Each needs to understand and respect the world of the other, and organizations should place a high value upon and do much to facilitate the working through of the differences which come into sharp focus at interfaces such as these.

Away from Utilizing an Individual Primarily with Reference to His Job Description Toward Viewing Him as a Whole Person

People get pigeon-holed very easily, with job description (or expectations of job performance) typically becoming the pigeon hole. A cost accountant is hired, and from then on he is seen and dealt with as a cost accountant. Our view is that people generally have much more to contribute and to develop than just what is expected of them in their specific positions. Whole persons, not parts of persons, are hired and available for contribution. The organizational challenge is to recognize this fact and discover ways to provide outlets for the rich, varied, and often untapped resources available to them.

One of many personal examples that could be cited within TRW Systems is that of a person trained as a theoretical physicist. Having pursued this profession for many years, he is now effectively serving also as a part-time behavioral science consultant (a third-party process facilitator) to the personnel organization within the company. This is an activity for which he had no previous formal training until a new-found interest began asserting itself. The organization has supported him in this interest, has made a relevant learning opportunity available to him, and has opened the door to his performing an additional function within the organization.

An organizational example involves the question of charters that are defined for particular sub-elements of the organization: divisions, staffs, labs, etc. What are their functions? What are they supposed to do? To state the extreme, an organizational unit can have very sharply defined charters so that each person in it knows exactly what he is supposed to do and not do. This can lead to very clean functional relationships. Another approach, however, is to say that the *core* of the charter will be very clear with discrete responsibilities identified, but the outer edges (where one charter interacts with others) will not be sharply defined and will deliberately overlap and interweave with other charters. The latter approach assumes that there is a potential synergy within an organization which people can move toward fully actualizing if they can be constructive and creative in their interpersonal and intergroup relations. Very different charters are produced in this case, with very different outcomes. Such charters must, by definition, not be clean and sharply described, or the innovative and coordinated outcomes that might come about by having people working across charter boundaries will not occur.

Away from Walling-Off the Expression of Feelings Toward Making Possible Both Appropriate Expression and Effective Use

In our culture, there is a pervasive fear of feelings. From early childhood, children are taught to hide, repress, or deny the existence of their feelings, and their learnings are reinforced as they grow older. People are concerned about "losing control," and organizations seek rational, proper, task-oriented behavior, which emphasizes head-level as opposed to gut-level behavior. But organizations also seek high motivation, high morale, loyalty, team work, commitment, and creativity, all of which, if they are more than words, stem from personal feelings. Further, an individual cannot be a whole person if he is prevented from using or divorced from his feelings. And the energy dissipated in repression of feelings is lost to more productive endeavors.

We appreciate and are not afraid of feelings, and strongly believe that organizations will increasingly discover that they have a reservoir of untapped resources available to them in the feelings of their members, that the repression of feelings in the past has been more costly, both to them and to their members, than they ever thought possible.

One of the relevant questions to ask within an organization is how well problems stay solved once they are apparently solved. If the feelings involved in such problems are not directly dealt with and worked through, the problem usually does not remain solved for very long. For example, if two subordinates are fighting about something, their supervisor can either intervene and make the decision for them or arbitrate. Both methods can solve the immediate difficulty, but the fundamental problem will most likely again occur in some other situation or at some other time. The supervisor has dealt only with the symptoms of the real problem.

The direct expression of feelings, no matter what they are, does typically take place somewhere along the line, but usually not in the relevant face-to-face relationship. A person will attend a staff meeting and experience a great deal of frustration with the meeting as a whole or with the behavior of one or more persons in it. He will then talk about his feelings with another colleague outside the meeting or bring them home and discuss them with or displace them on his wife or children, rather than talking about them in the meeting where such behavior might make an important difference. To aid communication of feelings, participants at a given staff meeting could decide that one of the agenda items will be: "How do we feel about this meeting; how is it going; how can it be improved?" They could then talk face-to-face with each other while the feeling is immediately relevant to the effective functioning of the staff group. The outcomes of the face-to-face confrontation can be far more constructive than the "dealing-with-symptoms" approach.

Away from Maskmanship and Game-Playing Toward Authentic Behavior

Deeply rooted in existing organizational lore is a belief in the necessity or efficacy of being what one is not, both as an individual and as a group. Strategy and outmaneuvering are valued. Using diplomacy, wearing masks, not saying what one thinks or expressing what one feels, creating an image—these and other deceptive modes are widely utilized. As a result, in many interpersonal and intergroup relations, mask faces mask, image faces image, and much energy is employed in dealing with the other person's game. That which is much more basically relevant to the given relationship is often completely avoided in the transaction.

To be that which one (individual or group) truly is—to be authentic—is a central value to us. Honestly, directness, and congruence, if widely practiced, create an organizational atmosphere in which energies get focused on the real problems rather than on game-playing and in which individuals and groups can genuinely and meaningfully encounter each other.

Recently, two supervisors of separate units within an organization got together to resolve a problem that affected both of them. At one point in their discussion, which had gone on for some time and was proving not to be very fruitful, one of them happened to mention that he had recently attended a sensitivity training laboratory conducted by the company. At that point, the other one mentioned that sometime back he had also attended a laboratory. They both quickly decided "to cut out the crap," stop the game they were playing, and really try to solve the problem they had come to face. Within a very short period of time, they dramatically went from a very typical organizational mode of being very closed, wearing masks, and trying to outmaneuver each other, to a mode of being open and direct. They found that the second mode took less energy and that they solved the problem in much less time and were able to keep it solved. But, somehow, at least one of them had not felt safe in taking off his mask until he learned that the other one had also gone through a T-Group.

When people experience difficulty with others in organizations, they quite often attribute the difficulty to the fact that the other person or group is not trustworthy. This attitude, of course, justifies their behavior in dealing with the other. On numerous occasions within TRW Systems, groups or individuals who are experiencing distrust are brought together and helped to articulate how they feel about each other. When the fact that "I do not trust you" is out on the table, and only then, can it be dealt with. Interestingly, it turns out that when the feeling is exposed and worked through, there are not really very many fundamentally untrustworthy people. There certainly are all kinds of people continuously doing things that create feelings of mistrust in others. But these feelings and the behavior that triggers them are rarely explored in an effort to work them through. Instead, the mistrust escalates, continues to influence the behavior of both parties, and becomes self-fulfilling. Once the locked-in situation is broken through and the people involved really start talking to each other authentically, however, trust issues, about which people can be very pessimistic, become quite workable. This has happened many, many times in organizational development efforts at TRW Systems.

Away from Use of Status for Maintaining Power and Personal Prestige
Toward Use of Status for Organizationally Relevant Purposes

In organizations, particularly large ones, status and symbols of status can play an important role. In too many instances, however, they are used for narrowly personal ends, both to hide behind and to maintain the aura of power and prestige. One result is that dysfunctional walls are built and communication flow suffers.

We believe that status must always be organizationally (functionally) relevant. Some people know more than others, some can do things others cannot do, some carry more responsibility than others. It is often useful for status to be attached to these differences, but such status must be used by its holder to further rather than to wall off the performance of the function out of which the status arises. An organization must be constantly alert to the role that status plays in its functioning.

It is relatively easy to perceive how status symbols are used within an organization, how relatively functional or dysfunctional they are. In some organizations, name dropping is one of the primary weapons for accomplishing something. A person can go to a colleague with whom he is having a quarrel about what should be done and mention that he had a chat with the president of the organization yesterday. He then gets agreement. He may or may not have talked with the president, he may or may not have quoted him correctly; but he is begging the question by using a power figure in order to convince the other person to do it his way. In other organizations, we have observed that people very rarely work a problem by invoking the name of a senior executive, and that, in fact, those who do name-drop are quickly and openly called to task.

At TRW Systems, with only minor exceptions, middle- and top-level executives, as well as key scientists and engineers, are typically available for consultation with anyone in the organization on matters of functional relevance to the organization. There is no need to use titles, to "follow the organization chart," to obtain permission for the consultation from one's boss or to report the results to him afterwards. As a result, those who can really help are sought out, and problems tend to get worked at the point of interface between need on the one hand and knowledge, experience, and expertise on the other.

Away from Distrusting People Toward Trusting Them

A corollary of the view that man is basically bad is the view that he cannot be trusted. And if he cannot be trusted, he must be carefully watched. In our judgment, many traditional organizational forms exist, at least in part, because of distrust. Close supervision, managerial controls, guarding, security, sign-outs, etc., carry with them to some extent the implication of distrust.

The increasing evidence available to us strongly suggests that distrusting people often becomes a self-confirming hypothesis—distrusting another leads to behavior consciously or unconsciously designed by the person or group not trusted to "prove" the validity of the distrust. Distrust begets distrust. On the other hand, the evidence also suggests that trust begets trust; when people are trusted, they often respond in ways to merit or justify that trust.

Where distrust exists, people are usually seen as having to be motivated "from the outside in," as being responsive only to outside pressure. But when trust exists, people are seen as being motivated "from the inside out," as being at least potentially self-directing entities. One motivational device often used in the outside-in approach involves the inculcation of guilt. Rooted in the Protestant ethic, this device confronts the individual with "shoulds," "oughts," or "musts" as reasons for behaving in a given way. Failure to comply means some external standard has not been met. The individual has thus done wrong, and he is made to feel guilty. The more trustful, inside-out approach makes it possibly for the individual to do things because they make sense to him, because they have functional relevance. If the behavior does not succeed, the experience is viewed in positive terms as an opportunity to learn rather than negatively as a reason for punishment and guilt.

Organizations which trust go far to provide individuals and groups with considerable freedom for self-directed action backed up by the experience-based belief that this managerial value will generate the assumption of responsibility for the exercise of that freedom. In California, going back about 27 years, a forward-looking director of one of our state prisons got the idea of a "prison without walls." He developed and received support for an experiment that involved bringing prisoners to the institution where correctional officers, at that time called guards, carried no guns or billy clubs. There were no guards in the towers or on the walls. The incoming prisoners were shown that the gate was not locked. Under this newer organizational behavior, escape rates decreased, and the experiment has become a model for many prisons in this country and abroad.

An organizational family embarked upon a two-day team-development lab shortly after the conclusion was reached from assessment data that the partial failure of a space vehicle had resulted from the non-functioning of a subsystem developed by this team. At the outset of the lab, an aura of depression was present but there was no evidence that the team had been chastised by higher management for the failure. Further, in strong contrast with what most likely would have been the case if they had faced a load of guilt generated from the outside, there was no evidence of mutual destructive criticism and recriminations. Instead, the team was able in time to turn its attention to a diagnosis of possible reasons for the failure and to action steps which might be taken to avoid a similar outcome in the future.

During a discussion which took place between the head of an organization and one of his subordinates (relating to goals and objectives for that subordinate for the coming year), the supervisor said that one of the things he felt very positive about with respect to that particular subordinate was the way he seemed to be defining his own set of responsibilities. This comment demonstrated the large degree of trust that was placed in the subordinates of this particular supervisor. While the supervisor certainly made it clear to this individual that there were some specific things expected of him, he consciously created a large degree of freedom within which the subordinate would be able to determine for himself how he should spend his time, what priorities he ought to have, what his function should be. This is in great contrast to other organizations which define very clearly and elaborately what they expect from people. Two very different sets of assumptions about people underlie these two approaches.

Away from Avoiding Facing Others with Relevant Data
Toward Making Appropriate Confrontation

This value trend is closely related to the one of "from maskmanship toward authenticity," and its implementation is often tied to moving "from distrust toward trust."

In many organizations today there is an unwillingness to "level" with people, particularly with respect to matters which have personal implications. In merit reviews, the "touchy" matters are avoided. Often, incompetent or unneeded employees are retained much longer that is justified either from the organization's or their own point of view. Feelings toward another accumulate and at times fester, but they remain unexpressed. "Even one's best friends won't tell him."

Confrontation fails to take place because "I don't want to hurt Joe," although in fact the non-confronter may be concerned about being hurt himself. We feel that a real absurdity is involved here. While it is widely believed that to level is to hurl and, at times, destroy the other, the opposite may often be the case. Being left to live in a "fool's paradise" or being permitted to continue with false illusions about self is often highly hurtful and even destructive. Being honestly confronted in a context of mutual trust and caring is an essential requirement for personal growth. In an organizational setting, it is also an important aspect of "working the problem."

A quite dramatic example of confrontation and its impact occurred in a sensitivity training laboratory when one executive giving feedback to a colleague said to him that he and others within the organization perceived him as being ruthless. This came as a tremendous jolt to the person receiving the feedback. He had absolutely no perception of himself as ruthless and no idea that he was doing things which would cause others to feel that way about him. The confrontation was an upending experience for him. As a result, he later began to explore with many people in the organization what their relationship with him was like and made some quite marked changes in his behavior after getting additional data which tended to confirm what he had recently heard. In the absence of these data (previously withheld because people might not want to hurt him), he was indeed living in a fool's paradise. A great deal of energy was expended by other people in dealing with his "ruthlessness," and a considerable amount of avoidance took place, greatly influencing the productivity of everyone. Once this problem was exposed and worked through, this energy became available for more productive purposes.

Away from Avoidance of Risk-Taking Toward Willingness to Risk

A widely discernable attribute of large numbers of individuals and groups in organizations today is the unwillingness to risk, to put one's self or the group on the line. Much of this reluctance stems from not being trusted, with the resulting fear of the consequences expected to follow close upon the making of an error. It often seems that only a reasonable guarantee of success will free an individual or group to take a chance. Such a stance leads to conformity, to a repetition of the past, to excessive caution and defensiveness. We feel that risk-taking is an essential quality in adaptable, growthful organizations, taking a chance is necessary for creativity and change. Also, individuals and groups do learn by making mistakes. Risk-taking involves being willing "to take the monkey on my back," and it takes courage to do so. It also takes courage and ingenuity on the part of the organization to foster such behavior.

At TRW Systems, the president and many of the senior executives were until recently located on the fifth floor of one of the organization's buildings, and part of the language of the organization was "the fifth floor," meaning that place where many of the power figures resided. This phrase was used quite often in discussion: "the fifth floor feels that we should . . ." In working with groups one or two levels below the top executives to explore what they might do about some of the frustrations they were experiencing in getting their jobs done, one of the things that dominated the early discussions was the wish that somehow "the fifth floor" would straighten things out. For example, a group of engineers of one division was having problems with a group of engineers of another division, and they stated that "the fifth floor" (or at least one of its executives) ought to go over to the people in the other division and somehow "give them the word." After a while, however, they began to realize that it really was not very fruitful or productive to talk about what they wished someone else would do, and they began to face the problem of what they could do about the situation directly. The discussion then became quite constructive and creative, and a number of new action items were developed and later successfully implemented—even though there was no assurance of successful outcomes at the time the action items were decided upon.

Away from a View of Process Work as Being Unproductive Effort Toward Seeing it as Essential to Effective Task Accomplishment

In the past and often in the present, productive effort has been seen as that which focused directly on the production of goods and services. Little attention has been paid to the processes by which such effort takes place; to do so has often been viewed as a waste of time. Increasingly, however, the relevance to task accomplishment of such activities as team maintenance and development, diagnosis and working through of interpersonal and intergroup communication barriers, confrontation efforts for resolution of organizationally dysfunctional personal and interpersonal hangups, and assessment and improvement of existing modes of decision-making is being recognized. And, in fact, we harbor growing doubts with respect to the continued usefulness of the notion of a task-process dichotomy. It seems to us that there are many activities which can make contributions to task accomplishment and that the choice from among these is essentially an economic one.

Within TRW Systems, proposals are constantly being written in the hope of obtaining new projects from the Department of Defense, NASA, and others. These proposals are done under very tight time constraints. What quite often happens is that the request for the proposal is received from the customer and read very quickly by the principals involved. Everybody then charges off and starts working on the proposal because of the keenly felt time pressure. Recently, on a very major proposal, the proposal manager decided that the first thing he should do was spend a couple of days (out of a three month period of available time) meeting with the principals involved. In this meeting, they would not do any writing of the proposal but would talk about how they were going to proceed, make sure they were all making the same assumptions about who would be working on which subsystem, how they would handle critical interfaces, how they would handle critical choice points during the proposal period, and so on. Many of the principals went to the meeting with a great deal of skepticism, if not impatience. They wanted to "get on with the job," which to them meant writing the proposal. Spending a couple of days talking about "how we're going to do things" was not defined by them as productive work. After the meeting, and after the proposal had been written and delivered to the customer, a critique was held on the process used. Those involved in general reported very favorably on the effects of the meeting which took place at the beginning of the proposal-writing cycle. They reported things such as: "The effect of having spent a couple of days as we did meant that at that point when we then charged off and started actually writing the proposal, we were able to function as if we had already been working together for perhaps two months. We were much more effective with each other and much more efficient, so that in the final analysis, it was time well spent." By giving attention to their ways of getting work done, they clearly had facilitated their ability to function well as a team.

Away from a Primary Emphasis on Competition
Toward a Much Greater Emphasis on Collaboration

A pervasive value in the organizational milieu is competition. Competition is based on the assumption that desirable resources are limited in quantity and that individuals or groups can be effectively motivated through competing against one another for the possession of these resources. But competition can often set man against man and group against group in dysfunctional behavior, including a shift of objectives from obtaining the limited resource to blocking or destroying the competitor. Competition inevitably results in winners and losers, and at least some of the hidden costs of losing can be rather high in systemic terms.

Collaboration, on the other hand, is based on the assumption that the desirable limited resources can be shared among the participants in a mutually satisfactory manner and even more important, that it is possible to increase the quantity of the resources themselves.

As organizational work becomes more highly specialized and complex, with its accomplishment depending more and more on the effective interaction of individuals and groups, and as the organic or systems views of organizational functioning become more widely understood, the viability of collaboration as an organizational mode becomes ever clearer. Individuals and groups are often highly interdependent, and such interdependency needs to be facilitated through collaborative behavior rather than walled off through competition. At the same time, collaborative behavior must come to be viewed as reflecting strength rather than weakness.

In organizations which have a high degree of interdependency, one of the problems people run into regarding the handling of this interdependency is that they look for simple solutions to complex problems. Simple solutions do not produce very good results because they deal with the symptoms rather than with real problems. A major reorganization recently took place within TRW Systems. The president of the organization sketched out the broad, general directions of the reorganization, specifying details only in one or two instances. He assigned to a large number of working committees the development of the details of the new organization. The initial reaction of some people was that these were things that the president himself should be deciding. The president, however, did not feel he had enough detailed understanding and knowledge to come up with many of the appropriate answers. He felt strongly that those who had the knowledge should develop the answers. This was an explicit, conscious recognition on his part of the fact that he did indeed need very important inputs from other people in order to effect the changes he was interested in making. These working committees turned out to be very effective. As a result of the president's approach, the reorganization proceeded with far less disruption and resistance than is typically the case in major reorganizations.

Another example involved a major staff function which was experiencing a great deal of difficulty with other parts of the organization. The unit having the trouble made the initial decision to conduct briefings throughout the organization to explain what they were really trying to accomplish, how they were organized, what requirements they had to meet for outside customers, and so on. They felt that their job would be easier if they could solicit better understanding. What actually took place was quite different. Instead of conducting briefings to convince the "heathen," the people in this unit revised their plan and met with some key people from other parts of the company who had to deal with them to ask what the unit was doing that was creating problems at the interface. After receiving a great deal of fairly specific data, the unit and the people with whom they consulted developed joint collaborative action items for dealing with the problems. This way of approaching the problem quickly turned interfaces that had been very negative and very hostile into ones that were relatively cooperative. The change in attitude on both sides of the interface provided a positive base for working toward satisfactory solutions to the problems.

Some Implications of These Values in Transition

Many people would agree with the value trends stated in this paper and indeed claim that they use these guidelines in running their own organizations. However, there is often quite a gap between saying that you believe in these values and actually practicing them in meaningful, important ways. In many organizations, for example, there is a management-by-objectives process which has been installed and used for several years—an approach which can involve the implementation of some of the values stated earlier in this paper. If, however, one closely examines how this process takes place in many organizations, it is in fact a very mechanical one, one which is used very defensively in some cases. What emerges is a statement of objectives which has obtained for the boss what he really wants, and, at the end of the year, protects the subordinate if he does not do everything that his boss thought he might do. It becomes a "Pearl Harbor file." The point that needs emphasis is that the payoff in implementing these values by techniques is not in the techniques themselves but in how they are applied and in what meaning their use has for the people involved.

To us, the implementation of these values clearly involves a bias regarding organizational development efforts. Believing that people have vast amounts of untapped potential and the capability and desire to grow, to engage in meaning-ful collaborative relationships, to be creative in organizational contexts, and to be more authentic, we feel that the most effective change interventions are thera-peutic in nature. Such interventions focus directly on the hangups, both personal and organizational, that block a person from realizing his potential. We are re-ferring to interventions which assist a person in breaking through the neurotic barriers in himself, in others around him, and in the ongoing culture.

We place a strong emphasis on increasing the sanity of the individuals in the organization and of the organization itself. By this we mean putting the individ-uals and the organization more in touch with the realities existing within them-selves and around them. With respect to the individual, this involves his under-standing the consequences of his behavior. How do people feel about him? How do they react to him? Do they trust him? With respect to the organization, it involves a critical examination of its culture and what that culture produces: the norms, the values, the decision-making processes, the general environment that it has created and maintained over a period of time.

There are obviously other biases and alternatives available to someone ap-proaching organizational development work. One could concentrate on struc-tural interventions: How should we organize? What kind of charters should people in various functional units have? The bias we are stating does not mean that structure, function, and charters are irrelevant, but that they are less impor-tant and have considerably less leverage in the early stages of organizational de-velopment efforts than working with the individuals and groups in a therapeutic manner. Furthermore, as an individual becomes more authentic and interperson-ally competent, he becomes far more capable of creative problem-solving. He and his associates have within them more resources for dealing with questions of structure, charters, and operating procedures, in more relevant and creative ways, than does someone from outside their system. Such therapeutic devices include the full range of laboratory methods usually identified with the National Train-ing Laboratories: sensitivity training, team building, intergroup relationship building, etc. They also include individual and group counseling within the or-ganization, and the voluntary involvement of individuals in various forms of psychotherapy outside the organization.

In order to achieve a movement towards authenticity, focus must be placed on developing the whole person and in doing this in an organic way. The program cannot be something you crank people through; it must be tailored in a variety of ways to individual needs as they are expressed and identified. In time, therapy and individual growth (becoming more in touch with your own realities) become values in and of themselves. And as people become less demotivated and move toward authenticity, they clearly demonstrate that they have the ability to be creative about organization matters, and this too becomes a value shared within the organization. Once these values are introduced and people move towards them, the movement in and of itself will contain many forces that make for change and open up new possibilities in an organization. For example, as relationships become more trustworthy, as people are given more responsibility, as competition gives way to collaboration, people experience a freeing up. They are more apt to challenge all the given surroundings, to test the limits, to try new solutions, and to rock the boat. This can be an exciting and productive change, but it can also be troublesome, and a variety of responses to it must be expected.

Therapeutic efforts are long-term efforts. Movement towards greater authenticity, which leads to an organization's culture becoming more positive, creative, and growthful, is something that takes a great deal of time and a great deal of energy. In this kind of approach to organizational development, there is more ambiguity and less stability than in other approaches that might be taken. Patience, persistence, and confidence are essential through time if significant change is to occur and be maintained.

For the organizational development effort to have some kind of permanency, it is very important that it becomes an integral part of the line organization and its mode of operating. Many of the people involved in introducing change in organizations are in staff positions, typically in personnel. If, over time, the effort continues to be mainly one carried out by staff people, it is that much more tenuous. Somehow the total organization must be involved, particularly those people with line responsibility for the organization's success and for its future. They must assimilate the effort and make it a part of their own behavior within the organization. In other words, those people who have the greatest direct impact on and responsibility for creating, maintaining, and changing the culture of an organization must assume direct ownership of the change effort.

In the transition and beyond it, these changes can produce problems for the organization in confronting the outside world with its traditional values. For example, do you tell the truth to your customers when you are experiencing problems building a product for them, or do you continue to tell them that everything is going along fine? For the individual, there can be problems in other relationships around him, such as within his family at home. We do not as yet have good methods developed for dealing with these conflicts, but we can certainly say that they will take place and will have to be worked out.

As previously stated, the Career Development program at TRW Systems, now in its fifth year of operation, is an effort in which both authors have been deeply involved. We feel it is one of the more promising examples of large-scale, long-term, systematic efforts to help people move toward the values we have outlined.[4]

One question that is constantly raised about efforts such as the Career Development program at TRW Systems relates to assessing their impact. How does one know there has been a real payoff for the organization and its members? Some behavioral scientists have devised rather elaborate, mechanical tools in order to answer this question. We feel that the values themselves suggest the most relevant kind of measurement. The people involved have the capacity to determine the relevance and significance to them and to their organizational units of what they are doing. Within TRW Systems, a very pragmatic approach is taken. Questions are asked such as: Do we feel this has been useful? Are these kinds of problems easier to resolve? Are there less hidden agenda now? Do we deal more quickly and effectively with troublesome intergroup problems? The payoff is primarily discussed in qualitative terms, and we feel this is appropriate. It does not mean that quantitative judgments are not possible, but to insist on reducing the human condition to numbers, or to believe that it can be done, is madness.

The role of the person introducing change (whether he is staff or in the line) is a very tough, difficult, and, at times, lonely one.[5] He personally must be as congruent as he can with the values we have discussed. If people perceive him to be outside the system of change, they should and will reject him. He must be willing and able to become involved as a person, not merely as the expert who will fix everybody else up. He, too, must be in process. This is rewarding, but also very difficult.

Introducing change into a social system almost always involves some level of resistance to that change. Accepting the values we have described means that one will not be fully satisfied with the here and now because the limits of man's potential have certainly not been reached. All we know for sure is that the potential is vast. Never accepting the status quo is a rather lonely position to take. In effect, as one of our colleagues has put it, you are constantly saying to yourself, "Fifty million Frenchmen are wrong!" From our own experience we know that this attitude can produce moments when one doubts one's sanity: "How come nobody else seems to feel the way I do, or to care about making things better, or to believe that it is possible to seek improvements?" Somehow, these moments must be worked thorugh, courage must be drawn upon, and new actions must follow.

We are struck with and saddened by the large amounts of frustration, feelings of inadequacy, insecurity, and fear that seem to permeate groups of behavioral science practitioners when they meet for seminars or workshops. Belief in these values must lead to a bias towards optimism about the human condition. "Man does have the potential to create a better world, and I have the potential to contribute to that effort." But in addition to this bias towards optimism, there has to be a recognition of the fundamental fact that we will continuously have to deal with resistance to change, including resistances within ourselves. People are not standing in line outside our doors asking to be freed up, liberated, and upended. Cultures are not saying: "Change us, we can no longer cope, we are unstable." Commitment to trying to implement these values as well as we can is not commitment to an easy, safe existence. At times, we can be bone weary of confrontation, questioning, probing, and devil's-advocating. We can have delightful fantasies of copping out on the whole mess and living on some island. We can be fed up with and frightened by facing someone's anger when we are confronting him with what is going on around him. We can be worn out from the continuous effort to stretch ourselves as we try to move towards living these values to the fullest.

On the other hand, the rewards we experience can be precious, real, and profound. They can have important meaning for us individually, for those with whom we work, and for our organizations. Ultimately, what we stand for can make for a better world—and we deeply know that this is what keeps us going.

Notes

1. McGregor [5].
2. This contention is supported by the further discussion of Theory Y by McGregor [6]: by the discussion of System 4 by Likert [4]: and by the discussion of 9.9 management by Blake and Mouton [2].
3. On reading an earlier draft of this paper, a corporation executive commented: "I think the perspective is wrong when the impression is created that these values are widespread. They are probably spreading from an infinitesimal fraction of the world's population, but at an accelerating rate."
4. This program is described in detail in Davis [3].
5. Each Winter Quarter, UCLA's Graduate School of Business Administration offers a residential program in Organizational Development for individuals instrumental in the change activities of their organizations.

References

[1] Bennis, W. G. *Changing Organizations.* New York, McGraw-Hill, 1966.

[2] Blake, R. R., and Mouton, J. S. *The Managerial Grid.* Houston, Gulf, 1964.

[3] Davis, S. A. "An Organic Problem-Solving Method of Organizational Change," *Journal of Applied Behavioral Science,* Vol. 3, no. 1 (1967), pp. 3-21.

[4] Likert, R. *The Human Organization.* New York, McGraw-Hill, 1967.

[5] McGregor, D. M. *The Human Side of Enterprise.* New York, McGraw-Hill, 1960.

[6] McGregor, D. M. *The Professional Manager.* New York, McGraw-Hill, 1967.

THE ETHICS OF ORGANIZATIONAL DEVELOPMENT*

Richard E. Walton and Donald P. Warwick

Over the past decade the concept of organization development (OD) has gained great currency and the ranks of its practitioners (ODPs) have swelled. Although there are no precise data, we estimate that the number of external consultants claiming to practice OD (as distinct from in-house practitioners) is between 500 and 1,000 for the U.S. alone. OD was first initiated in business, later in government and education, and more recently in work organizations as diverse as military units, hospitals, and religious groups. Today it is an international phenomenon.

The rapid expansion of both practice and practitioners in an uncharted field raises numerous ethical questions. Who are its clients and what are its power implications? What norms of professional responsibility should govern the work of the ODP? What are the rights of OD participants, particularly when their power position is weak, vis-à-vis these initiators of change? Is OD a morally neutral tool applicable to any organizational setting, or are there situations in which its use is ethically questionable?

*Reproduced by special permission from *The Journal of Applied Behavioral Science.* "The Ethics of Organization Development," by Richard E. Walton and Donald Warwick, Volume 9, Number 6, pp. 681-698. Copyright © 1973 NTL Institute. This article grew from two separate papers presented by the authors (see Reference list) at the Conference on the Ethics of Social Intervention, Battelle Seattle Research Center, May 1973. Warwick's contribution was completed while he was a Visiting Fellow at Battelle from June-August, 1973.

Our aim in this paper is to stimulate reflection on and discussion of these questions among applied behavioral scientists and other parties interested in or affected by OD. We would hope, in fact, to provoke comment not only from ODPs but from employees, representatives of unions, and other potential beneficiaries or casualties of OD. Although we will raise more questions than we answer, we suggest a number of tentative ethical guidelines. Our own experience with OD has been somewhat different but complementary. Walton has worked as a practitioner, primarily in business organizations but also in government and other settings. Warwick comes from a background of research on and occasional consulting with organizations, and has participated in evaluations of OD efforts in the U.S. Department of State and The Agency for International Development. We both believe that there is a great potential for good as well as harm in OD, and that the realization of the former will be enhanced by increased sensitivity to ethical concerns.

What Is OD?

Consider two value orientations which may guide an external professional engaged in changing organizations:

First, the person may seek improvement in the organization's capacities to achieve its goals: e.g., profit in a business firm, delivery of services in a government agency. This orientation to *organizational achievement* is essentially an identification with the traditional concerns of managers themselves.

Second, the person may seek to improve the *quality of work life* for members of the organization in order to increase their individual self-esteem and personal development, to ensure justice, and so on. This represents a particular application of a growing concern in our society with the quality of human experience.

The dominance of the first orientation in OD is reflected in the way the field is defined. For example, Beckhard (1969) defines OD as:

> . . . an effort (1) *planned,* (2) *organization-wide,* and (3) *managed* from the *top* to (4) increase *organization effectiveness* and *health* through (5) *planned interventions* in the organization's processes, using *behavioral science* knowledge (p. 100).

The question of values surfaces immediately in this definition. Why should organizational change be managed from the top? This approach may give the ODP maximum leverage but it also tends to align his (or her) influence pattern with the influence mechanisms that already characterize the organization and his thinking with top management's views of "problems," needs, and purposes. The practitioner should be clear about the full implications of top-down OD.

Then, again, what is organizational "health"? Here, as with the notion of "mental health," the term obscures basic value judgments. While a broad spectrum of observers would acknowledge that certain conditions are undesirable or even pathological, there is far less agreement on what constitutes the positive end of the health pole. Words such as "health," "growth," and "maturity" do not obviate the need to examine value judgments. Both theorists and practitioners need to be more explicit about the ideal end-states toward which their work is directed, and the supporting evidence or rationale for their choice.

For Burke and Hornstein (1972) the ultimate goal of OD is a self-renewing organization. The "social technology of OD" is used to enhance the "social functioning of organizations" and "for adapting to needed changes on a day-to-day basis." Further, ". . . the primary focus in OD is normative change; individual change is simply a by-product" (p. xi). These statements also indicate that OD and its methodology reflect a primary concern with organizational effectiveness, including organizational performance and survival.

Schmuck and Miles's (1971) definition also emphasizes the effectiveness of the *system*: "OD can be defined as a planned and sustained effort to apply behavioral science for system improvement, using reflexive, self-analytical methods" (p. 92). However, in detailing "system improvement" by OD the authors identify "the integration of individual and organizational goals" as one element of concern.

As persons and as professionals, many OD practitioners are deeply concerned about the quality of working life—certainly more concerned than their own definitions would signal. Both their initial values on entering the field and their professional socialization lead them to prefer authenticity and openness in human encounters, whether or not these patterns enhance effectiveness. The practitioner's ethical and value dilemmas arise from the need to be simultaneously a management consultant, with a primary concern for effectiveness, and a social reformer, striving to increase humanistic values in the work place.

Many of the ethical dilemmas in OD fall under three generic headings: power, freedom, and professional responsibility. Although these issues are tightly interwoven in any concrete intervention, the ethical problems which they present are sufficiently distinct to merit separate attention. Our treatment of these issues reflects the authors' judgment that the interests and rights of sponsors, but especially the targets of OD, deserve more consideration than they typically receive.

Power

The question of power relations in OD raises two ethical questions in itself, and provides an important backdrop for the discussion of freedom and professional responsibility.

The first question is one of justice. Is it fair that those who already possess power and control wealth have much more access in our society to the "social technology" of OD than do others? This is particularly important because effective OD interventions will almost always change or reinforce the balance of power, influence, and authority in a system. For example, the leadership positions of incumbents are often strengthened, though sometimes weakened, by an OD exercise. The pattern of data-gathering and testing before decisions are made is often modified, strengthening the influence of some members relative to others.

A critical and obvious factor shaping the structure of OD is the immediate source of sponsorship and the ultimate point of accountability. With few exceptions, the ODP gains access to the organization through management, which also pays for his services. While many ODPs argue that they are working for the entire organization, the fact remains that they enter the system as *management* consultants. Without stereotyping a wide variety of situations, it is fair to say that in most OD interventions, issues of sponsorship, point of entry, and accountability are far from inconsequential.

The second question centers on the degree of openness regarding the power implications of an OD effort. Are the power consequences of OD acknowledged —or (as is often the case) are interventions characterized as benign, neutral exercises in "participation" or "team building"? Our implicit premise is that the power consequences of OD are ethically more acceptable if the game is played in the open so that all participants can make informed moves.

The following are some ways in which OD may affect power relations and raise the questions of justice and openness.

Definition of the Change Problem

A core component of OD is the collective identification of one or more problems as the focus of subsequent action. *What* gets defined as a problem is thus one of the most crucial and politically salient aspects of OD. There are two common patterns of problem identification, both of which influence whether this problem will be defined in a way congenial to the ODP's sponsor.

First, the ODP may simply accept the definition provided by the sponsor. Beckhard (1969, pp. 45-56) describes a case illustrating this approach. At issue was an attempt to change a family-owned and managed organization to one which was professionally managed. Following several years of deterioration in the company's market position, a progressive and influential family member called on an OD consultant to provide a strategy for achieving the change. However, "most of the management and work force were long-term employees and were generally satisfied with this state of affairs" (that is, the "royalist" pattern, with family members in all top positions). The ODP further found: (a) "The change in management would be very dramatic and probably traumatic for a number of management people." (b) "It would be necessary to prepare the division-management group for the change, to get out some of their feelings and attitudes toward the new leadership, and to find ways of getting their commitment to making the new mode work." The ODP did not take responsibility for the problem definition, but rather defined his role as that of a helper in implementing the change chosen by his sponsor.

Second, the ODP may serve as a midwife in helping the organization or some part of it to define the problem. As a skilled group leader, he can exert a strong influence on the outcome of this process. He can channel attention in certain directions and away from others by raising certain questions, reinforcing some kinds of comments, and ignoring others. The concerns of his primary contact in the organization often set the direction for his work.

Choice of Target for Intervention

Decisions about where precisely to intervene in OD depend partly on the definition of the problem and partly on strategic considerations—where can the change realistically be brought about with maximum benefit and minimum damage? In the case cited earlier, if the problem was a deteriorating market position, it did not follow that shifting the structure of management from the family to professionals was the only possible approach to change. Closer analysis might have shown that the market position could be improved by less drastic means.

Intelligence-Gathering

OD often involves gathering data on the political life and emotional underbrush of an organization. Diagnosis considers such conditions as openness, trust, or communication. But these benign terms are applicable only in benign situations. Under other conditions, particularly during times of internal crisis or external attack (a normal state in some government agencies), the information obtained by OD may be a tool of administration or repression. Interviews, problem-identification sessions, and confrontation meetings—the stock-in-trade of OD—quickly uncover pockets of discontent or inept leadership in the system. Organizational surveys may further show which managers are liked or hated by their subordinates, which units are judged to be efficient or effective, and where morale is sagging.

In the typical OD scenario, such information is to be collected in an atmosphere of trust, where no one will be harmed by his honesty or by revelations made about him by others. But trust has its limits and administrators are human. If the data from OD show that three division chiefs are evident roadblocks to effectiveness, transfer or dismissal rather than rehabilitation may result. More seriously, if the entire OD effort collapses, the data may be used for less than benign purposes. The chances for such abuses are particularly great in organizations such as the State Department, which are run on a top-down, chain-of-command basis and are constantly subject to external attack. And even with the best intentions and the most careful preparations, the trust built up during the data-collection stage may be shattered by a change in top management.

The ethical dilemma of internal consultants is heightened by the fact that they gather data over longer periods of time, and therefore come under more pressure to share their knowledge.

Appraisals

Not infrequently a manager will invite an ODP to help him in assessing a subordinate. A few ODPs will not decline this bid, which not only runs the risk of violating confidentiality, but also serves to strengthen the power position of his advisee by communicating privileged information and opinion.

"Cooling Out" and Stabilization

Critics of OD have sometimes argued that it serves an inherently conservative function, either by "cooling out" potential opposition in an organization or by working in other ways to stabilize the system. The possibility of cooptation arises when the ODP is brought in to mediate conflicts or improve cross-cultural communication. For example, one of the authors participated in a problem-solving workshop on border disputes in the Horn of Africa (Walton, 1970), which was viewed by a few participants as potentially stabilizing conservative national systems. The participants believed that the resolution of the disputed national boundaries would delay the development of the revolutionary front in the area which they supported, at least intellectually.

A case study published by Golembiewski et al. (1972) also illustrates the possibilities for "cooling out":

> As part of a broader reduction-in-force, 13 regional managers from the marketing department of a major firm were given a choice of accepting demotion to senior salesmen or terminating. The demotees were a heterogeneous lot . . . the managers ranged in age from 33 to 55; they had been with the company from nine to 24 years; and they had been managers for periods ranging from six months to 17 years. Moreover, although most of the demotees could suffer a major reduction in salary, reductions would range from less than $1,000 to approximately four times that amount (p. 37).

The 11 who accepted demotion were required to participate in an OD experience. Two stated purposes of this exercise were to ease the pain for the men themselves and to preserve valued resources for the organization. The intervention was also intended to build on the values of the laboratory approach, develop linkages between the people involved, and provide data on the difficulties of adaptation.

The ODPs raised no questions about the fairness of the decisions leading to the demotions—including questions about the decision criteria and the appeal mechanisms, if any, which were used. They focused their attention on "integration" and on avoiding "anti-goals," specifically "obsessiveness and postponement of the unavoidable facing-up to new work demands. . . ." Commenting on this case, Kramer (1972) writes:

> And does the morality of making decisions less painful convert the applied social scientist into an agent of management, or a "cooling out" functionary? Does conversion of group demotion into a "more/ more" proposition create a tenuous illusion that ought to be challenged? In addition, tactical questions such as "Who was the client?" also need to be made clearer (p. 63).

In their reply to Kramer, the original authors confirm the pertinence of the above questions, but assure us that they had no intentions of "cooling out" anyone (Golembiewski, Carrigan, & Blumberg, 1973).

In another case (Beer & Huse, 1972) involving the redesign of work, OD has been accused of being an instrument for solidifying and legitimating existing organizational arrangements by making authority relations or job assignments more palatable to workers (Brimm, 1972).

Each of the above interventions illustrates the *potential* use of OD to achieve stability where forces at play might otherwise produce change in the service of justice. The most general question raised by this discussion is whether the participants in OD, such as the demotees, are adequately informed of the power dimension at stake and its consequences. This facet is frequently obscured by the neutral, technological language of OD such as "problem-solving workshop" and job redesign and by the therapeutic overtones of terms such as "integrative experience."

Freedom

Some of the most serious ethical questions about OD lie in the area of personal freedom and the related value of individual welfare. A person can be said to be free when he has the capacity and the opportunity to make reflective choices and to act on those choices (Warwick, 1971, p. 14). The essential ingredients of freedom are an awareness of options for choice, knowledge of their consequences, and the ability to act upon a decision. Freedom may be reduced or destroyed by coercion, environmental manipulation, psychic manipulation, and certain kinds of deceptive persuasion (cf. Warwick & Kelman, 1973). All of these conditions arise in OD efforts, with varying degrees of severity. The following example will illustrate some of the more common problems.

Kuriloff and Atkins (1966) report a case in which they employed T-Group methodology to improve interpersonal skills and relationships in the top work team of a small manufacturing firm. Kuriloff was the chief executive, and Atkins was one of two OD consultants in this exercise. When Kuriloff became president he found a lack of trust and confidence among three of his key subordinates— Rod, the chief engineer; Hans, the production manager; and Earl, the purchasing manager. After five months he concluded that "the time was ripe for a more intensive and powerful attempt to resolve the problems of interpersonal conflict" (Kuriloff & Atkins, 1966, p. 66). Kuriloff reports on how the subordinates were approached:

> When the time came to tell my people about the T Group, I ap-proached each person individually. "We've got a chance to go through special training, paid for by the company. It'll be partly on company time, partly on your own. We'll go for five days straight, from three in the afternoon 'til ten at night, with an hour break for dinner. The objective is to help us learn how we appear in the eyes of others, so we can improve our ability to get along with one another and improve our business.
>
> "Attendance is voluntary, and if you choose not to come, it won't be held against you" (Kuriloff & Atkins, 1966, p. 67).

Atkins then describes many of the interpersonal episodes which occurred during the five days of team building and training. The stage was set by the physical context, the expectations of the two consultants, and their introduc-tory statement of ground rules:

> Fifteen brave people would be confronting one another in this circle, finding it very difficult to hide, even behind silence or bright, facile talk. The wide space in the center of the circle would be the dumping ground for people's misconceptions, for untested assumptions about one another that caused confusion, for unstated resentments. . . .
>
> Jack, the co-trainer, a tall, slow-speaking, mild-mannered man of few words, explained that the purpose of our getting together was to ex-plore our feelings and relationships. Projecting a quiet strength, he said, "It's important to express feelings about one another, including us trainers. No holds are barred." He added, "However, everyone should also feel free *not* to respond if it becomes too difficult or too uncomfortable. Openness is valued, but so is the right of privacy" (Kuriloff & Atkins, 1966, pp. 70-71).

This and other examples illustrate four ethical problems related to personal freedom and welfare: (1) informed consent, (2) coercion, (3) manipulation, and (4) misuse of information arising from OD.

Informed Consent

We would question whether most OD participants, particularly in programs involving some version of sensitivity training, are adequately informed about the nature or consequences of these activities. In the Kuriloff-Atkins case few of the members had been through anything resembling OD. Only those who had at least attended a T Group with strangers would have been in a position to anticipate what they were getting into.

The authors do not indicate any serious effort to describe the processes and the range of potential consequences for the invitees—a minimum step necessary for informed choice. From our observation, many employees have only the vaguest notion of what OD means at the time they agree to or are persuaded to participate, even after some discussion. Thus, the ODP in one way or another solicits an act of faith in his own skills or the good intentions of management, engages in an exercise of power ("the boss wants you to join in this"), or practices a kind of seduction, telling the employee enough to draw him in but not enough to frighten him away.

There are no easy solutions to the problem of informed consent, either here or in other areas of applied behavioral science. Nevertheless, we offer the following tentative guidelines. First, serious attention should be devoted to a more accurate "labeling" of OD services, including both its ingredients and the possibly harmful effects of particular interventions. Second, both informed consent and voluntary participation are more likely when the targets of change have had a voice in the decision about whether OD should be undertaken. While it may be difficult to say "no" to a session ultimately proposed by the boss, the early expression of reservations can, on the one hand, alert the superior to sensitive areas and, on the other, give the employee greater confidence in holding back. Third, where advance and direct participation is less important or more difficult to achieve, OD programs can use pilot projects. In other words, they can be "market tested" for employee response. If reactions are, on balance, neutral or negative, management and the ODPs could decide not to extend the process, or even to eliminate it in the pilot unit.

Coercion

Whether or not an employee is adequately informed about the nature and effects of OD, he can be coerced into participating. In the Kuriloff-Atkins case, participants were not really able to make a free choice about whether or not to sign up. Kuriloff wanted attendance to be voluntary, but admitted that there was coercion in the situation. It was very difficult for a subordinate to imagine that there would be no penalty for declining to participate. No matter how Kuriloff wanted and phrased it, the situation had the earmarks of a command performance. Interestingly, he interpreted the fact that all key managers and supervisors showed up as confirming evidence of trust and noncoercion. The case would have been much stronger, if some subordinates had felt free to *decline.*

Another form of coercion, endemic to the federal government and traditional line organizations, is pressure from senior administrators on middle-level managers to allow OD to take place. Consider the following example from the U.S. government:

> The Director of [Unit A] accepted OD readily and this influenced selection of his division as an initial target. The Deputy Director of [Unit A], heavily involved in daily operations of the Office, perceived himself as "shut out" of the OD process. Whether this was actually the case is now difficult to verify, but his perception strongly influenced his attitude toward the Director's mandate. OD became identified as the Director's pet project, a serious handicap when he was succeeded by the Deputy in March. . . .

> When the former Deputy became Acting Director, he immediately indicated his lack of interest in pursuing the OD effort. The consultants ceased work in March, 1971 and did not return until September when, as Director, he responded to a strong suggestion by his superiors and permitted them to return (American Technical Assistance Corporation, 1972).

This situation is most likely to arise in line organizations where promotions depend heavily on "cooperation" with senior managers rather than on measurable aspects of output.

Manipulation

This term refers to deliberate attempts to change personal qualities or the structure of the physical or social environment, without the knowledge of the individuals involved.

The use of group manipulation in OD is well illustrated in the Kuriloff-Atkins example. The material quoted earlier referred to a wide circle which provided an emotional dumping ground for misconceptions and resentments. Once the discussions were underway, various tactics were used to bring in one of the key members who had chosen not to attend. This individual, Hans, had been the target of considerable resentment for being a "Nazi-like, unfeeling, relentless man who would hurt people to advance his own interests" (Kuriloff & Atkins, 1966, pp. 74-75). Hans's absence from the sessions on the first two days caused obvious discomfort in the group and led to a discussion about how to bring him in. Hans appeared on the third day. When finally confronted, he revealed his own personal background and suffering in a way that enabled others to empathize with him. According to this account he was emotionally liberated by his revelations and by the group's acceptance of them.

The ethical problems in this example are acute. There was a clear discrepancy between the norms of freedom established at the outset by Jack, the trainer, and the realities of group pressure. Jack had said: ". . . everyone should feel free *not* to respond if it becomes too difficult. . . . Openness is valued, but so is the right of privacy." Yet in Hans's absence the group agreed to pressure him into attendance and to confront him with their biting resentment. When he did not show up for the second session, it was assumed that he was exercising a choice not to attend—and yet they set out after him.

Within the sessions themselves, ODPs often engage in manipulation to encourage or force participants to "open up." This strategy—unsuccessfully employed—was seen in the example. The consultant reports:

> I asked Bob why he felt so responsible for everyone—Helen, the men in the field, production, engineering. Giving my further impression, I said to Bob that it appeared to me that he had a strong fear of failure and shouldered responsibility that was not rightly his. "Why do you try to make everything perfect?" I asked.
>
> "That's enough, laddie. I've said my piece," Bob concluded with finality. "No more. I have to leave for school in a few minutes and now I'm all upset."
>
> I backed off . . . (p. 78).
>
> Bob had missed out on yeaterday's session with Hans, but he had been told. He seemed cold and disconnected from the warmth of the group. I tried to help him back in by reflecting this.
>
> Giving warning, Bob said, "Don't try to pull your tricks on me again, laddie. I won't fall for it!" (p. 81).

Despite the warning, the consultant continued to try his techniques, including an emotional statement about his own frustration with Bob's silence. There is little doubt that the trainer pursued him relentlessly. Hence the earlier promises of privacy and freedom not to participate seem empty and deceptive.

Misuse of Information

As suggested in the example, a basic component of many OD exercises is the use of group processes to elicit the expression of hostility, anxiety, and resentment, as well as positive feelings. In the name of "authenticity" and "trust," participants are encouraged to open up to others. Moreover, a good ODP is typically skilled in encouraging a person to lower his defenses. The open expression of negative feelings in OD, as in sensitivity training, raises two major ethical problems, one concerning the impact of the revelations on the revealer, the other concerning the impact of "overload" on the target of hostility.

While self-disclosure may have net positive value to the person, as apparently happened with Hans, it may also bring him harm. One problem arises when the ODP or the group go too far in eliciting expressions of feelings. The temptation to "open up" is reinforced by the sense of relief which commonly occurs after the person ventilates strongly felt, but previously unstated, emotions and opinions. Later, however, he may feel anxiety at having said too much or chagrin at revealing what he did about himself. Ethical questions arise when the participant is essentially seduced or pressured into self-revelations which he later comes to regret.

An equally serious problem created by induced honesty is the potential backlash effect of hostile or critical reactions to others in the same workgroup. Differences of power and authority give some members of the system the opportunity to retaliate later for unpleasant revelations or attacks. In a situation such as the U.S. Foreign Service—where status differences are accentuated, promotion depends heavily on the favorable opinions of supervisors, and transfer to other organizations in the same career line is difficult—the effects of honesty can be devastating.

Related ethical issues arise with "overload"—a situation in which an individual receives more aversive feedback than he has bargained for or can handle. The result may be increased psychological pain for the person, a loss of esteem in the eyes of the others, and a deterioration in organizational performance without other redeeming features. Some diagnostic insights may be useful for the organization as a whole, but not necessarily for the work team; others may help the total team, but damage particular members. The borderline between useful feedback and psychic battering is often a fine one, and should be carefully watched.

Some of these difficulties can be avoided or reduced by greater practitioner insight into the practical and ethical issues of open expression. Many ODPs alert clients to these issues from the beginning and encourage them to monitor their own involvement. It is also useful to have the participants themselves engage in occasional disucssion about the limits of self-revelation and feedback, and even about the ethical questions at stake. It is inconsistent with the general philosophy of OD to entrust the entire task of ethical monitoring to the practitioner.

Professional Responsibility

The last set of ethical issues are those arising from the ODPs obligations as a professional. ODPs working as external consultants typically hold doctoral degrees

in a discipline such as psychology or a professional field such as business administration, and are often affiliated with a university. One might be tempted to say
that problems of professional ethics could properly be resolved by adhering to
the canons of one's own discipline. But most codes of ethics in the relevant
disciplines either do not take account of the exigencies of OD or are phrased at
such a broad level that they provide little concrete guidance. Some of the problems of professional responsibility, such as excessive client dependency, are familiar enough in fields such as clinical psychology, but others are relatively specific
to OD. The most salient issues include questions of professional competence,
client dependency vs. ODP commitment, role contamination, and violations of
confidence.

Competence

It is the basic ethical responsibility of any professional to apply the body of knowledge and skills in his field in the proper way and to avoid exaggerated claims about
what can be accomplished. An occasional difficulty in OD practice arises when an
ODP allows a client to expect more than can be delivered. The ODP who creates,
or knowingly allows the client to have, such exaggerated expectations is behaving unethically.

A more subtle but no less significant problem of competence arises from the
practice of force-fitting interventions. In this case, the ODP may be competent
in a particular specialty but fails to tailor the intervention to the needs of the
situation. The practitioner who relies heavily on preprogrammed or prepackaged
interventions may unwittingly define the problem in ways that meet his own constraints of time and competence. Unfortunately, this abuse is not uncommon in
OD. Some practitioners almost reflexively recommend either team-building interventions or intergroup confrontation, regardless of the problem. The blame also
rests in part with OD clients, who often want to bypass the diagnostic step or believe that there is a simple, patent remedy.

From both an ethical and a practical standpoint it is essential to study each
situation on its own terms and to be alert to distinctive features of the organization or its environment. For example, most observers would agree that the OD
effort undertaken in the U.S. Department of State from 1965 to 1967 failed to
take account of some unique features of the federal bureaucracy. One such feature is the transitory character of the senior political leadership. The ODP working in this setting should be aware that the median tenure of political executives
(Assistant Secretaries, Under Secretaries)—who are often the sponsors or protec-
tors of OD—is about two years. A related factor common to rotating top leaders
is a tendency to be a new broom for a few months, sweeping out the pet reforms
of their predecessors in order to establish their own authority. The permanent im-

permanence of this echelon also breeds suspicion, wariness, and passive resistance in the middle and bottom levels. A crucial practical implication, which may escape the ODP entering this system from a background in industry, is that career officials may well see efforts initiated at the top as short-term flings by the latest Johnny-come-lately, while interventions originating in the middle may be killed at the top or swept out by the next rotation. Lest this point seem overly abstract, we quote from former Deputy Under Secretary of State William Crockett, the initiator of OD in the State Department:

> The rotation of top officials in State . . . does produce casualties in programs left by an outgoing official, especially if the program is either difficult to carry out, controversial, or in trouble. . . . If we can't command the time frame to get it in place then we should think carefully about starting it in the first place. At least this is the way I feel now, but I frankly didn't even think of this matter at the time.*

Crockett speaks from the sad experience of having a large OD effort which he launched completely scuttled by his successor, who found it too controversial and "out of line" with the demands of government service.

Other failures of competence are seen in projected or distorted diagnoses. The problem in this case arises from a confusion of the ODP's own needs with the realities of the client's situation. Some practitioners seem to *project* their own preferences for openness, affection, affiliation, and the like onto the clients or target groups, and then design OD to meet those needs. Others seem to create a stage for *acting out* their own needs. In a case observed by Walton, an internal OD consultant habitually arranged for confrontations between subordinate groups and superiors, and then played an active role in challenging the latter's authority. From all indications, he was acting out his own needs. Projection, other distorted diagnoses, and acting out are less likely to occur when practitioners develop insight into their own needs, when they understand the practical necessity (which some seem to forget) of denying themselves some self-expression, and when they work in teams with each member alert to the other's biases.

Client Dependency vs. ODP Commitment

The brief history of OD suggests two extremes in the ODP-client relationship which are ethically questionable. The first is an *insufficient* commitment by the ODP to the client, i.e., a smaller commitment than is necessary to accomplish mutually established. goals. From our observations, a significant fraction of trainers are attracted to temporary systems, preferring short, intensive experiences in which (a) they are highly needed or have high influence, and (b) there

*From personal correspondence to Warwick, 1971.

develops a climate of affective intimacy. The problem of insufficient commitment was more serious in the 1960s as increasing numbers of sensitivity trainers moved over into OD. When they began to apply their skills in organizational rather than laboratory settings, some of these professionals did not modify the time frame of their commitment. Where one or two weeks might be adequate to accomplish the goals of sensitivity training, the life span of OD efforts must usually be measured in months and years. Hence there were complaints from clients that ODPs created strong dependencies within the organization, and then did not follow through. Although this problem seems to have diminished, we would suggest that if an ODP does not have the ability or interest to commit himself for the time period required for an intervention, he should make this clear at the beginning.

Now that OD has become an established and well-paying profession, a greater ethical difficulty seems to be *excessive* client dependency. This can occur as either economic or psychic exploitation, the latter involving continued gratification of the ODP's need to be needed, when the original aims of OD have been satisfied. This abuse can be minimized when both consultants and clients arrive at explicit understanding about the conditions under which the relationship will be ended or phased out, and when they build automatic review dates into their agreement.

Role Contamination: Consulting vs. Research

There are potential ethical dilemmas for behavioral scientists whose interests embrace both generating new knowledge and engaging in OD in the same organization. The first risk is that research will lead to a neglect or distortion of the goals of OD. This problem can be reduced by keeping the research and consulting roles separate in any given setting, or by a clear understanding that one is practicing OD unless he specifically announces that he is "putting on his research hat."

The second danger is that a concern about the welfare of the client-subject or about continuation of the consulting contract will produce distortion in the research findings. This risk is especially great if the behavioral scientist deals with material which could be highly damaging to the image of the organization or could otherwise jeopardize the consulting relationship. The temptation in this case is to avoid sensitive subjects, though they may be central to an understanding of the organization, soft-pedal the more damaging findings, or not publish the findings at all.

Violations of Confidentiality

As in the doctor-patient and lawyer-client relationship, there should be norms about confidentiality in OD. Given the fact that the ODP is typically brought in by management, it is particularly important that all parties concerned—including management—have the same understanding of the ground rules governing sensitive information generated in OD. Sometimes the ODP's sense of responsibility to the larger client system, such as the firm that hired him, overrides his commitment to a particular individual with whom he has worked. One ODP related a case to Walton in which the evident incompetence of a manager was largely responsible for the failure of a division in the company. Although the manager was crippling his entire team, his superiors did not recognize his weaknesses. The ODP felt a mounting responsibility to bring these weaknesses to the attention of management. Yet he recognized that in doing so he would be perceived as the perpetrator of a "hatchet job," and would thus have reduced access and effectiveness in his continued OD work.

As a general principle, we would argue that the ODP should establish clear understandings from the outset to cover such developments, and hold strictly to them. Passing over from a consulting to an intelligence role not only jeopardizes the immediate OD program but damages the integrity of the entire profession.

In conclusion, although we are personally and professionally concerned about ethical abuses in OD, we would not argue for a moratorium on practice until these matters can be resolved. A more fruitful avenue to ethical understanding and solutions is continued practice coupled with greater self-analysis and dialogue. Specifically, we would advocate more frequent publication of case studies that facilitate ethical discussion *in concreto,* and greater candor among ODPs in raising questions of concern in their own practice. In the long run, it is incumbent on the profession itself to develop a code of ethical conduct. To be useful and acceptable, however, that code will have to be based on the experience and insights of the group who know the field best—OD practitioners.

References

American Technical Assistance Corporation. *Organization development in AID: An evaluation.* Washington, D.C.: the Corporation, 1972.

Beckhard, R. *Organization development: Strategies and models.* Reading, Mass.: Addison-Wesley, 1969.

Beer, M., & Huse, E. F. A systems approach to organization development. *Journal of Applied Behavioral Science,* 1972, **8,** 79-101.

Brimm, M. When is change not a change? *Journal of Applied Behavioral Science,* 1972, **8,** 102-107.

Burke, W. W., & Hornstein, H. A. *The social technology of organization development.* Fairfax, Va.: NTL Learning Resources Corporation, Inc., 1972.

Golembiewski, R. T., Carrigan, S., Mead, W. R., Munzenrider, R., & Blumberg, A. Toward building new work relationships: An action design for critical intervention. *Journal of Applied Behavioral Science,* 1972, **8**, 135-148.

Golembiewski, R. T., Carrigan, S. B., & Blumberg, A. More on building new work relationships. *Jouranl of Applied Behavioral Science,* 1973, **9**, 126-128.

Kramer, H. Letter to the editor. *Journal of Applied Behavioral Science,* 1972, **8**, 630.

Kuriloff, A. H., & Atkins, S. T group for a work team. *Journal of Applied Behavioral Science,* 1966, **2**, 63-93.

Schmuck, R. A., & Miles, M. B. *Organization development in schools.* Palo Alto: National Press, 1971.

Walton, R. E. A problem-solving workshop on the border disputes in Eastern Africa. *Journal of Applied Behavioral Science,* 1970, **6**, 453-496.

Walton, R. E. Ethical issues in the practice of organization development. Paper presented to Conference on the Ethics of Social Intervention, Battelle Seattle Research Center, May 1973.

Warwick, D. P. Freedom and population policy. In Population Task Force, *Ethics, population and the American tradition.* Hastings-on-Hudson, N.Y.: Institute of Society, Ethics, and the Life Sciences, 1971.

Warwick, D. P. Organization development: Freedom, power and responsibility. Paper presented to Conference on the Ethics of Social Intervention, Battelle Seattle Research Center, May 1973.

Warwick, D. P., & Kelman, H. C. Ethical issues in social intervention. In G. Zaltman (Ed.), *Process and phenomena of social change.* New York: John Wiley, 1973. Pp. 377-417.

WHY ORGANIZATION DEVELOPMENT HASN'T WORKED (SO FAR) IN MEDICAL CENTERS*

Marvin R. Weisbord

Understanding and helping improve medical organizations has become a passion for many behavioral scientists, including me. It is a passion matched only by that of health administrators to have their organizations improved. On my pessimistic days, our mutual frenzy reminds me of a story the late Saul Alinsky liked to tell. It concerns a bitch in heat parading up and down behind a screen door, while a neighbor's hound scratches to get at her.

"That's a laugh," says the bitch's owner. "Your hound's fixed. Even if he got in here he couldn't *do* anything."

"You don't understand," replied the neighbor. "My dog's a consultant!"

Though many of us have pawed through the screen door, we find medical centers peculiarly impregnable, at least with our present equipment. On the one hand there's a vast descriptive literature of health organizations.[1] On the other, there exists little practical data on how to use this knowledge effectively. In my interviews with health center managers, I note a mounting despair over trying to organize what seems, increasingly, a bottomless pit.

If those who are not "hands on" providers of health services wish to have useful impact on the functioning of health delivery organizations, we must start by owning up that certain management methods, no matter how valued in other settings are—by any standard of scientific objectivity—not working very well in medicine.

*Reprinted from *Health Care Management Review,* Vol. 1, Spring, 1976, pp. 17-28.

In this article, I want to provide, from the standpoint of a student of organizational behavior, a new diagnosis of what ails medical centers. Using this diagnosis, I will explain why one elixir for which I have had high hopes—organization development (OD)—is, for now, not even a good placebo. My central thesis is that medical centers, unlike industrial firms, have coordination problems not subject to rationalization even by "state-of-the-art" administrative practice. I think advocates of other management technologies will find this explanation relevant too.

I see three major reasons OD works better for industry than medicine:

1. Medical centers have few of the formal characteristics of industrial firms, where OD, like all management science, was first recognized, tested, and developed.[2]

2. Physicians and scientists are socialized to a form of rational, autonomous, specialized, expert behavior, which is antithetical to the organization of any but the most narrow individualized pursuits.[3]

3. Medical centers, therefore, require three different social systems, not one, as in industry. The links among the *task* system which administrators manage, the *identity* system which undergirds professional status, and the *governance* system, which sets standards, are extremely tenuous.

Therefore, it is hard to achieve a "good fit" between individual and organization. Medical centers represent what the late psychologist A. H. Maslow called "low synergy institutions"[4]—that is, while the systems are extremely interdependent, people do not act that way. This is the opposite of business, where productivity improves measurably when people learn to work together better.

OD is hard to use in low-synergy situations, because it is based on an assumption not widely shared in our culture: that it is possible, through trial and error, to discover *organizational* procedures that enhance both productivity and self-esteem. In industry, people recognize a common stake in the discovery, even while skeptical of its worth. In medicine, professionals believe in their bones that procedures an organization needs for its survival will be inimical to theirs.

We need a new, non-industrial model for what constitutes a good individual/organization fit in medical centers. Industry has not been a very good teacher, for professionals experience "business-like" methods as threatening to their self-esteem. Why should coordination be more threatening in medical centers than in business firms?

OD Is Industry Specific

Nearly all organization development theory and research derive from industry, which sponsored the seminal work of Argyris, Beckhard, Blake and Mouton,

Herzberg, Laurence and Lorsch, Likert, McGregor, Trist and many others. Firms like Esso Standard Oil, Texas Instruments, TRW Systems Group, Union Carbide provided clinical test sites for theories about the relationships between human satisfaction and productivity.[5] This is probably because OD is intended to help organizations balance, better than they often do, the need for structural constraints and the need for creativity. Such constraints exist to a greater degree in industrial organizations than elsewhere.

Structure is important because it is the creation of rational, systematic relationships which constitute the essence of an "organization." Organizations make it possible for people to do things they value and cannot do alone. But, no matter how innovative, organizations perform if—and only if—they achieve a balance among four key structural features, which restrain individual behavior:

Task interdependence

Concrete goals

Performance measures

Formal authority.

The co-existence of these structural constraints makes an organization sensitive to improvement through focus on its informal system, for people either carry out or subvert goals through their normative behavior.

Historically, industrial firms were structured following the theories of church and military thinkers. To them, authority, goals, and interdependence were central; today, bureaucracy as a structural mode pervades our society. In the 19th Century technologies and performance measures made possible the marriage of bureaucracy to production. Management, as a profession, was born.

Bureaucracy's strength lies in certainty and order. However, its practices, like many industrial products, do not age well. In no time managers discovered that bureaucratic processes have built into them an intractable rigidity. This works against optimal performance. More, at some point the constraints of order outweigh the benefits, restricting personal judgment so that output suffers—and along with it people's self-esteem and morale.

In industry, behavioral scientists using OD provide exactly the right medicine. We introduce counter-bureaucratic values and practices, making it legitimate to do things not a part of everyday work. This includes examining group problem solving, how people express and act on feelings ("personal style"), norms, policies, way of handling conflict—anything that might conceivably impact on the performance of work.

Organizational development methods go under names like "teambuilding," process consultation, intergroup problem solving, survey, data feedback. All of them help people understand, express, learn about, and free themselves from their more irrational constraints. They can then achieve a better balance among goals, authority, task interdependence, and measures. Having done it together, they are more likely to feel committed to making things work, and given recognition for their efforts, their morale improves.

Health Care Professionals Are Socialized Differently

Science-based professional work differs markedly from product-based work. Health professionals learn a rigorous scientific discipline as the "content" of their training. The "process"—not explicit—inculcates a value for autonomous decision-making, personal achievement, and the importance of improving their *own* performance, rather than that of any institution.

In consequence physicians identify much less with a specific institution and more with the culture of medical science. This constitutes a set of values, skills, and knowledge quite independent of any work setting. The rewards of major significance to them—respect, reputation—may come more from this larger arena than from their institutional affiliation.

Medical Centers:
Three Systems, Not One

Both health care and industry require financing; both have customers; each has inputs and outputs, environmental constraints, physical facilities, technologies, employment contracts, managers. At the same time, much important medical center activity does not seem connected to its administrative machinery.

Professionals are enmeshed in the three social systems—Task, Identity, Governance—that pull and tug at each other. Health administrators operate the least influential of the three, quite the reverse of the situation of the industrial manager.

The Task system refers to a specific work organization, which seeks to coordinate three tasks: patient care, education and research. The Identity system refers to the professional development, or career track, in medical science, on which the status and self-esteem of health professionals depends. The Governance system is the network of committees, boards, and agencies, within and without task systems, which set standards for the profession.

Each system has its own ground rules and membership requirements. Each is necessary to the others. Health center professionals belong to all three. Yet the Task system is, in many ways, at odds with the Identity and Governance systems, and vice versa.

The Task System

In industry the Task system is called "management." In health care it's called "administration." I use the generic term Task system to mean either one.

Health care professionals do one or more of four tasks requiring coordination: (1) Patient Care; (2) Education; (3) Research; (4) Administration. Each task is independently valuable to a reasonably complete health care system. These tasks constitute the work of medical centers, hospitals, clinics, and health maintenance organizations.

Patient care, education, and research superficially resemble business functions like production, marketing, or research and development. These superficial similarities encourage the use of industry-based technologies, like program planning and budgeting, management by objectives, and organizational development.

These create an illusion of rationality that disappears quickly when scrutinized, for there are radical discrepancies between industrial and medical Task systems. They lack commonality *exactly* on the four features that make industry such a fertile laboratory for OD.

In industry, management attempts to obtain organizational support for a common definition of interdependence, authority, goals, and measures, while avoiding financial loss. But as Figure 1 shows, in complex medical centers goals

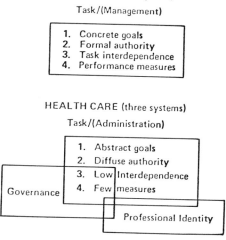

Figure 1   Differences between industrial and health care systems. Overlapping Identity and Governance Systems function to thwart the application of goals, authority, interdependence, and measures in the Task System.

tend to be abstract, authority diffuse, interdependence low, measures few and controversial. Since there are three systems, not one, it is extremely hard to achieve organizational support, and even harder to avoid financial loss. Let us discuss each of the four features in turn.

Task Interdependence

Industrial managers each do one task at a time in an enterprise of any size. A person works in production, marketing, sales, or finance, for example, and while a manager might build a sequential career in various functions, none would conceive of trying to perform these tasks all at once. Nevertheless, the functions are interdependent. The organization requires all to be performed well if it is to be successful. This mixing requirement—called "task interdependency"—rests on two concepts: the differentiation of function, and the integration of functions towards specific goals.

Lawrence and Lorsch demonstrated empirically how these two concepts complement each other in high-performing business.[6] They showed that people need different social/emotional orientations for different tasks. Differences that make a difference include Time horizon—how fast the feedback?; interpersonal relations—how important?; goals—how precise?, and so on. Such matters seem to vary with environmental complexity and rate of change. Successful managers recognize this.

Of course these differences, however necessary, create conflict because different groups in the organization have necessarily different goals. The more productive managers were found not only to differentiate skillfully, but also to integrate or manage effectively conflict between diverse functions. Examples of integrative mechanisms, as opposed to people, include information, cost control, budgeting, and planning systems.

Now, consider problems of differentiation and integration in health centers. First, health centers are differentiated primarliy by specialty. Each specialty runs its own little "business" called a service. Within each service, several tasks may go on simultaneously: patient care administration, teaching and research. Moreover, these tasks are *all* performed by people wearing multiple hats. Few health center professionals do only one of the major tasks, for to do a single task seriously hampers status and mobility in the other two systems. The most complex example is a one-person entity called a "department chariman" in a medical school whose title masks the fact he is often, not only, doing all four major tasks, but managing many other people who also do two, three, or four things at once.

To make sense out of this reality, Lawrence, Charns, and I found we had to turn Lawrence-Lorsch theory upside down.[7] Imagine the organizational confusion when task differences exist not only between functions, but also within

INDUSTRIAL FIRM

Sales	Production	Research

3 People, 3 Hats
Problem: Integration. What's the strategic goal?

MEDICAL CENTER

Patient Care	Teaching
Research	Administration

1 Person, Many Hats
Problem: Differentiation. Who's doing what? Are the goals compatible?

Figure 2   Two different organization problems.

each individual. As Figure 2 demonstrates, coordination is often left to the whim of the individual.

How can one manage such a system? With difficulty. The reason it runs at all is because individuals are so adept at differentiating and integrating what they do. Health professionals identify much more task conflict "in general" than they do "in my own work."[8]

To me this means multiple hats are not so much a personal problem as an *organizational* one. Task system managers do not know what to do if they can not predict how much of each task is being performed on a given day, the strategic goals this work supports, how much it will cost, and who will pay for it.

This fact accounts for much conflict between administrators and professionals. The one tries to coordinate towards institutional goals, and the other sees this effort, given their personal goals, as bureaucratic constraint which hinders, not helps, their performance and reduces their autonomy.

Concrete Goals

Setting priorities, upon which rational resource management depends, is central to industry. "Only if targets are defined," writes Peter Drucker, "can resources be allocated to their attainment, priorities and deadlines set, and somebody held accountable for results."[9]

Health priorities are hard to set, for everything seems equally urgent. Hospital managers consider patient care central, medical deans education, clinicians their own specialty. For many teachers research matters most, because academic advancement, peer recognition, and personal satisfaction are wrapped up in it.[10]

Three-Legged Stool

The famous "three-legged stool"—equal commitment to service, research, teaching—permits each person to defend whatever he does as high primacy of one or another task at any point in time. Besieged on all sides to accommodate every social and political need, a service institution, writes Drucker, "cannot concentrate; it must try to placate everyone." Thus, the critical question for medical centers is: Can we pay for it? The organizational question is: Does it make sense for us to do it?

One way out of this intolerable goal dilemma is to specify which services or customers come first. Narrowing goals makes coordination with existing technologies more feasible. This strategy had made limited service private hospitals a successful growth industry while local medical school affiliates are going broke.

It is much easier to run a "businesslike" operation when profit is predicated on treating selected diseases, while limiting or eliminating teaching and research entirely. At the same time, there is a professional cost in this. Physicians attracted to academic medical centers wish to choose for themselves which mix of tasks they need to do to remain at the cutting edge in their fields. They resist the implication they could learn, grow, create, and contribute if limited to working on one task at a time.

This obstacle, however, is not insurmountable. Task differences are subject to rational analysis, even without forcing people to take off some hats. For example, it is possible to write separate contracts for each hat a person wears, instead of lumping tasks into one undifferentiated person labelled "Professor and Chairman."

Performance Measures

In industry, accountability hinges on managing to a set of numbers. Having goals, dividing up and coordinating work, seem pointless unless you can track progress and make course corrections. Business firms use three major indices: Costs, productivity, and profitability.

Customers are the judges who enforce accountability. Their behavior affects the numbers by which managers manage. Customers can go elsewhere, lobby Congress, write Ralph Nader, picket, boycott, in short make life as miserable for a firm as its faulty products do for them. Health care customers—patients, students—have fewer options. They can do the above, but they are fighting three systems, two of which have cultural/international roots, rather than a single entity with offices somewhere.

The health care Task system uses three major indices, each measuring quite different dimensions: (1) size of budget; (2) space; (3) salaried "full-time equivalents." More of each is held to constitute good performance, and less equals bad, because, as Drucker says, "No institution likes to abandon anything it does."

Quality control, while an issue for administrators, is very difficult for them to manage; for quality standards come not from customer to manager to organization, but from the Governance system to the manager to the customer. Given the nature of medicine, public expectation, and physician training, it is physicians who set and enforce quality standards.

Until recently this has been an extremely individual, rather than organizational, act. "Such evaluation," writes the Joint Commission on Accreditation of Hospitals, "isn't done systematically . . . in a way that reflects the bulk of care given in a hospital." Therefore, the "onus is on the reviewer rather than the system," making it hard for the institution to learn and perform differently.[11]

Thus, while most physicians have and practice high standards, there are few organizational procedures for connecting standards, good or bad, to dollars, space, and staffing decisions. The JCAH's new focus on outcome audits (how well did the patient do?) is a step in the direction of better organization—if such data can be linked to Task system decisions, and not just to physician competence. But so long as the two sets of standards are managed independently of each other, health costs will continue to spiral.

Formal Authority

To enforce and link Governance with Task system measures requires not only a cognitive act but decisiveness. Industrial managers are acknowledged to have the right to decide, even when people question their good sense. The marketplace, in the long run, determines whether they are right or wrong.

In industry, it requires formal authority to sanction "teambuilding," a democratizing process which spreads influence to those who have had too little. In addition, the formal boss-subordinate relationship provides a setting that permits the scrutiny of dynamics important for task accomplishment: anxiety; group collusion to maintain problems; unrealistic expectations for the boss, and vice versa; intolerance of mistakes; reluctance to speak candidly; and the impact of interpersonal feedback on working together.

Health administrators are not exempt from these dynamics. Many have legal responsibility for the consequences. Their formal authority, though, extends in practice only to nurses, aides, technicians, service employees, and other administrators. It excludes physicians and scientists. In this situation business tools and training have limited utility. Health administrators find themselves more often playing the political game of engineering consent rather than the managerial game of implementing decisions.

Lawrence, Charns and I have asked hundreds of medical school faculty to

whom they were responsible when wearing each of their medical task hats. From
20+ percent for undergraduate education, to 55 percent in patient care, to 70
percent on research have said "no one," or left the item blank, or named a person or group outside their medical center. While accountability is a much discussed and much valued concept, when applied to others, a great many medical
faculty cannot imagine Task system accountability at all. For them, it is purely
a Governance matter, based on setting standards for the identity system.[12]

The Identity System

It is the salience to the doctor of the physician Identity system that is key to
understanding why health care is so hard to organize. There is a complex interplay of forces: The medical personality, how doctors are socialized, what society
expects of physicians. All of these forces reinforce a physician self-concept based
largely on the technical expertise needed to diagnose and treat disease, and the
mental toughness to make life-and-death decisions alone. This symbolic system
exists inside each physician. It is based on public recognition of professional
credentials which confer status and a sense of self-worth. Four binds result from
this emphasis.

The Self-Concept Bind

The scientific definition of knowledge relevant to disease is extremely limited.
All data outside a medical model of life are difficult for many doctors to internalize, let alone act upon. This in no way denies the impressive achievements of
modern medicine. It does result in doctors paying a high price, internally, to
maintain identity. Most consider task-related feelings, for example, as irrelevant.
Some grow quite emotional at the suggestion emotions constitute "scientific"
data worthy of study, codification, understanding, and integration with whatever specialty they practice. Many share, in the extreme, a common cultural
belief that to show feelings is an unprofessional retreat from reason and a sign
of weakness.

They tend to see no middle ground of choice between uncontrolled, hys-
terical catharsis and extreme self-control. Yet few people do work that continually stirs up so much anger, fear, and helplessness. Thus, physicians have few
ways of using their emotions constructively toward the solution of problems, in
the same way they use their expertise. This seriously limits the degree to which
they can invest in joint work with others, and in the utility of their contributions when they do.

This bind extends to positive feelings too. To a great extent trust, in such
a disorderly system as health care, is a valuable commodity. Often one's good

feelings about another provide a reliable indicator of relevant expertise; many physicians use personal relationships and intuitive trust as important variables in their professional judgments.

Medical theories cannot easily accommodate this fact. Unless your conceptual frame includes (a) a sense-making view of the interplay among feelings, behavior, and relationships, and (b) the impact of these on medical practice, you cannot utilize such data systematically. In fact, a high percentage of important medical decisions are made from such a framework—which constitutes, by formal standards, an extremely unscientific view of medicine.

The Accountability Bind

Doctors do not judge each other's work publicly. However valued the concept, it is difficult to practice it. This makes sense where identity is so closely linked to narrow expertise. Only those with equivalent specialized knowledge are presumed to be able to judge one's work. Moreover, at least until recently, such judgments—even when made formally, as part of a hospital audit—were based on "How I would have handled this case," rather than the result for the patient and the impact on the hospital.[13]

Paradoxically, each physician has strong opinions about health system goals, and what roles *all others* (non-physicians) should play in achieving them. They "often regard themselves as expert in medicine at large," writes a public health school dean, which "includes all parts of the hospital . . . and, beyond that, the community, since so many aspects are 'health related.' "[14]

"Catch-22" of Medicine

Accountability is the Catch-22 of medicine. The demonstration of expertise in one specialty, which is critical to self-esteem, is taken as admission of incompetence in all other areas. Thus, physicians accept administrator claims to management expertise—so long as no clinical matters are involved.

The trouble is that in hospitals nearly everything is health related. Yet accountability—for the system as a whole—is extremely fragmented. Though most physicians care very much about quality, they have few procedures for linking this concern to institutional management.

The Knowledge Bind

Identity hinges on state-of-the-art skills and knowledge. Yet nobody can keep up any more. "If I did nothing but read journals all day," one doctor told me,

"I'd just fall behind at a slower rate." To maintain status, doctors must maintain an illusion of keeping up. Knowing the impossibility of doing this, they do the next best thing. They narrow their focus and become sub-specialists.

This has a curious organizational consequence. It cannot be predicted when a new technique, piece of equipment, or care concept will be developed. It *can* be predicted at what point in time physicians will pressure their medical facility to acquire an innovation: at once. From an Identity system perspective this makes sense. Whether it makes sense from a patient care or teaching or institutional management standpoint varies considerably from place to place.

To put it another way, knowledge is piling up at a rate beyond the ability of anybody to assimilate it—and it is easier for physicians to blame bureaucracy for their inability to keep up than to accept their own human limitations.

The Task Interdependence Bind

The only reason to be organized is that the problems you are trying to solve require it. Certainly this is true of complex health facilities. At the same time, organizations, for optimal performance, require some cooperation—which implies give and take. Physicians, caught in their other binds, feel compelled to direct, control, decide and be responsible for every patient and patient decision within their purview. It is hard for doctors to share life-and-death risks with anybody, even the patients themselves. What is more, this bind is growing tighter. A growing number of malpractice suits seem based on the premise that infallibility, rather than best effort, should be the minimum standard.

Physician identity has serious consequences for medical organizations. It is the department, rather than an institution, which undergirds Identity. Medicine is organized by specialty to a greater degree than generic tasks like service, teaching, research. Specialty is so pervasive that without the label it is difficult to achieve status in a medical center. Budgets tend to flow through departments. Programmatic activity—integration of knowledge around patient problems—often suffers.

Except for science-based R&D, there is nothing in industry remotely comparable to the medical Identity system. To a remarkable degree industrial managers measure self-esteem and organizational achievement together. They feel good about themselves when the numbers improve, and badly when they do not. The needs of Task and Identity systems work hand in glove. Enhancing one will also enhance the other. It is this chance that makes organization development valuable and welcome.

The Governance System

The Governance system sets and maintains health and medical practice standards. It is the "appreciative" mechanism, in Vickers' phase, which performs the valuing function that makes the Identity system so potent.[15]

Governance exists both in and outside institutions. Inside, it includes trustees, hospital and medical boards, audit committees, and—in medical schools—faculty senates, executive faculty (chairmen), task forces, and committees on everything from admissions to curriculum and grading. Outside are professional societies, specialty boards, accrediting groups, granting agencies, and government. These influence admission to the field, ethical practice, funding, and educational, clinical, and research criteria.

Governance, in its own terms, is the best organized of the three systems. From the standpoint of health care systems, however, Governance mechanisms tend to have three flaws:

Licensure by a Governance group, not an employment contract, undergirds Identity. It is not necessary to demonstrate competence in working with others, nor an understanding of organizational complexity, to achieve status in medicine. Moreover, it is not necessary to demonstrate achievement in a particular Task system. Once technical competence is certified, all else is assumed.

Governance systems tend to be more closed than the Task system, which requires daily interaction with patients, students and the public. There have been few pipelines into health policy which lay people can use, although this is changing.

In addition, links between Governance and Task systems are spotty, rather than well-institutionalized. In most hospitals, for instance, utilization review, under cost pressure from third party payers, is an important Task problem. Meanwhile, hospitals are also under pressure to phase-in outcome audits, as a means of insuring uniform, high quality care. The latter is a Governance function. As hospitals are presently structured, whether physicians will have an opportunity to analyze with managers the relationship between both sets of data and their impact on goals and costs is questionable. Another result of this is that administrators are called upon to implement standards which they are not considered competent to judge. This exacerbates still more the inherent conflict between physicians and managers.

Governance systems work against interdependency. Internal committee meetings, by far the most frequent type in medical centers, tend to be long, frustrating, and often non-productive. Department loyalties are more intense than loyalty to the whole which Governance represents. Without concrete institutional goals, it is hard to favor anything except what will be least restrictive of one's own freedom of action.

The High Costs of Poor Linkage

Throughout, I have tried to show the significance of the lack of links between Task, Identity, and Governance systems, and to demonstrate how this works against rational management and incurs costs.

This lack of links among the three systems requires more Task system administrators. This drives up fixed costs, which are then squeezed from professional budgets as a sort of "coordination tax." Despite this, integration remains elusive. It takes place in a vacuum. Toward what ends is the system being integrated? If ever there was a cat chasing its tail, it is the addition of administrative systems in the absence of goals that professionals share.

Second, is cost in alienation. An anomaly of medical centers is the degree to which the Task system so slavishly imitates industry's least appropriate bureaucratic mode. Functional specialization defines status in health, despite a crying need for programs integrated on behalf of whole people—patients, students, communities, the professionals themselves.

To cite one example, consider a connection between deteriorating doctor-nurse relationships and rising hospital costs. There are in the main three things hospital patients need: Clinical care, personal attention, and help in getting a complex system to focus on their own case. Doctors provide the first service. Increasingly, aides do the "hands-on" care, clerks the paperwork, allied technicians the clinical tests, and ombudsmen the patient advocacy. Nurses, who might provide a link between clinical and administrative tasks are being squeezed out. RN's often don't want the narrow jobs, for they are trained to greater responsibility.

They cannot use their knowledge well in the present setup, despite the fact that they spend more time with patients, and often understand better than anyone the complex relationship among physical, emotional, social, and administrative problems.[16] With clinical and administrative training, they might make excellent hospital integrators—much better, in fact, than doctors or administrators. Instead, they are opting for the Identity game—seeking to become nurse practitioners—because nobody, themselves included, can visualize a more appropriate use for their training.

Why OD Hasn't Worked—So Far

Since face-to-face interdependence is so important for solving medical center problems, it seems plausible that applied behavioral scientists, with OD skills, would have some useful procedures. Alas, we have our binds too.

First, our knowledge is inadequate. Though we have some ideas about how to coordinate the major tasks, industrial theories shed no light at all on how to link the three systems in ways so that both individuals *and* organization are enhanced. They do not, in particular, account for the consequences of a highly competitive Identity system, based entirely on individual achievement.

Second, our structure-reducing, interdependence-enhancing technologies do not work where there is no organizational payoff for interdependent behavior. To practice structure reduction in such a competitive environment is to raise professional anxieties even higher, for these technologies seek to improve a set of conditions physicians do not value to begin with.

The OD repertoire needs structure-*creating* interventions, consistent with our humanistic values. Yet we share with health professionals a profound mistrust of mindless bureaucracies.[17] To the extent we can find no middle ground between free-flowing "organic" relationships and industrial constraints, we may resist the persistent—not intermittent or temporary—commitment that the invention of innovative structures calls for.

The Health Manager's Bind

The risk for all of us is falling prey to what Maslow called "the dangers of unrealistic perfectionism."[18] It is this syndrome which probably accounts in part for the short half-life of deans, chiefs, chairmen and administrators. Knowing the scene firsthand, many go into management believing they, unlike their predecessors, will avoid the big mistakes.

They see the pitfall—there is little evidence to the contrary—as personalities, not systems, and soon discover they can not easily change others. Instead, they seek to change themselves, in the same mode that made them competent physicians or scientists—by acquiring new skills and knowledge. They study MBO, PPBS, and the more adventurous OD, as if these were anatomy courses through which the system, once understood, can be manipulated. However, the courses are based on industrial practice and deal with a very different anatomy.

Where their industrial counterparts use technology strategically, they use it *ad hoc,* to patch up this situation, to damp down that one. They find themselves constantly saying No to people they like, rejecting ideas they value, holding the creativity of others at bay, unappreciated for the good things they have done, attacked for the numberless things others think they *should* have done. Only a few redefine the problem as something beyond technology: how to discover/translate/invent wholly new modes.

How can this be done? The paradox is profound. Though the Identity system names the game, and the Governance system makes the rules, the Task system is the playing field. Those who play by technical expertise alone win only at the expense of many others, jeopardizing an already fragile system. A critical variable is cognition of the missing linkages, for managerial changes which lack Governance sanctions or threaten Identity are not likely to be stable.

Paradoxically, to introduce a new management practice sensitive to all three systems requires, in the absence of relevant organization theory, innate political and interpersonal skills. These skills, though in short supply, are not lacking entirely. Some administrators with whom I have been privileged to work over the years are doing things worth studying:

> Budgeting both by department *and* program to encourage integrative activity
>
> Clarify the center's institutional and departmental goals
>
> Involving professionals in managerial tasks
>
> Planning resource management more deliberately
>
> Bringing physicians and scientists into institutional budget discussions
>
> Educating others to the complexity of these tasks.

Judging the efficacy of these efforts by "all-or-nothing" medical standards seems inappropriate, for no one knows what "all" looks like, and "nothing" is unacceptable in a system strangling for lack of organizational innovations equal to those of medicine.

A sensible goal for health managers, it seems to me, is to try to make small improvements, say 10 percent, in the congruity of goals, interdependence, authority, and measures. Small rationalizations, sanctioned by Governance, mindful of Identity, contribute importantly to more humane medical centers.

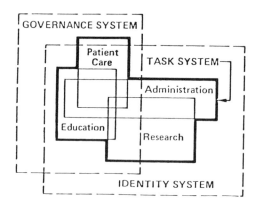

Figure 3 Systems link-up needed in medical centers. 1. Task system itself requires coordination of major tasks—the target of management technologies. 2. In addition, links are needed with Governance and Identity systems. Theory is inadequate to this.

Figure 3 charts the complex interdependencies I think must be taken into account in any new theory of individual/organization fit in medical centers. Present technologies seek to rationalize the task system (solid lines). Whether they also can be used to link the three systems is one test of their practicality. Those unwilling to experiment with new structural relationships cannot facilitate change, for the changes called for may be the very ones they resist. If that is an exaggeration, the changes called for are certainly structures of a different sort than any of us know much about. They are structures that encourage, support, and utilize creative individualistic, and idiosyncratic behavior for socially desirable ends.

If we can own up to our ignorance, and to our values in such matters, then I believe we are ready to have the "right" problem: how to create, in health-care-specific situations, a better fit between people and work.

References

1. Georgopoulos, Basil S. (Editor), *Organization Research On Health Care Institutions.* Institute For Social Research, The University of Michigan, Ann Arbor, Michigan, 1972.

2. Friedlander, Frank, "OD Reaches Adolescence: An Exploration of Its Underlying Values." *The Journal of Applied Behavioral Science,* Vol. 12, No. 1, 1976.

3. Freidson, Eliot, *Professional Dominance: The Social Structure Of Medical Care.* Aldine Publishing Co., Chicago, Illinois, 1970.

4. Maslow, A. H. "Synergy in the Society and in the Individual," Chapter 14, *The Farther Reaches of Human Nature.* The Viking Press, New York, 1972, pp. 199-211.

5. French, Wendell L. and Cecil H. Bell, Jr., "A History of Organization Development," *Organization Development.* Prentice-Hall, Inc., Englewood Cliffs, New Jersey, Chapter 21, pp. 21-29, 1973.

6. Lawrence, Paul R., and J. W. Lorsch, *Organization and Environment.* Homewood, Illinois: Richard D. Irwin, Inc., 1969.

7. Lawrence, Paul R., Marvin R. Weisbord, Martin P. Charns, "The Organization and Management of Academic Medical Centers: A Summary of Findings." Unpublished Report to Four Medical Schools, Organization Research & Development, 1974.

8. Lawrence, Weisbord, Charns, op cit., page 7.

9. Drucker, Peter F., "Why Service Institutions Do Not Perform," *Management—Tasks—Responsibilities—Practices.* Harper & Row, 1974, Chapter 12, pp. 137-147.

10. Lawrence, Paul R., Marvin R. Weisbord, and Martin P. Charns. *Academic Medical Center Self-Study Guide,* Report to Physicians' Assistance Branch, Bureau of Health Manpower Education, National Institutes of Health, 1973.

11. Jacobs, Charles M., J.D. *Procedure for Retrospective Patient Care Audit in Hospitals,* Joint Commission on Accreditation of Hospitals, Third Edition, 1973.

12. Lawrence, Weisbord, Charns, op cit., page 6.

13. Jacobs, op cit.

14. Lynton, Rolf P., "Boundaries in Health Care Systems" (Backfeed Section), *Journal of Applied Behavioral Science,* Volume 11, No. 2, 1975, page 250.

15. Vickers, Sir Geoffrey, *The Art of Judgment,* Basic Books, New York, New York, 1965.

16. Charns, Martin P., "Breaking the Tradition Barrier: Managing Integration in Health Care Facilities," *Health Care Management REview,* Winter, 1976.

17. For a sensible, humane statement see, Culbert, Samuel A., *The Organization Trap and How to Get Out of It.* Basic Books, Inc., New York, 1974.

18. Maslow, A. H., op cit., p. 217.

INDEX

Acceptant interventions, 33-38
Action-research model, 107-108, 210
Agreement, crisis of:
    causes of, 177-179
    symptoms of, 172-177
    treatment of, 180-189
Aluminum Company of Canada, 213
Atomic Energy Commission, U.S., 53
Authority, concept of:
    revisions required by OD, 109-
        112, 116-121
    traditional, 105-107, 115-116,
        118-121

Behavioralism as predecessor of OD,
    105-108
Booz, Allen, and Hamilton, 45

Catalytic interventions, 38-41
Change:
    and ethics, 232-247
    in individuals, 15-16
    Lewin's three-stage model of,
        75-81
    and management of transitions,
        191-205
    models of, 20-21, 77-98
    new cognitive structure in, 94-95
    in organizations, 75-77
    and role of self-esteem, 90-94

[Change]
    and "unfreezing," 75-77
Change agent:
    and consultation strategies, 31-55
    and ethics, 232-247
    insider/outsider varieties of, 68-69
    intervening in neurotic organiza-
        tions, 172-189
    range of interventions by, 33-48
    useful perspectives for, 17-21
Change, Lewin's three-stage model of,
    75-81
Conflict as inherent in organizations,
    50-53, 112
Confrontation designs, 211
Confrontation interventions, 42-45
Consent, informed, 240-243
Consultation, strategies for:
    and crisis of agreement, 172-189
    and ethics, 232-247
    matrix of, 31-33
    in neurotic organizations, 172-189
    varieties of interventions in, 33-55
"Cooling out," 237-238
Coping with transition management,
    191-205
Cultures in organizations, 192-195,
    203-204
"Cycle of accumulating human exper-
    ience," 15-16